PDT Program
LCSC
Return to HR

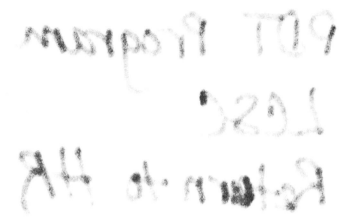

FOLLOWERSHIP

LEADERSHIP FOR THE COMMON GOOD

HARVARD BUSINESS PRESS

CENTER FOR PUBLIC LEADERSHIP
JOHN F. KENNEDY SCHOOL OF GOVERNMENT
HARVARD UNIVERSITY

The Leadership for the Common Good series represents a
partnership between Harvard Business Press and the
Center for Public Leadership at Harvard University's
John F. Kennedy School of Government. Books in the series aim
to provoke conversations about the role of leaders in business,
government, and society, to enrich leadership theory and
enhance leadership practice, and to set the agenda for
defining effective leadership in the future.

OTHER BOOKS IN THE SERIES

Changing Minds
by Howard Gardner

Predictable Surprises
by Max H. Bazerman and
Michael D. Watkins

Bad Leadership
by Barbara Kellerman

Many Unhappy Returns
by Charles O. Rossotti

Leading Through Conflict
by Mark Gerzon

Five Minds for the Future
by Howard Gardner

The Leaders We Need
by Michael Maccoby

Through the Labyrinth
by Alice H. Eagly and
Linda L. Carli

*The Power of
Unreasonable People*
by John Elkington and
Pamela Hartigan

FOLLOWERSHIP

How Followers Are
Creating Change and
Changing Leaders

Barbara Kellerman

HARVARD BUSINESS PRESS
BOSTON, MASSACHUSETTS

Library of Congress Cataloging-in-Publication Data
    Kellerman, Barbara.
        Followership: how followers are creating change and changing leaders / Barbara
    Kellerman.
            p.   cm.
        Includes bibliographical references.
        ISBN-13: 978-1-4221-0368-5
        1. Leadership. 2. Organizational behavior. I. Title.
        HD57.7.K4477 2008
        302.3'5—dc22

                                                                                            2007031572

For my father,

Ernest F. Kellerman

Young Alexander conquered India.
He alone?
Caesar beat the Gauls.
Was there not even a cook in his army?
Philip of Spain wept as his fleet
Was sunk and destroyed. Were there no other tears?

—BERTOLT BRECHT

Contents

Acknowledgments

Jonathan Greenwald and Samir Randolph were indispensable from day one. Peter Pollard and Dave Simonson searched so I could find—none better. Rod Kramer, Joseph Nye, Todd Pittinsky, and Seth Rosenthal provided valuable feedback. And when I had questions, Nathanial Fick, Leonard Grob, Michele McAloon, and Todd Rogers gave me good answers.

Introduction

"Shooting an Elephant"

In the mid-1930s George Orwell published a story about a British police officer stationed in Burma, when it was one of the jewels in the British crown. Responsible for maintaining law and order, the officer was held in contempt by the Burmans for whom he was officially responsible, which further fueled his belief that "imperialism was an evil thing."[1] Inexperienced and still ignorant of the ways of the world, he detested his job, the more so because the town where he was situated seethed under British rule.

One day the young officer, who was Orwell, received a call. A few miles away an elephant that was normally tame had briefly gone wild (as elephants apparently are disposed to do), ravaging the bazaar and killing one man. The expectation was that Orwell would come immediately, take charge, and somehow repair the situation.

As soon as Orwell appeared on the scene, a mass of Burmans gathered, roused by the prospect that he, now toting a rifle under his arm, would provide entertainment by killing the elephant. But Orwell was not inclined to shoot. Moreover, by the time he, along with the rapidly growing crowd, had located the elephant, it had returned to its normally peaceable state, "tearing up bunches of grass, beating them against his knees to clean them, and stuffing them into his mouth."

Orwell writes that as soon as he saw the elephant, he "knew with perfect certainty" that he ought not to kill it. Not only was it a serious matter to kill a working elephant, but Orwell makes clear that he did not have the stomach to shoot an animal now appearing "no more dangerous than a cow." His plan was to make certain that the elephant was once again calm, and then to go home.

But the crowd right behind and in hot pursuit had grown—now it was some two thousand strong. "All happy and excited over this bit of fun," they were convinced that the elephant should and would be shot, and that it was Orwell who should and would be the shooter. In this instant, it seemed to Orwell the situation had changed. Now there was no choice: he had to kill the elephant. Although the one in the position of authority, the one in possession of the large rifle, Orwell felt powerless, completely unable to stop, "two thousand wills, pressing me forward, irresistibly."

As the story comes to its inexorable conclusion, the stark differences between Orwell and the Burmans are heightened still further. In the end Orwell feels it would be "murder to shoot the elephant." But at the same time, he senses that if he fails to do what is expected of him, or even if he bungles the job, "those two thousand Burmans would see me pursued, caught, trampled on and reduced to a grinning corpse."

So he pulls the trigger and shoots the beast, describing with enormous sensitivity and in great detail the slow, dreadful death. It would take several more shots to finally finish the elephant off. But even before the "tortured gasps" that "continued steadily as a ticking clock" had ceased, Orwell, who could not stand it any longer, left the scene.

On one level Orwell's narrative is political—about one nation subjugating another, an act of imperialism that he had come to believe was abhorrent. But on another level it is a gripping parable about ordinary people trapped in a complex relationship—between those who ostensibly have power, authority, and influence, and those who do not. "Shooting an Elephant," an apparently simple story of a man in over his head, is in the end a cautionary tale in which complex, if conventional, wisdoms are upended. The man in the position of authority, and who had firepower to boot, was unable to do what he wanted to do. Conversely, those who lacked authority as well as power of any kind had their way. They wanted Orwell to shoot the elephant, and they got Orwell to shoot the elephant.

But whatever the might that made right in this case, it was not might as it is usually conceived. This was the might of the many, of subordinates who, by mobilizing as a mob, obliged their superior to bend to their will.

On the one hand, Orwell's short story is typical in that he, the British police officer, the authority figure, is the protagonist. On the other, it is atypical because in just a few strokes he paints a picture in which the slaughter of the elephant—an act that finally assumes near-mythical significance—is ordained not by the British police officer officially in charge, but rather by those ostensibly beneath him. Similarly, on the one hand, Orwell's narrative would seem to suggest that the triumph of the powerless over the powerful is rather a natural phenomenon, albeit one not usually anticipated. But on the other, "Shooting an Elephant" can be read as a story about deviance, with a surprise ending fully intended to unsettle.

This book on followers, on followership, bears some resemblance to Orwell's cautionary tale. It deliberately departs from the leadercentric approach that dominates our thinking about how power, authority, and influence are exercised. It claims that to obsess about superiors at the expense of subordinates is to distort the dynamic between them. And it sends a message: to underestimate, or to undervalue, the importance of those whom Shakespeare once referred to as underlings is to disempower them. So long as we fixate on leaders at the expense of followers, we will perpetuate the myth that they don't much matter.

During the last quarter of the twentieth century, the idea of leadership gained fresh currency. First in the military (which had long since paid attention), next in corporate America, and finally in the public and non-profit sectors, we became persuaded that good leadership was of signal importance. We became further persuaded that good leadership can be taught—that is, that people can be taught to be good leaders. Just a few years ago, in fact, the investment in leadership education and development was said to approximate some $50 billion.[2] All this theory and all this practice triggered an explosion of interest—it triggered what I call the *leadership industry*, in which, among other things, a good number of people make a good amount of money.[3]

At the same time, the concept of followership languished. This is not to say that leadership scholars in particular failed to acknowledge that leadership is a relationship between a leader and at least one follower. Rather it is to point out that, overwhelmingly, even now, we overemphasize the former and underemphasize the latter. Leaders are presumed to be so much more important than followers that our shared interest is in *leadership*, not in *followership*. In fact, the word itself, *followership*, remains suspect. Look up the word in your dictionary, and it's as likely as not to be missing. Type the word into your computer, and it's as likely as not to be rejected, either as misspelled or as not even in the English language.[4] Search the Web, and the results are similarly telling: maybe a few hundred thousand results for *followership*, compared with a billion or more for *leadership*. The bottom line: for all the lip service paid to the importance of the relationship between leaders and followers, the message we receive is that the former belong front and center and the latter off to the side.

In titling this book *Followership: How Followers Are Creating Change and Changing Leaders*, I am staking a claim. I am claiming that followers are important—every bit as important as are leaders. But there's one small problem. As Orwell's tale makes plain, exactly who are the leaders and who are the followers is not always completely clear. How can the Burmans who insisted the elephant die be considered *followers* in any conventional sense of this word? Whatever their rank, it was they, not the man ostensibly in charge, who effected the outcome. Where, then, do we draw the line between those designated leaders and those designated followers?

Here is a similar, much more recent story. Lawrence Summers became president of Harvard University in 2001. While personally unpopular nearly from the start, Summers nevertheless led the university with some measure of success during his first few years in office. But when he made the mistake of suggesting there might be, could be, "intrinsic" reasons why women were less successful in science and engineering than were men, a group of faculty was outraged to the point of rebellion. Thirteen months later the objections to his presidency had become so strong and so insistent that Summers finally felt he had no choice but to step down.

Members of the faculty are not *followers* as this word is usually understood. Among other things, tenured faculty cannot ordinarily be fired. Still, this is a story somewhat analogous to the one told by Orwell: the putative leader lost control because those who were expected to go along refused to do so. Usually, university presidents govern, and usually, members of the faculty are content to be governed. But in this case the situation was reversed. In this case the president of Harvard University was obliged to bow to the most defiant among Harvard's faculty.

This book has stories about all sorts of followers, from those who stand by and do nothing to those who are agents of change. Still, who exactly is a follower remains vague, which is why some clarifications are in order at the start.

- Followers can be defined by their *rank*: they are subordinates who have less power, authority, and influence than do their superiors.

- Followers can also be defined by their *behavior*: they go along with what someone else wants and intends.

In general, rank and behavior coincide. That is, in general, those who are in subordinate positions go along with those who are in superior ones. But as we have just seen, sometimes rank and behavior deviate from one another. Sometimes those ranked as superiors follow, and those ranked as subordinates lead. President George W. Bush was portrayed repeatedly, especially during his first term and with regard to the war in Iraq, as Vice President Dick Cheney's puppet. Cheney's lower rank notwithstanding, he was seen as pulling the strings, while Bush, his ostensible superior, danced to the tune of his puppeteer.

The distinction between rank and behavior is an important one. To take another example of the complexities involved, consider the case of the whistle-blower. On the one hand, *rank* dictates that whistle-blowers are followers. That is, by being located somewhere in the organizational hierarchy that is other than at the top, they are expected to go along with those who rank higher than they. But on the other hand, by refusing to comply with their leaders and managers whom they view as incompetent, immoral, or both, whistle-blowers do not *behave* like followers at all. In fact, if they successfully stage the organizational equivalent of a palace coup, rank is trumped by behavior. In other words, successful whistle-blowers are followers no longer. By creating change, they have morphed into leaders.

To avoid confusion, and for the purposes of this book, I define followers by rank: *followers are subordinates who have less power, authority, and influence than do their superiors and who therefore usually, but not invariably, fall into line.* Sometimes followers are formally designated, as in organizational

hierarchies in which those at the bottom and in the middle are clearly subordinate to those higher up. Sometimes they are informally designated—for
example, the American people generally go along with the president of
the United States, even when they disagree or disapprove. And sometimes
followers become something else altogether—they become agents of change.
In this book I discuss all three—that is, followers as they are formally ascribed, followers as they are informally understood, and followers who
end up with more power and influence, if not authority, than their leaders.
The point, in any case, is this: I define followers broadly, as "unleaders," if
you will. They are without particular power, without positions of authority, and without special influence.

This returns us to *followership*. More particularly, how do I define the
word earlier described as "suspect"? We know there is no widely accepted
definition of *leadership*. As one scholar put it, "There are almost as many
different definitions of leadership as there are persons who have attempted
to define the concept."[5] Even as apparently straightforward a noun as
leader is used by different experts in different ways. For example, some define leader by rank: leaders are people in positions of authority. Others
consider that the word has a moral imperative: leaders engage their followers in influence relationships. And still others define leaders as the few
who get the many to do what they want and intend, by any means necessary. In my own recent book on bad leadership, I considered Stalin and
Saddam, although tyrannical and cruel, and Bernard Ebbers and Dennis
Kozlowski, although greedy and corrupt, to be leaders.[6]

Given these differences, devolving from terms as well known and frequently used as *leader* and *leadership*, what can reasonably be said about *followership*, a word out of the gate only recently? As I use it in this book,
followership is the response of those in subordinate positions (followers) to
those in superior ones (leaders). *Followership implies a relationship (rank),
between subordinates and superiors, and a response (behavior), of the former to
the latter.*

Up to now the problems associated with the word *follower* have de-
terred us from our work. These problems include the conventional wisdom that followers are less important, *much* less important, than leaders;
the confusion between rank and behavior; and the fear of being called a
follower: a mindless member of a mindless herd, a sheep.[7] Now, though,

it's time, it's past time, to face facts. As "Shooting an Elephant" eloquently testifies, people without obvious sources of power, authority, and influence are far more consequential than we generally assume, and they are ubiquitous. To give them short shrift is to shortchange our understanding of both leaders and followers, however easy the appeal of the former and however elusive the attractions of the latter.

In fact, as the result of changes now converging, followers are more important than ever before. And leaders nearly everywhere are more vulnerable to forces beyond their control, including those from the bottom up. As Howell Raines (former executive editor at the *New York Times*), Riccardo Muti (former conductor at Milan's La Scala opera house), Gray Davis (former governor of California), Michael Eisner (former CEO of Disney), Carly Fiorina and Patricia Dunn (former CEO of Hewlett-Packard and former chair of the board, respectively), Leonid Kuchma (former president of Ukraine), Robert Nardelli (former CEO of Home Depot, albeit resurrected rather rapidly as CEO of Chrysler), and Paul Wolfowitz (former president of the World Bank) can testify, the days when people in high places can sit pretty and do what they want how they want are over. For reasons to be seen, followers the world over are getting bolder and more strategic. They are less likely now than they were in the past to "know their place," to do as they are told, and to keep their opinions to themselves. This change, this small but potentially seismic shift in the balance of power between leaders and followers, constitutes a caution: leaders who ignore or dismiss their followers do so at their peril.

This book, then, departs from the leadercentric approach that dominates our work on leadership and management. Focusing on followers enables us to see the parts they play, even when they do little or nothing. And it empowers them, which is to say that it empowers us.

Let me, though, make clear even now that this book was written for leaders, every bit as much as for followers. First, as we know from our own experience, the line that separates superiors from their subordinates is often blurred. Sometimes leaders and managers follow; and sometimes followers lead. In addition, the line between them tends to shift. Some of us are followers most of the time and leaders some of the time. Others are the opposite: leaders most of the time and followers some of the time. Finally, many of us are superiors and subordinates simultaneously. For example, middle managers or even highly placed executives have people who are below them on the organizational ladder, and they have people above them at the same time.

The second reason the book pertains to both leaders and followers is that we are all, every one of us, followers first. We are followers first in infancy and childhood of the adults on whom we depend, and then later in life we follow leaders before we lead followers. Jean-Jacques Rousseau went so far as to argue that learning to lead requires learning to follow: "Much trouble, we are told, is taken to teach young princes the art of reigning; but their education seems to do them no good. It would be better to begin by teaching them the art of obeying . . . Reigning is a science we are never so far from possessing as when we have learnt too much of it, and one we acquire better by obeying than commanding."[8]

The book to come is divided into three parts. Part I explores the phenomenon of followership: fictions about followers and truths about them; relationships between followers and leaders; and the ways in which followers differ, one from the other. Part II consists of stories about followers who range from being completely complacent to completely committed. And part III looks to the future—a future in which followers will have more of an impact than ever before.

As a longtime student of leadership, I have known all along that leaders and followers are enmeshed, entwined. But there's knowing and knowing. Until I wrote my most recent book, *Bad Leadership: What It Is, How It Happens, Why It Matters,* I did not have a visceral feeling for how important was the follower to the leader. Bad leaders, I now understand, cannot possibly do what they do without bad followers. They depend on them absolutely. This book, then, is a product of its immediate predecessor. It points to the roles followers play. And it reminds us of what on some level we already know: better followers beget better leaders.

Orwell understood that power in the hands of the apparently powerless is difficult to detect. "Here was I," he wrote, "the white man with his gun, standing in front of the unarmed native crowd—seemingly the leading actor of the piece." But, he went on, "in reality I was only an absurd puppet pushed to and fro by the will of the yellow faces behind." His point was plain: to fixate on one and slight all the rest is to misread the story and the message it sends.

PART I

Seeing Followers

*We who give you our advice ought to be resolved
to look rather further into things than you
whose attention is occupied only with the surface.*

—THUCYDIDES

CHAPTER 1

Fictions

BEGINNING IN 2002 an ad agency by the name of McKinney & Silver rolled out a slogan that caught on fast. Hired to persuade people in the market for premium cars that Audi cars were better than their competition, the agency created a tagline—"Never Follow."

The "Never Follow" print ad was striking. One two-page spread had a shot of most but not all of a sleek, gray Audi A6 Avant on the left-hand side, and on the right a picture of the front of the car, the nose, along with the words *Never Follow* etched in fine white letters. These glossy, minimalist ads were so effective that in short order "Never Follow" was transformed from a routine promotional campaign into a "multi-tiered communications program honoring innovators in the fields of music, film, literature and sports." Celebrities such as rock legend David Bowie and actor William H. Macy were held up as exemplars of Audi's "Never Follow philosophy"— as talented performers who "embraced a Never Follow approach."[1]

In time the tagline was associated with all Audi automobiles and in fact was finally abandoned only in 2007. The question is, What accounted for its remarkable longevity? Why did this particular slogan, which admonished us *never* to follow, last so long when so many others come and go? Because "Never Follow" tapped into a fear rooted deep in the American psyche. It reflected our aversion to being, or to be seen as being, one among many in a meek and mindless herd.[2] The word *never* says it all. It says plainly that

3

there is no conceivable circumstance under which we should fall so low as to fall into line. And it says equally plainly that to be a follower rather than a leader is to be second best.

Americans are not the only ones quick to deny they are followers. On announcing he was stepping down as prime minister, Tony Blair made it a point to declare that "Britain is not a follower. It is a leader."[3] But Americans have had an antiauthority, "Never Follow" mind-set from the beginning, going all the way back. In 1683 a Flemish missionary monk observed of Native Americans, they "think every one ought to be left to their own opinion, without being thwarted." Another added there was "nothing so difficult to control as the tribes of America." They do not know what is "meant by the bridle and bit." In turn, Native Americans were apparently aghast at the European habit of hierarchies, in which those on the lower rungs of the ladder deferred to those higher up.[4]

Until the mid-1700s most European Americans assumed their way of doing things would never be challenged. They were content with strati-fied societies, in which some were rich and some poor, some honored and some obscure, some powerful and some weak. But the Revolutionary War changed everything. As historian Bernard Bailyn wrote, it "brought with it arguments and attitudes bred of arguments endlessly repeated, that under-mined [the] premises of the *ancient regime*."[5] There could be no clinging to a strictly stratified society during a decade in which defiance of the highest constituted powers "poured from the colonial presses and was hurled from half the pulpits of the land. The right, the need, the absolute obligation to disobey legally constituted authority had become the universal cry." Rather than *obedience*, it was *resistance* that became a "doctrine according to godli-ness."[6] In other words, rather than following, it was refusing to follow that was considered at the time to be necessary and appropriate.

Once religious dissent joined political dissent—in New England a scion of the church went so far as to negate "all human authority in mat-ters of faith and worship"—it became commonplace, commendable even, to challenge people in high places and to be in obvious ways defiant.[7] It was this antigovernment, antiauthority attitude that over the years came to be considered quintessentially American. As political scientist Samuel Huntington has observed, the ideas that constitute the American Creed—equality, liberty, individualism, constitutionalism, and democracy—clearly demonstrate that "opposition to power, and suspicion of government as the most dangerous embodiment of power, are the essential themes of American political thought."[8] In other words this was a political culture in which anything was better than being, merely, a follower.

The culture of capitalism further fed the habit of resistance. In nineteenth-century America, Alexander Hamilton's grand capitalist dream fused with Thomas Jefferson's democratic idealism. "The result was to electrify the democratic individual with a passion for great achievement and to produce a personality type that was neither Hamiltonian nor Jeffersonian but a strange mixture of them both: the heroes of Horatio Alger."[9] Alger wrote hugely popular rags-to-riches stories, in which young boys, whose only resources were their own determination and drive, advanced from poverty to wealth and acclaim. The moral of each story was obvious: the rewards of success go to those who are individualistic go-getters, not to those who are content to conform. Put another way, it now seemed America's economic system went hand in glove with its political system. Both valued the entrepreneurial individual more than the group as a whole.

Our reluctance to go along complicates the lives of leaders—and those of followers as well. Moreover, it puts on them, on us, an onus. For in a country that since its revolutionary inception has honored those who resist people in positions of authority, there is no glory to be had in toeing the line. In fact, the American Revolution, or, more precisely, the ideas that inspired it, created a culture in which even now, at least under certain circumstances, civil *dis*obedience is more admired than is civil obedience. This is not to suggest that Americans ordinarily honor those who break the law. As we have just seen, constitutionalism and the rule of law that it implies are among our core beliefs. But it is to point out that we do not place an especially high value on convention and conformity. Recall the American archetype: he is not the common man content with the commonplace. Rather, he is the cowboy, who prefers to be alone rather than comply with the conventions of others.

Alexis de Tocqueville observed in his classic, *Democracy in America*, that Americans did not "recognize any signs of incontestable greatness or superiority in any of their fellows." Rather, they relied on "their own judgment as the most apparent and accessible test of truth." While the independence to which Tocqueville alludes is generally considered admirable, it does not make it easy to govern, to lead. In fact, in a national culture in which, again in Tocqueville's words, there "is a general distaste for accepting any man's word as proof of anything," the exercise of leadership is destined to be difficult.[10] But the implication of the resistance to which Tocqueville alludes is even more fundamental and far-reaching. For not only are the roles and reputations of leaders at stake, so are the roles and reputations of followers. To refuse to recognize "incontestable greatness or superiority" in anyone else is to put a premium on individuality and independence. Anything less is to be a follower—anything less is to be a sheep.

Fear of Following

Since the word *follower* is considered something of an insult, certainly in the United States, it has been shunned by those in the leadership field. For example, leadership expert John Gardner so disliked the word *follower* that he chose simply not to use it. "The connotations of the word 'follower' suggest too much passivity and dependence to make it a fit term for those who are at the other end of the dialogue with leaders," Gardner wrote. "For this reason I shall make frequent use of the word 'constituent.'"[11] Other students of leadership have similarly distanced themselves, on the presumption that to be a follower is to be somehow diminished. So, in addition to *constituent*, euphemisms such as *associate* or *member* or *subordinate* have been used.[12] The Wharton School's Michael Useem went even further. Although one of his books was clearly intended for those in subordinate positions, as opposed to those in superior ones, he titled it *Leading Up: How to Lead Your Boss So You Both Win.* The point of *Leading Up* was to urge people to "come forward [even] when an organization or superior does not encourage it."[13] But since "leading" of any kind is better than "following" of any kind, Useem made his case by embracing the former and rejecting the latter.[14]

Even when *follower* has been used, there was a strong sense that somehow it had to be justified, explained away. In *Leadership for the Twenty-First Century,* Joseph Rost insisted that although others might find it condescending, he had "no trouble with the word *followers*."[15] But then he went on to disassociate himself from the idea that followers were "passive." This, he insisted, was an old-fashioned way of thinking, one that reflected the dynamics of decades past in which leaders were directive and active, and followers were "submissive and passive." Now, Rost argued, things were different. Since leaders are no longer equated with being superior, followers should no longer be equated with being subordinate.

Rost was typical of leadership experts more generally: under no circumstance did they, we, want to be seen as callous calculators of a dynamic in which one party was destined always to be dominant, and the other always to be dominated. For most of the last two decades, the period during which leadership education and development became big business, this was the prevailing sensibility. While on the one hand we were obsessed with leaders, on the other we did not want to appear to diminish followers.

In the last couple of years, our reluctance to use the word *follower* has receded—somewhat. We are more willing now than we were before to acknowledge that followers are integral to the leadership process, and to use the word without worrying that we are being condescending. As one scholar noted, "An increasing number of writers argue that 'exemplary,' 'courageous,' and 'star' followers are a precondition for 'successful' organizations." Rejecting the common stereotype of followers as "timid, docile sheep," these experts claim that good followership matters—a great deal.[16]

Still, the fear of following has precluded us from exploring followership in full—and deluded us into thinking that power between leaders and followers is easily shared, which it is not. In corporate America especially, we are loath to admit the obvious: those high on the organizational ladder generally dominate those lower down. To obscure the unpleasant truth that power relationships persist, we use language that lulls us into thinking things are different from what they really are.[17] Words and terms recently in fashion, especially in corporate America, including *empowerment, participation, teams,* and *distributed leadership,* all suggest rather a level playing field, which by and large is false. While many if not most organizational hierarchies have been flattened in recent years, leaders and managers generally remain in control. Whatever the jargon, the fact is that most organizations still have systems and structures in which superiors control their subordinates.

Joanne Ciulla has suggested that the word *empowerment* is the most insidious. Employers who empower their employees "to be leaders in their own way" are presumed to be those who are the most enlightened, the most willing to blur the distinction between those at the top and those at the bottom of the organizational hierarchy. The trouble is, the promise of empowerment is often empty, bogus.[18] Rather than being indicative of genuine power sharing, the very use of the word *empowerment* is often manipulative, intended to keep subordinates in line by deluding them into thinking that in some fundamental way their relationship to their superiors has changed.

Again, this is not to suggest that to speak of empowerment is by definition to be inauthentic. In their recent book, *True North*, Bill George and Peter Sims clearly mean it when they ask, "If mutual respect provides the foundation for bringing out the best from people, what are the steps needed to empower them?"[19] Rather, it is to point to the persisting gap between what is promised and what is delivered. To take perhaps the most glaring example of how the most fundamental power relationship in corporate America has not really changed, there is this simple statistic: during the three-year period 2003 to 2005, more than 4.25 million American workers were involuntarily separated from their jobs. So, at a minimum, we can say this: in those situations in which superiors have the right to dismiss their subordinates, words like *empowerment* and *distributed leadership* are more in the realm of fantasy than of fact.

So keen are we to avoid the very idea of followership that sometimes even our reasoning is tortuous. "Followers do not do followership," Rost wrote. "They do leadership. Both leaders and followers form one relationship that is leadership. There is no such thing as followership in the new school of leadership."[20] Where is the logic in this? How can there be leadership but no followership? How can followers not "do followership"? What does it mean to speak of a "new school of leadership" if the dynamics of power, authority, and influence are endemic to the human condition? It is telling, is it not, that by his own testimony, each and every one of William Styron's novels focused on one recurrent theme: "the catastrophic propensity on the part of human beings to attempt to dominate one another."[21]

I have colleagues who, when I told them I was writing a book about followers, insisted there was no such thing. Every leader is a follower, they argued, a point with which I agree. But then they went on to claim that every follower is also a leader, a point with which I emphatically disagree. It is true that those at the top of the greasy pole are vulnerable to being bumped off. Thus they have no choice but to track, to follow, if you will, their followers, if only to ensure that they stay in line. The converse, though, is not true. While in some circumstances it is possible for followers to exercise leadership, to "lead up," in other circumstances it is not. Sometimes followers are in every way and at every moment subordinate to, or even at the mercy of, those who are in positions of power and authority. We must conclude, then, that however endearing the idea that subordinates can freely and easily impact on their superiors, it is mostly misguided.

THE IMPORTANCE OF BEING A FOLLOWER

Notwithstanding the obvious—that leaders generally have more power, authority, and influence than do followers—we still overestimate the importance of the former and underestimate the importance of the latter. Undeterred by the fact that leaders and followers are inextricably enmeshed, each defined by and dependent on the other, we continue to dwell on the first and dismiss the second.

This disposition affects not only how we perform in the present but how we perceive the past. To take one of the most obvious and extreme examples, while there have been a few excellent books on Germans who fueled the machine that was Nazi Germany, the explanatory paradigm that still prevails is Hitler. It is Hitler who is held responsible for the Second World War, and for the genocide that was part of it. But there is no evidence that, although many millions died, including 6 million Jews alone, Hitler personally killed even a single one. Instead, Europe's Jews were massacred by Hitler's followers, who, in the words of Daniel Jonah Goldhagen, were his "willing executioners."[22]

This all-important truth does not deter those who insist, "no Hitler, no Holocaust."[23] Milton Himmelfarb, for example, argued that the genocide had to be viewed through the lens of a single man. "Hitler willed and ordered the Holocaust, and was obeyed," he wrote. "Hitler murdered the Jews because he wanted to murder them."[24] While I do not deny the importance of leadership, or suggest that Hitler was anything other than the driving force behind the war and the Holocaust, there is a big difference between assuming that one individual explains all and granting that a situation is far more complex than the "great man" theory of leadership would suggest. In fact, Himmelfarb used two verbs—*ordered* and *obeyed*—that undermine his own argument. When leaders give orders, they are, by definition, engaging their followers in the task at hand. Therefore, every German who obeyed Hitler and his deputies, as opposed to defying them, was somehow implicated in the murder and the mayhem. In short, while "no Hitler, no Holocaust" may be a necessary formulation, it is not a sufficient one.

Our tendency to see great change through the prism of great leaders is not confined to our reflections on the past. Even now we are told, repeatedly, that we should aspire to leadership, to becoming a leader. What accounts for the widely held belief that leaders dictate the course of human history? How has it happened that there is a "leadership industry" in which followers are in effect invisible? And if everyone is educated to lead, who exactly is supposed to follow?

There is more than one reason for this skewed view of human affairs. At this point I will focus on one in particular, on what has been called the *romance of leadership*.[25] We fixate on leaders to the exclusion of nearly everyone else because leaders help us order a world that otherwise is hopelessly confusing.[26] The capacity of the human mind is finite—coming at us from all sides is more information than we can possibly absorb. Leaders, then, provide a convenient solution to an obvious problem: how to perceive and then process what is happening in the world in which we operate. A leader like Bill Gates helps us to understand the remarkable story of Microsoft, even though the full truth is much more complicated than the easy attribution to one man would seem to suggest.[27]

Attribution theory explains why we have the mistaken belief that individuals, leaders in particular, have more power than they really do. We assume the all-importance of leaders, even when the assumption is demonstrably false, as in blaming Hitler for in effect single-handedly murdering 6 million Jews. Of course, on some level we know full well that the story of Hitler cannot be told out of context, separate and distinct from the story of what was happening more generally in Germany in the 1920s and 1930s. Nor can we leave on the cutting-room floor the story of Hitler's followers, ranging from early and enduring acolytes such as Joseph Goebbels and Hermann Goering to ordinary Germans, most of whom stood by and did nothing while people and places burned. Still, we prefer to keep it simple. We prefer to look at leaders because they provide an easy explanation. They provide an observable someone who appears to account for what happened.[28] Recall Orwell's making this point plain: although "seemingly the leading actor of the piece," in reality he was no more than "an absurd puppet pushed to and fro" by untold numbers of others.

Richard Hackman has written about what he calls the "leader attribution error." As a student of teams, and as an admirer of teams that energize, orient, and engage the talents of their members, Hackman is demonstrably put off by our tendency to assume that team leaders, more than team members, deserve credit for the group's accomplishments. "When we think about a great team," Hackman writes, "the image we conjure up almost always includes a great leader." For example, when the final chords of Mahler's "Resurrection" Symphony reverberate in the concert hall, "the conductor, exhausted but beaming, turns to accept the applause of the audience." By the same token, the standard remedy for an athletic team that is losing rather than winning is to fire the coach, on the expedient but often mistaken assumption that replacing the designated leader will solve the problem.[29]

Our tendency to make the leader attribution error is especially strong when the leader is especially strong. For example, the story of the Sunbeam Corporation under the leadership of Al Dunlap became one and the same as the story of Dunlap himself. So large and fearsome a figure was "Chainsaw Al" that the fate of the company was thought to be in the hands of this one man. Dunlap, of course, was notorious for being the world's worst boss. He was known for being mean and nasty even when he was CEO at Scott Paper, and by the time he got to Sunbeam, his reputation was that of a "street fighter with a sharp blade." With regard to layoffs in particular, "he always cut big, deep, and a little wild."[30] Moreover, Dunlap had a fearsome temper that intimidated even his closest aides. Sunbeam's corporate culture was a "culture of misery"; Sunbeam's work environment was one in which "the pressure was beyond tough. It was barbarous."[31]

One consequence of Dunlap's tyranny was that he overshadowed everyone else. None of the other players seemed to us to play any kind of meaningful role. But even in this case, in which one man so dominated, it is a mistake to attribute to him all the credit for what went right at Scott Paper (the stock price in particular) and all the blame for what went wrong at Sunbeam (it finally ran aground). Dunlap got away with outrageously bad behavior at Sunbeam because those around and beneath him tolerated it. On the one hand, then, this is the story of a powerful leader. But on the other hand, it is, equally, the story of submissive followers, who were unwilling or unable to stop him from leading badly.

This was not a case in which just a few people did nothing to save the day. Rather, it was one in which large numbers of stakeholders freely followed their leader over a cliff. For example, until nearly the end of his reign, members of Sunbeam's board supported Dunlap. They were not especially interested in what he was doing, nor did they seek to interfere with how he ran the business, even in those cases in which large layoffs made the headlines. In fact, no matter how draconian his proposed measures, Sunbeam's board unanimously approved Dunlap's plans for restructuring. Those beneath Dunlap on Sunbeam's corporate ladder offered equally little resistance. To be sure, rank and file employees in particular typically think of themselves as powerless. But this was a case of downsizing in the extreme, and still there was no screaming and yelling, and no organizing to protest what turned out to be widespread layoffs. Finally, there was Dunlap's management team, his closest aides, every one of whom was craven, who did as he was told, no matter how mean the message or the messenger.

The fact is that no one had the fortitude to call Dunlap privately or publicly to account, either as chief executive of a company in trouble or as leader of a business on which many thousands depended for their livelihoods. Nor did anyone who was anyone dare take a stand by resigning in protest.[32] Clearly, this was not for lack of options. Members of his management team and members of the board especially could have chosen another course, such as quitting Sunbeam altogether or trying their utmost to modify Dunlap's behavior from within.[33] The fact that they did nothing to stop or at least slow Dunlap's bad leadership made virtually certain it would continue until both he and the company tanked.

The importance of being a follower notwithstanding, the popular leadership literature still suggests that leaders matter and followers do not. As earlier indicated, this does not mean that followers are in any obvious way put down. In fact, in keeping with the point I made about words like *empowerment*, leaders are encouraged now to take their followers into account and to treat them well. They are further encouraged to gain voluntary, as opposed to forced, compliance. When Daniel Goleman and his colleagues write, "Great leaders move us. They ignite our passions and inspire the best in us," that's what they have in mind: followers who follow because following is what they want to do.[34] But let's be clear: since the leadership industry sells to those who would be leaders, not followers, its products are crafted so as to attract this particular customer base. The title of Goleman's book is *Primal Leadership*—not *Primal Followership*. And, as the book jacket makes clear, the intended audience is the "leader in any walk of life," not the follower.

In fact, the appetite for books on leadership and management is now so great that many if not most have the sexier of the two words, *leadership*, right in the title. And many if not most imply, if they do not so say outright, that if you read this book, you will increase the likelihood of your becoming a leader—or you will increase the likelihood of your becoming a better leader than you are now. While the focus on leadership and management began during the first half of the twentieth century, with writers and thinkers like Mary Parker Follett, Chester Barnard, and Peter Drucker paving the way, the outburst of interest is more recent, beginning only in the 1980s. This was the decade during which books with the word *leader* or *leadership* directly in the title began to flood the marketplace (my own included)—for example, Warren Bennis's *On Becoming a Leader* and John Kotter's *The Leadership Factor*. Both books distinguished between leaders and managers; and both similarly claimed the first were more important than the second.[35] A decade or so later, the literature on leadership expanded still further, now including, among countless others, Ronald Heifetz's *Leadership Without Easy Answers* and James Kouzes and Barry Posner's *The Leadership Challenge*. Both of these books dealt of course with leaders, but also with the contextual complexities of exercising power, authority, and influence.[36] More recently, practitioners have climbed on the bandwagon. To take just one of many examples, Rudolph Giuliani wrote *Leadership*, in which he claimed, among other things, that leadership is a capacity that can be acquired. "Leadership does not simply happen," Giuliani wrote. "It can be taught, learned, developed."[37]

As noted, there has been a slight shift: followers are finally getting more attention. In particular, there is a gradually growing interest in the leader-follower relationship, as opposed to an interest in leaders only. Still, much more often than not, the work in this general area is leadercentric. The question that still seems most to interest us is how leaders can impact on their followers, not the other way around. By making followers the effect rather than the cause, one could reasonably argue that experts contribute considerably to the conventional wisdom that leaders are all-important, while followers are unimportant.[38]

My intention is not to diminish the leadership literature or the leadership schools, institutes, centers, courses, seminars, workshops, and programs this literature sustains. Rather, it is to point out that the canvas on which we paint is simply too small. It should hold more than a single looming figure, the leader. It should be enlarged to accommodate followers as well.

Focus on Followers

We know that during roughly the first half of the twentieth century, the gradually developing literature on leadership and management presumed that superiors did, and should, control their subordinates. While the growth of large organizations gave rise to an increasing interest in how those with power, authority, and influence related to those without—particularly in the workplace—no one questioned the pecking order. Rather, the ranks and roles associated with organizational hierarchies were seen as the natural order of things.

To be sure, some early students of leadership and management, Follett and Barnard, for example, were concerned about the general welfare, as opposed to the welfare of only a few.[39] Moreover, several social science experiments in the late 1930s and early 1940s explored the different effects of democratic and authoritarian leadership styles on the behaviors of group members.[40] So it is not as if followers were excluded from the discussion altogether. Still, to prompt serious study of followers in their own right, it took another kind of circumstance altogether. It took genocide to get scholars systematically to consider this question: Why do followers follow their leaders?

Professor Stanley Milgram was once asked why he conducted his famous—or, maybe more accurately, infamous—experiments on obedience to authority. He said it was the Holocaust that made him want to understand better how ordinary people could act so "callously and inhumanely." As he put it years later, the question that haunted him was, "Under what conditions could a person obey, when commanded, actions that went against conscience?"[41]

The murder of millions by the Nazis during the Second World War motivated some of America's most prominent social scientists, Milgram among them, to study man's inhumanity to man. They recognized what I earlier described as the not-so-obvious: that, our obsession with Hitler notwithstanding, the Holocaust was not his handiwork alone. Rather, it was the consequence of orders obeyed, directly and indirectly, by millions of apparently ordinary Germans.

Obedience is not by definition something to be abjured. To the contrary: some measure of obedience or at least compliance is necessary for the effective performance of nearly all groups and organizations. Moreover, under certain circumstances, in the heat of battle, for example, near-blind obedience is essential. But as the Nazi regime receded into the past, the question of how it happened that one of the most highly educated and culturally sophisticated peoples in the world "supported and even cheered the bestial schemes of their deranged leaders" became more compelling.[42] In addition, it had become glaringly apparent perhaps for the first time that those who obey orders play as important a role in human affairs as those who issue them.

Milgram's experiments on obedience, conducted mainly in the early 1960s, are the most important ever conducted on followership. But the interest in the Holocaust—and in Germans more particularly—began years earlier. In America during the 1940s, probably the best-known book on the subject was Erich Fromm's *Escape from Freedom*.[43] Fromm, himself an émigré from Nazi Germany, developed a theory of the "sado-masochistic character" as it related to totalitarian leadership. His basic notion was that since the demise of the medieval church-state, which dominated the social order in the Middle Ages, Europeans especially were searching for a new source of authority. In other words, the rhetoric of the enlightenment notwithstanding, Fromm argued that people did not necessarily want to be free. Above all, and particularly during hard times, they wanted to be taken care of, to be protected. This, he maintained, is why Germans in the early 1930s, beset first by their defeat in World War I and then by the Depression, followed Hitler, no matter where he led.[44]

Another important book on this general subject was *The Authoritarian Personality*.[45] Published in 1950, it made an argument similar to Fromm's. Using social scientific tools such as interviews and attitude scales, the authors developed a measure that tested people for potential fascism, and found there was an authoritarian "pattern," not very different from Fromm's sadomasochistic character. In other words, both of the above-mentioned books described followers who achieved their "social adjustment by taking pleasure in obedience and subordination."[46]

Years later the two books came under attack for various reasons, above all for what came to be seen as the simplistic and even dangerous suggestion that there were personality types such as "sadomasochistic" and "authoritarian," and that these could be broadly associated with a particular people—for example, the Germans.[47] But their intellectual impact was considerable—and they certainly set the stage for Milgram's study of obedience.

There were other reasons Milgram conducted his experiments in the early 1960s. They coincided roughly with the trial in Israel of Nazi war criminal Adolph Eichmann and with the publication of Hannah Arendt's controversial but important book on the subject, *Eichmann in Jerusalem*.[48] Arendt insisted that Eichmann and his ilk were not monsters or aberrations of any kind. Rather, she claimed, they were more or less ordinary bureaucrats who murdered Jews not because they were virulently anti-Semitic, but because they were doing what they were told to do—they were following orders. Hence Arendt's famous phrase, "the banality of evil."

Milgram's experiments have been widely described in the social scientific literature; and there is a film that shows the experiments as they were actually being conducted.[49] Here, then, I will describe his work—undertaken initially at Yale University but eventually repeated in different places and involving more than a thousand participants—only briefly.[50]

The setup was simple. Two people came to a lab to take part in what they were told was a study of memory and learning. One was designated the "teacher" and the other the "learner." The experimenter, properly dressed for the occasion in a white lab coat, proceeded to describe the study, which ostensibly was about the effect of punishment on learning. Then the learner was led into a room and seated in a chair. His arms were strapped to prevent excessive movement, and an electrode was attached to his wrist. He was told that he was to memorize a list of word pairs, but that whenever he made an error, he would receive electric shocks of increasing intensity.

However, the real focus of the experiment was the teacher. After watching the learner being strapped into place, the teacher was led from the room and seated before a large shock generator. He was told that the thirty switches in front of him, over which he would have complete control, could inflict on the learner shocks of increasing intensity, all the way up to 450 volts. What the teacher did not know was that the learner was really an actor, who in fact would be receiving no shocks at all. As Milgram put it, the purpose of the experiment was "to see how far a person will proceed in a concrete and measurable situation in which he is ordered to inflict increasing pain on a protesting victim."[51] In other words, at what point, if any, would people follow the dictates of their own conscience and defy the man in the position of authority, the experimenter?

The results of Milgram's experiments were appalling. Not one of the subjects refused to administer a shock. And a substantial proportion were willing to administer the last shock on the generator, even though what they were hearing from the other room, from the presumed learners, were escalating cries of pain and discomfort that ended finally either in agonizing screams or in a deadly silence. To be sure, the shocks were not lightly inflicted. Many of the subjects experienced intense conflict between wanting to quit and wanting to continue, if only because the experimenter was enjoining them to do so. Nevertheless, what became terribly clear is that under the "right" circumstances only a few of us have what it takes to defy authority. What this meant to Milgram was that "ordinary people, simply doing their jobs, and without any particular hostility on their part, can become agents in a terrible destructive process."[52]

We now know that under ordinary circumstances followers tend to obey their leaders. What we know as a result of Milgram's experiments is that under *extraordinary* circumstances followers tend to obey the orders of their leaders—even when they consider such orders to be badly misguided or morally wrong. As a result of other studies along similar lines—such as the well-known Stanford Prison Experiment, conducted in 1971 by Philip Zimbardo, in which within days some college students were turned

into brutal guards while others became weak and despondent prisoners—
we know that perfectly natural patterns of dominance and deference can
be downright disheartening. In short, what we have learned is that certain
social settings, from Auschwitz to Abu Ghraib, contaminate both superiors
and their subordinates.[53]

TIMES CHANGE

Both before and after the Second World War, the most important question
in the field of leadership and management was, How can superiors get
their subordinates to do what they want them to do? While the leadership
field has now distanced itself from hierarchical models that assume command and control, it still remains stuck on leaders.

But in the real world, the world outside the academy and outside the
leadership field, there are signs of change. These signs of change—Zbigniew Brzezinski refers to a "global political awakening"—are so significant that those of us with any interest at all have no choice but to pay
attention.[54] *The fact is that followers are gaining power and influence while leaders are losing power and influence.* Which brings us to why: what is it about
this moment in time that favors those of lower rank over those of higher?
Before I turn to this question, which I do in the next chapter, here are just
a few examples of what I have in mind.

The first is from Israel. The second intifada—yet another wave in the
cycle of violence between the Israelis and Palestinians—began in September
2000. One of its characteristics was the use of suicide bombers by the
Palestinians against the Israelis, to which the Israelis responded by engaging
in "targeted killings," to eliminate the most militant leaders in the West Bank
and Gaza Strip. While the Israeli military usually carried out such attacks
without any repercussions, in 2002 there was an incident that aroused
public ire. An Israeli Air Force plane dropped a one-ton bomb on the house
of a particular target, killing him, his family, and some neighbors as well.
In all, fourteen Palestinians died in the attack, eight of whom were children.

In the wake of the civilian casualties, and in response to the public
condemnations, the chief of the Israeli Air Force, General Dan Halutz,
publicly defended his pilots. In an interview he said to his men, "Your ex-

ecution was perfect. Superb . . . You did exactly what you were instructed to do."[55] But, however well intended, Halutz's comments were judged a callous and even arrogant response to what the Americans call "collateral damage." So after another similar incident, in which more innocent civilians died, twenty-seven Israeli Air Force pilots had enough. They came to the conclusion that since targeted killings were imprecise, such attacks should be considered "immoral and illegal."

Israeli pilots are typical in that they are part of a strict military hierarchy: they are expected to obey the orders of their superiors, especially in times of crisis. But in response to the collateral killings, the twenty-seven pilots drafted a "moral statement." It was directed at Halutz and was intended to bring to an end "the turning of pilots into controlled machines and into criminals." Moreover, they used the media to make their case to the people, affirming their deep loyalty to the state of Israel while at the same time declaring they would neither "harm innocent civilians" nor carry out orders that were "blatantly illegal."

The response was predictable. The military angrily defended its position. Left-wing activists supported the pilots. And politicians on the right condemned them. To this response from the right, however, there was a striking exception: Prime Minister Ariel Sharon.

Sharon did not by any means bestow on the pilots his blessing. In fact, he called their resistance a "very grave matter." Moreover, in the short term, several pilots paid a heavy price for breaking the rules, including expulsion from the military for refusing to obey orders to engage in more targeted killings. However, over the long term, the twenty-seven pilots had an impact far greater than they could have expected. While it is impossible to say exactly what determined Sharon's stunning decision several months later to disengage from Gaza by the summer of 2005, there seems to be a connection. In explaining Sharon's outright reversal of a policy he had long championed, one of his closest advisers, Dov Weisglass, said that by the fall of 2003 Sharon had come to see Israel as "stuck." The economy was stagnating, and relations with Palestinians were continuing to deteriorate. Then, Weisglass continued, "We were hit with letters of officers and letters of pilots and letters of commandos." These men were not "weird kids with green ponytails and a ring in their noses who give off a strong odor of grass." Rather, they were Israel's "finest young people," young people who had reached a breaking point.[56] In other words, by refusing to go along, and by using clever tactics such as standing together, going public, and making their case on moral grounds, these subordinates affected their superiors.

Of course followers who break rank are hardly typical—most go along with what their leaders want and intend. But this single story is emblematic. And it substantiates one of the claims I make in this book: *those who lack obvious sources of power, authority, and influence are not usually helpless. Many can and do find ways of being heard.*

Here are some other examples, indicators of how times are changing in the United States. The first is the story of what happened at the 2006 graduation ceremonies of New School students. A vocal minority protested in anger that Senator John McCain was keynote speaker, particularly because of his support for the war in Iraq. Who really upset them, though, was not McCain, but New School President Bob Kerrey, who had the temerity to choose McCain without consulting them. As one of the students put it, "This invitation was a top-down decision that did not take into account the desires and interests of the student body on an occasion that is supposed to honor us all."[57] This student protest paled in comparison with those taking place at about the same time at Gallaudet University. Many months of campus unrest, started by students but not confined to them, finally obliged members of the university's board to withdraw their choice of a new president, of whom they strongly disapproved. While there had been some students and faculty on the search committee, they claimed they were ignored. And so they vowed to fight to the finish, until the board's decision was reversed. They did—and it was.

Then there is the story of what happened in 2007 to talk show host or, if you prefer, shock jock Don Imus. He had long been outrageous, but on this one occasion he was more outrageous than usual. By referring to the Rutgers women's basketball team as "nappy-headed ho's," he offended nearly everyone, and women and African Americans in particular. Still, for a couple of days nothing much happened. It seemed as if his remark would go largely unnoticed and certainly unpunished. But then the tide turned. Within a few more days, after the video and transcript were posted on the Web and played over and over and over again, and after an e-mail blast was sent to several hundred reporters, and after bloggers started to weigh in, the "digital brush fire" could no longer be contained.[58] In spite of his apologies, Imus was under relentless attack—by swarms of people with far less power and influence than he. Staffers at NBC, who were unexpectedly angry and outspoken, led the charge to "dump Don." As one NBC News executive put it, "We went out and created diversity in our newsrooms and we empowered employees to say what they think. And they're telling us."[59]

Don Imus was not, of course, a leader in the conventional sense of this word. But he was an opinion leader or, as *Newsweek* put it, "one of the media powerhouses of the age." Nevertheless, those who wanted him down and out came together in various ways—literally, virtually—so as to give Imus's employers nearly no choice but to get rid of him immediately. Lesson learned? "In earlier eras he would almost certainly have withstood the storm, but 2007 is a different time."[60]

Finally there was the time the "grass roots roared, and an immigration plan fell."[61] Monique Thibodeaux was an example of an ordinary citizen who joined with countless other ordinary citizens to defeat, if only temporarily, an immigration bill that was so contentious it motivated legions of angry voters in some way to act. An office manager at a towing company in suburban Detroit, Thibodeaux and many thousands like her decided in 2007 to get involved. They made calls and sent e-mail messages to senators around the country—and urged their friends to do the same. The idea that some 12 million illegal immigrants would be granted a path to citizenship was enough to spark what the *New York Times* called "a furious rebellion among many Republican and even some Democratic voters, who were linked by the Internet and encouraged by radio talk show hosts." Advocacy groups played their part as well. Groups such as NumbersUSA whipped up and organized their constituencies and managed to sign up seven thousand new members in a single week. For its part, Grassfire.org, a conservative Internet group, called for volunteers for a petition drive and instructed anyone with any interest on how to barrage lawmakers with telephone calls and e-mails. The result of this relentless offensive was to derail a bill that had been cobbled together only with great difficulty.

The fact that some of these same individuals and groups later reversed themselves, thereby managing to resurrect a measure already declared dead, only underscores the point: people power has the potential to be greater now than ever before. Within days it can, nearly single-handedly, turn things around. There is, in any case, a growing sense of entitlement, a growing sense that leadership should in fact be "distributed." In turn, there is the inevitable counterpart: leaders who are more vulnerable now to being pushed and pulled in every direction.

Nowhere is this as much in evidence as in America's corporate sector. In 2005 *BusinessWeek* ran a cover story that made the point. Titled "The Boss on the Sidelines: How Auditors, Directors, and Lawyers Are Asserting Their Power," the piece was about how players other than the CEO "are more powerful than ever." Whereas in the past, members of boards, for example, usually exercised their power as watchdogs only in moments of crisis, now times are different. Now the "chumminess and banter" of the past have given way to a "more adversarial attitude" that, in turn, has led to the toppling of top corporate leaders such as Fannie Mae CEO Franklin Raines, Boeing CEO Harry Stonecipher, Pfizer's CEO Hank McKinnell, and the legendary titan of AIG, Maurice "Hank" Greenberg. Of course, professionals including auditors, directors, and lawyers are not the only ones now intruding on chief executive officers. Shareholders have also become more restive, thereby threatening corporate leaders who in the past could afford to be nearly impervious to their preferences. The bottom line is that while CEOs remain in charge, their power is diminished. As *BusinessWeek* put it, the age of the corporate monarch is over.[62] No wonder that, for reasons both voluntary and not, CEO turnover is at an all-time record.[63] In fact, one 2007 estimate is that nearly half of American firms will have a new CEO in the next four years.[64]

Moreover, the impression that executives are increasingly beleaguered transcends the top office. Leaders and mangers at every level are being targeted by those around them, those above and those below. "Tough global competition, more diligent regulators, increasingly engaged boards of directors, and demanding investors have combined to create an environment in which new hires have to show results almost from Day One."[65] Leaders and managers are vulnerable even when the sin they commit would in years past be considered no more than a misstep. The chief executive of Home Box Office, Chris Albrecht, was forced to resign three days after he was accused of assaulting his girlfriend in a Las Vegas parking lot. Todd S. Thomson, the head of Citigroup's global wealth management group, was obliged to depart over questions about his relationship with CNBC anchor Maria Bartiromo. And Wal-Mart fired Julie Roehm, its high-powered marketing executive, over allegations that she had accepted gifts from agencies and had an affair with a coworker.[66] This, then, is the bottom line: that position no longer affords protection, or at least not as much now as it did in the past.

The leader attribution error explains why we believe that leaders matter and followers do not. But explanations can be plausible without being accurate. As we have already started to see, in the real world followers have an impact. They have an impact if the role they play is a supporting one, or if they break rank, or even if they do nothing. For this good and simple reason, thinking leadership without thinking followership is not merely misleading, it is mistaken.

CHAPTER 2

Facts

THIS IS THE TIME of the follower. It's not that over the course of human history those without power, authority, and influence have had no impact at all. In fact, some change has always been created by those in subordinate roles rather than by those in superior ones. Still, the twenty-first century is destined to be different. Instead of leaders calling most every shot, followers will have more of a say, more often, than they ever did before.

The point is that things change. There has been a historical progression from times past, when the "great man" theory generally did apply, to now, when leaders are less able than they were before to be in complete control. In the West, at least, the ideas of the Enlightenment; the American and French Revolutions; nineteenth-century claims by those lower down to better treatment by those higher up, workers in particular; and, in the United States, twentieth-century demands for equal rights by African Americans, Native Americans, women, and more recently gays and lesbians, constitute a clear trajectory. At different times, different people with less of everything have demanded greater equity from those who had more.

This is not to deny the obvious: there always has been and always will be a divide between the haves and the have-nots, between those who have resources such as power and money and those who do not. But the haves are more vulnerable now—especially leaders. Whereas in the past the advantages they had were generally safe and secure, in today's world these are more slippery commodities, more likely to be wrested away. Captains of industry are closely monitored and constantly scrutinized. And their political counterparts, presidents and prime ministers, are relentlessly reviewed, increasingly resisted, and even easily threatened by a few terrorists with a few explosives. Try as they might, even the members of China's ostensibly all-powerful ruling class cannot completely contain bloggers who challenge them in ways unimaginable even a decade ago. It is this changing relationship, between putative leaders and their putative followers, to which we now turn.

NEW AND DIFFERENT

Followers came increasingly into their own beginning in the 1960s. Why? Because during the last half century, there were two great changes, both favoring those of lower rank over those of higher.[1]

The World the Sixties Made

Some three decades after the social and political upheavals of the late 1960s and early 1970s, Todd Gitlin observed that all Americans, those on the right as well as those on the left, still stood on soil tilled during that time. In fact, we now take for granted many attitudes and behaviors first associated with the counterculture. Symbolized on the surface by telling details—still with us are ponytailed ranchers and matrons in jeans—the impact of these years is difficult to overestimate. Specifically, political activists brought to an end the war in Vietnam; and, over time, they also secured major changes in the lives of African Americans, women, and gays and lesbians.[2] More generally, the 1960s and 1970s reinforced the unbridled individualism that Tocqueville had described more than a hundred years before. Gitlin commented on the legacy of this period as follows: "Today, on every political and cultural front, the question is not whether to question authority, but which authority to question."[3] How similar this sounds to Tocqueville as earlier quoted: "There is a general distaste for accepting any man's word as proof of anything."

The sociopolitical turmoil during the 1960s and 1970s was nothing if not inclusive. Initially protesters marched for civil rights and against the war in Vietnam. But soon there were other initiatives that evidenced the sweeping demand for change—and the growing resistance to authority. In the early 1970s, General Motors employees in Lordstown, Ohio, members of United Auto Workers Local 1112, engaged in a sort of guerrilla warfare, intended to slow down production and oppose what they viewed as management by terror.[4] In the mid-1970s, the newly formed Clamshell Alliance engaged in massive civil disobedience to oppose the construction of a nuclear energy plant near Seabrook, New Hampshire.[5] In the late 1970s, in Philadelphia, a young, dynamic street vendor and state legislator by the name of Milton Street led the city's Ad Hoc Committee on Housing and Neighborhood Revitalization to fight for fair housing, in part by organizing well-orchestrated disruptions of meetings at City Hall.[6] Clearly, some of these initiatives had leaders—Street, for example—as this word is generally conceived. But such leaders as they did have were not people in positions of authority; in fact, up to then they had been followers. Or put another way, whatever the impetus for change, it came from the bottom up rather than from the top down.

Arguably, it was on college campuses all across America that these changes were the most insistent and visible. What some consider "the assault" on the university began in 1964, with the student revolt on the Berkeley campus of the University of California. Berkeley was followed by Columbia in 1968, Harvard and Cornell in 1969, and Yale and Kent State in 1970. In fact, "during this same period some three hundred universities were the scene of student sit-ins, building takeovers, strikes, riots, and other forms of rebellious behavior." Student protests were of course not something altogether new. But what distinguished these efforts from those in the past is that they came from within the university itself and met with amazingly little resistance from either professors or administrators.[7]

To the satisfaction of some and the dismay of others, America's institutions of higher education would never again be the same. The old ways of behaving—for example, students deferring without question to faculty— went out the window. Moreover, conceptions of what constituted an appropriate curriculum were democratized, some would argue to a fault; and policies such as affirmative action transformed the very notion of who should be attending college in the first place. Finally, the idea of the campus as a proper place for protest became entrenched. Although the first decade of the twenty-first century is not known for widespread student activism, in fact more than half of the 2006 graduating class of Columbia University reported having joined one or another protest during their years at college.[8]

The most recent of our cultural revolutions did not come out of thin air, any more than did those that preceded it. The history of the left in the United States has been cyclical: periods of flourishing activism typically followed by periods in which protest activity is almost invisible.[9] In addition, however egalitarian and empowering their messages, the sixties and seventies left a legacy that was challenged for years to come. Prominent critics such as Harvey Mansfield considered the upheavals and changes that were the result—the sexual revolution among them—"a comprehensive disaster for America."[10] More broadly, the revolution triggered a counterrevolution. That is, in the beginning the modern conservative movement was simply a reaction to the unsettling times that immediately preceded it.

Still, whatever the controversies, those who debate the sixties and seventies generally agree that they engaged the ideals of freedom and equality with a vigor that was rarely seen before and has not been seen since.[11] Moreover, the multiple challenges to the existing order were so pervasive, and so persuasive, that it finally became impossible simply to return to what was. It is not as if the relationship between those with power, authority, and influence and those without was turned on its head. But it was a time during which the playing field was leveled, at least somewhat. And it was a time during which, whatever the problems, obedience to authority was not among them, at least not in the West.

The Information Revolution

An expert on leadership and management by the name of Harlan Cleveland was among the first to explore the connection between leading and managing on the one hand and the information revolution on the other. In a pamphlet published in 1997, he was prescient about the degree to which, as a result of "ever-faster computers and ever-more-reliable telecommunications," power would be more diffuse. More precisely, it would trickle down, away from leaders and toward followers.[12]

Cleveland understood that information, not things, had become the world's most powerful resource. But unlike things—land, for example—

information is impossible to hoard. It expands as it is used. It is easily transportable. It is transparent. And it leaks—the more we have, the more of us have it. Here, according to Cleveland, are just some of the implications of the information revolution, for leaders and followers in particular.

- Nobody anywhere will be in complete charge of anything.

- Diversity will change our conception of who can, and should, lead.

- Claims by disadvantaged majorities around the world will no longer be so easily denied.

- Followers everywhere will "get to the policy answers before their leaders do."

Cleveland was persuaded that people power was more important than ever before in part because of what happened after the collapse of the Soviet Union. "Look around the world," he wrote. "In those many, surprisingly peaceful, revolutions since 1989, the impatient crowds in Europe and Asia have been moved . . . by rapidly spreading information about neighbors who were obviously getting goods and services, more fairness in distributing them, and firmer guarantees of human rights, than their own bosses and planners seemed able to deliver." It was, Cleveland concluded in bold type, "the spread of knowledge" that will enable followers to play a much more powerful role in the future than they did in the past.[13]

Cleveland built on a distinction that Peter Drucker had made in 1966, between what he labeled "manual workers" and "knowledge workers."[14] Manual workers are the old-fashioned kind. They work with their hands, and they produce "stuff." Knowledge workers, in contrast, are new and different. They work with their heads, and they produce ideas and information that, in turn, generate a whole new kind of economy, a knowledge economy. For our purposes, the key point is that in knowledge economies competence can and often does trump position as an indictor of who in fact is leading and who in fact is following. For both superiors and their subordinates, the importance of competence, of expertise, changes not only the dynamic between them but also our conception of what leading and following actually entail.

Let me be clear here: the importance of the information revolution does not supercede in importance the generational changes of the 1960s and 1970s. Rather, the second builds on the first, so that by now, well into the twenty-first century, power relationships really are different—leaders being somewhat less powerful and followers somewhat more.

The Internet in particular has changed the dynamic between those who hold positions of power and authority and those who do not. The evidence is everywhere—for example, in higher education, where e-mail has leveled even further relations between students and their professors. Not so long ago, the former dared to approach the latter only in special situations. Now, though, even the most formidable instructors are just a keystroke away—and they can be contacted 24/7.[15]

In the broader realm of information and ideas, the picture we have had in our mind's eye, of the individual expert as a figure of authority, is becoming similarly antiquated. In its place is what James Surowiecki has called the "wisdom of crowds," the idea that the many are smarter than the few. It is collective rather than individual expertise, Surowiecki claims, that now "shapes business, economies, societies, and nations."[16] For example, in order to harness our collective intelligence, Wikipedia, the online encyclopedia currently considered the best in the world, invites everyone to contribute.[17]

Along similar lines, bloggers are making more of a difference than we could have imagined just a few years ago. And they are multiplying, fast: approximately 120,000 new Web logs are created each day, and the number of blogs now exceeds 70 million.[18] As a result, leaders around the world and in every sector are obliged to play offense and defense simultaneously. "The CEOs of the largest 50 companies in the world are practically hiding under their desks in terror about Internet rumors," says one top crisis manager.[19] Moreover, as *BusinessWeek* points out, most companies are wholly unprepared to deal with the new online nastiness. "That's worrisome as the Web moves closer to being the prime advertising medium—and reputational conduit—of our time."[20]

Here's an example: e-mail protests are considered a "new force in advertising," which, in turn, can pressure even the most complacent of CEOs into full retreat.[21] A recent target was Dolce & Gabbana. The high-fashion house had run a print ad showing a bare-chested man pinning a glamorously dressed woman to the ground by her wrists, as three other men looked on. The ad drew widespread criticism from consumers in several countries, including the United States and Italy; as a result, within just a few short months, Dolce & Gabbana decided to withdraw it. Of course, consumers are not followers in the usual sense of this word. But in this day and age, they can constitute an advocacy group, enabled by the Internet to exert power and influence. In fact, advocacy groups or interest groups of all kinds "have become experts at using the Web to mobilize consumers or group members into action as a way to promote their issues or point of view."

The Web threatens big business in other ways as well. Historically, it was large companies that were able to afford the latest innovations, and that reaped the benefits of greater efficiency, higher sales, and expansions into distant markets. But now this pattern is being challenged by the second wave of Internet technologies. "That means a cost leveling that puts small companies on equal footing with big ones, making it easier for upstarts to innovate, disrupt industries and even get big fast."[22]

Of course, the information revolution has had every bit as much of an impact on the public sector as on the private one. Consider the trend in just two countries: China and the United States.

Although executives from Yahoo!, Google, Microsoft, and Cisco have been pilloried in recent years for cooperating with Chinese officials trying to crack down on political dissidents, the information they seek to control is, in any case, impossible for the state to contain completely.[23] By now the Internet is just too big and too complex. In China, in fact, the Web has already assumed to some extent the watchdog role filled in freer countries by the media.[24]

To be sure, the Chinese government is serious in its effort to suppress: it employs somewhere between thirty thousand and fifty thousand people to police the Internet, and everyone in China who has personal Internet access is required to register his or her name and phone number. Moreover, the government has sentenced for up to ten years some of the most conspicuous of the cyberdissidents.[25] Still, the pressures notwithstanding, savvy Chinese use proxy software to reach forbidden sites; and "hacktivists," some of whom are based abroad, know how to circumvent the system completely. One such group, "Freegate," constantly changes the address of its U.S. servers so that Chinese censors find it impossible to block the connection.[26] In any case, bloggers are finding ways to break through the barriers faster than they can be set up. By posting an open letter on his Internet blog, Zou Tao, a resident of Shenzhen, managed to launch a daring grassroots campaign to tamp down overheated property prices. He attracted attention across China, received tens of thousands of letters of support, and further inflamed already existing resentments against greedy developers and local authorities.[27] Similarly, bloggers were the first to draw attention to what ultimately became a big story about Wu Ping, a "simple homeowner" who "stared down" the forces of the large-scale developers sweeping across China.[28] The bottom line: text messages, instant messaging, Internet bulletin boards, and individual bloggers make it difficult, if not impossible, for Chinese officials to exert full control. The implication boggles the mind: those without formal sources of power and influence nevertheless now have access to both.[29]

The long-term effect of the Internet on American politics is less clear. What we can say though is this: since Howard Dean's campaign for president in 2004, which was the first to prove to the polity the power of the Internet, a transformation has taken place. Both Democrats and Republicans have sharply increased their use of technology—e-mail, interactive Web sites, candidate and party blogs, text messaging—in order to more effectively raise money, assemble crowds, and get out the vote.[30] In the early months of the 2008 presidential campaign, it was Barack Obama who capitalized on the new technology most effectively, which explains in good part why he was able to seriously challenge Hillary Clinton, who up to then was the clear front-runner. By April 2007 Obama had raised $6.9 million using the Internet, compared to only $4 million by the Clinton campaign.[31] Moreover, Obama did very well in cyberspace more generally. Not long after he announced he was running for president, some forty-eight thousand members of the wildly popular social-networking site MySpace had added Obama as a "friend," while only twenty-five thousand had "befriended" Clinton. While numbers like these might seem small, for those convinced of the Internet's long-term political importance, no Web trend, including YouTube, is too trivial to track.[32] The point, in any case, is this: in politics as in business, power and influence are flowing from the center to the periphery. The Internet in particular disadvantages those on top and out front, and advantages those who for one reason or another decide to take them on.

Finally, there is technology as a global phenomenon, spanning countries and cultures without regard for traditional boundaries of any kind. Case in point: a David by the name of Amit Srivastava, who works out of his small home in El Cerrito, California. Srivastava spearheads Global Resistance, an international web of activists who have challenged no less a Goliath than Coca-Cola, particularly its operations in India. With meager resources that include little more than a laptop, a fax machine, and a telephone calling card, Srivastava flagged a possible connection between Coca-Cola and the degradation of the Indian environment—for example, the water supply. As a result largely of his efforts (Srivastava's Web site draws more than twenty thousand visitors a month), Global Resistance has chalked up some major successes. Coca-Cola, in turn, has been forced to defend itself all across India, in courts and in legislatures.[33] So much for the great divide between those with power, authority, and influence and those without!

LEADERS LIVING DANGEROUSLY

In the spring of 2006 there was an article in the *New York Times* titled "It's Hard out There for a Leader in the West."[34] Illustrated by large headshots of President George W. Bush, Prime Minister Tony Blair, President Jacques Chirac, and Prime Minister Silvio Berlusconi, one appeared more tired and troubled than the next. No wonder. The point of the piece was that Western leaders across the board were suffering from "power fatigue." Faced with track records that were mixed at best, persisting problems nearly impossible to solve, and a series of embarrassing scandals, these leaders found no obvious solace. Above all, not one of the four was particularly well liked or even well respected. Whatever the various signs—approval ratings in steep decline, a series of humiliating defeats, protests in which hundreds of thousands took to the streets—they were not good.

To some degree, the public mood was the result of events beyond anyone's control. Bush had been slammed twice, first by Osama and then by Katrina. Blair faced fallout from his early alliance with the Bush administration, which was making one mistake after the next. Chirac inherited the problem of restless young people, both in France's immigrant suburbs and in its big cities. And Berlusconi was also faced with a problem that was not, or at least not entirely, of his own making: the underperforming Italian economy.

At the same time, each of the four leaders had a hand in his own plight. Bush's personal rigidity and at least intermittent incompetence had made two very bad situations—the war in Iraq and the aftermath of Katrina—even worse. Blair's unwavering loyalty to a man (Bush) and a cause (the war in Iraq) suggested a tin ear, at least so far as his own constituents were concerned. Chirac suffered a huge political defeat when he unnecessarily submitted Europe's draft constitution to a political referendum. And Berlusconi was known simply as the man of a thousand gaffes.

But whatever the circumstances, and however ineffectual were all four of these leaders some of the time, simultaneously they were situated in a larger context in which exercising leadership was hard, even harder than it used to be. We know, of course, that leadership, democratic leadership in particular, has never been easy to exercise. Most American presidents could readily testify to the fact that neither declines in approval ratings nor humiliating public defeats are unfamiliar. But what has changed is the time in which we live. First, leaders have been demystified, in part by the modern media, which demands grist for its mill 24/7; and in part by the modern culture, in which figures of authority are no longer exalted or even much respected. Second, because the line between the leader and the led has been blurred, the led have been emboldened.

This trend is everywhere in evidence, at home and abroad, in business and in government. Leaders at every level are more vulnerable now than they were in the past to forces beyond their control. And if they go wrong or do wrong, they are more prone to being punished and to being evicted from their position of power.

Case in point: the unhappy saga of former president of the World Bank, Paul Wolfowitz. Before taking over at the bank, Wolfowitz was deputy secretary of defense under Donald Rumsfeld, and strongly associated with President Bush's decision to invade Iraq. Given this history, and given the fact that many of the bank's employees are known to be liberal in their leanings, Wolfowitz had a problem from the get-go. But by all accounts, he compounded an already difficult situation by exhibiting a management style that was both insular and imperious. As a result, once it became known that he was involved in discussions on promotions and pay hikes for a previous bank employee, who just happened to be a woman with whom he was having a personal relationship, his goose was cooked. What made the story so compelling, so telling, is that on the one side there was Wolfowitz, a leader determined to cling to power in spite of what quickly became overwhelming opposition; and on the other side there were his subordinates, men and women at every level of the organization who refused to be quiet and go away until Wolfowitz was out.[35]

From day one those involved in what the *Financial Times* called a "staff rebellion" were not to be moved.[36] When the story broke, the World Bank Group Staff Association promptly issued a statement demanding of Wolfowitz that he step down: "The president must acknowledge that his conduct has compromised the integrity and effectiveness of the World Bank Group and has destroyed the staff's trust in his leadership. He must act honorably and resign."[37] Soon thereafter forty members of the bank's anticorruption team came out and declared that the controversy over Wolfowitz's behavior was making it difficult, if not impossible, for them to do their work. They flat out said to the bank's board that it should take "clear and decisive actions to resolve this crisis," which was undermining the bank's "credibility and authority to engage" on the corruption issue.[38] The attacks from below continued, including also a rebuke of Wolfowitz from the bank's most powerful oversight committee and a call for his resignation from one of his two top deputies. Finally, after six weeks of being publicly pilloried by those who were supposed to be following his lead, Wolfowitz gave up and agreed, however reluctantly, to resign.

To reiterate, some of this is cyclical. This is obviously not the first time in human history that those of lower rank have wrested power, authority, and influence from those higher up. In fact, there are some moments in time when the unrest is widespread, when it transcends groups, organizations, and even nation-states. In the late eighteenth century, the American and French Revolutions, although an ocean apart, broke out within just over a decade of each other. In the mid-nineteenth century, Karl Marx and Friedrich Engels published *The Communist Manifesto*; and at virtually the same moment (both appeared in 1848), Elizabeth Cady Stanton and others issued the *Declaration of Sentiments*. And in the mid-twentieth century, Martin Luther King's *Letters from a Birmingham Jail* appeared in the exactly the same year, 1963, as did Betty Friedan's *The Feminine Mystique*. There was no collusion here. Marx and Engels had no obvious connection with Stanton, nor did King in any way engage with Friedan. But when great minds think alike at virtually the same time, it's more than mere co-incidence. In all of these cases there was a *Zeitgeist*, a particular mood at a particular moment—here the insistence that power be more widely distributed.

While the twenty-first century is in some fundamental ways different from those that preceded it, it is also in some fundamental ways the same. Always the question is, How exactly do people with less power, authority, and influence wrest some away from those who have more? Are these commodities voluntarily redistributed? Or are they always taken by force, even if only by the force of public opinion?

As a general rule, power holders are not willing to share. The power they have they want to keep—to wit, Paul Wolfowitz. This means the re-distribution of power is a process, nearly always contested, in which those with less somehow oblige those with more to surrender at least some. It's a fight, sometimes, but not always, initiated and then led by a few individuals who play key roles. Obviously, King and Friedan played famously promi-nent parts in the modern American civil rights and women's movements, respectively. But at the start neither had much power or influence, and neither occupied a prominent position of authority. Rather, it was their willingness to resist the haves—whites and men, respectively—and their abil-ity to motivate others to do the same that over time created change.

Business

In times past, labor unions took on big business. During the late 1940s and 1950s, for example, many of America's top corporate leaders had no choice but to negotiate with their union counterparts, labor leaders who championed the interests of their constituencies. But by and large, unions failed to adapt adequately to the changing times, and so they are past their prime. In 2006 the president of the once powerful United Automobile Workers, Ron Gettelfinger, told his members that while bad management and falling auto sales had contributed to the decline of the automobile in-dustry, so did they. Among other things, the generous health-care benefits for which the union had fought so hard were contributing to costs now considered "unsustainable."[39]

To be sure, the American labor movement is not moribund. Some of the old unions still fight the good fight; and there are new ones, such as those representing white-collar professionals including physicians, nuclear engineers, psychologists, and judges.[40] But in the main, big challenges to big business now come from a series of stakeholders who, while previously content to go along, are now fed up. Above all, they are fed up with a corporate culture that since the 1970s has bred scandal; and that since roughly the same time has tolerated and even encouraged the redistribution of power and wealth from the many, workers and stockholders in particular, to the few, to those at the very top of the corporate ladder.[41] Lee Scott, for example, the president and CEO of Wal-Mart, has been earning roughly two thousand times the salary of the average Wal-Mart worker.[42]

During the last couple of decades, most CEOs had the benefit of free rein. Boards of directors were the most obvious sluggards, often failing to do what they were supposed to do: mind the man (rarely a woman) who was minding the store. In some cases the problem was board members too familiar and too friendly with top management. But in others it was sheer ineffectualness. For example, on the Enron and Tyco boards, "directors consistently deferred to company executives instead of challenging them." They discouraged debate and disagreement instead of cultivating it; and while in their own worlds these directors had strong opinions and a forthright manner, in a room together they were something else entirely. They were meek and they were mild.[43]

But in the last few years, things have changed, at least slightly. Many members of many boards, who once behaved like followers in thrall to their leaders, are no longer willing, nor do they any longer dare, to play that role. Consider the case of Conseco, in which board members have now taken it on themselves to use "tally sheets" to determine how much their CEO is really being paid. Or the case of Integral Systems, in which one board member, deeply offended by the company's policy on executive compensation, provided investors with a scathing paper trail that detailed in full her litany of complaints. Or the case of Tenet Healthcare, where a former director went public with his objections to the company's executive bonus program, declaring it would reward the CEO, even without "any improvement in results."[44] Or the case of Boeing, in which, to spare the company further embarrassment, the board unceremoniously dumped its chief executive officer, Harry Stonecipher, as soon as it became public that he was engaged in a personal relationship with a female executive, in spite of being married.

Note that these actions, however parallel in their general nature, are not the handiwork of a "great man," of a single individual leading the charge. Rather, they are the result of different people in different places deciding for different reasons at more or less the same time to refuse to roll over. Articles by the dozens—such as these in the *Wall Street Journal*, titled or subtitled "Independent Directors Strike Back," and "Move Over CEO—Here Come the Directors," and "What Boards Can Do to Ease Shareholder Anger Over Pay Packages"—testify to the fact that this movement is widespread and likely to have an impact on corporate governance for some time to come.[45]

I hasten to add that these changes are still too few and far between to transform the system altogether. Most CEOs, especially of major corporations, still earn enormous amounts of money, no matter their performance.[46] And some members of some boards have remained in place even after they were sued and publicly rebuked. Prominent directors of Hollinger International, for instance, such as Henry Kissinger and Richard Perle, stayed on the board after it was revealed how poorly they performed, with Perle in particular being accused of "abject failure to fulfill his fiduciary duties."[47] Still, it seems clear that more members of more boards are now determined to do the right thing. There are, of course, explanations for this shift in their position. Some have been publicly humiliated into taking action. Others, their consciousness now raised, are genuinely outraged by the systemic inequities. And still others fear being made in some way to pay if they fall down on the job. For example, shareholders irked with executive pay are increasingly taking it out on directors by "withholding" their votes for reelection from board members they hold responsible.[48] Sometimes the threat is direr: the former directors of WorldCom, who ultimately had to pay millions of dollars of their own money to settle with investors, set an example of what to avoid. The effect is the same: leaders on the line.

Shareholder activists, a term that just a few years ago was oxymoronic, have also evolved into a force more seriously to be reckoned with. On paper, of course, shareholders are the corporate owners to whom CEOs are ultimately accountable. But although in theory shareholders should all along have participated in some meaningful way at least in some aspects of the decision-making process, in practice they have famously followed where others, CEOs in particular, led. They failed even to rise up against "Soviet-style elections," which prohibited them from ousting directors, including those who were the most incompetent. Now, though, this is changing, again for several reasons, including technological innovations that enable individual shareholder activists to communicate and connect much more easily. There is, in any case, a surge in shareholder resolutions, and in companies that recognize that "the way the wind is blowing" favors shareholders who hang in and fight to be heard.[49] "Finally, Shareholders Start Acting Like Owners," trumpeted Gretchen Morgenson, financial columnist for the *New York Times*. In a 2006 column she noted that shareholders at no fewer than one hundred forty companies had finally claimed their right to be involved in the election of directors.[50] Challenges to executive pay are at an all-time high as well. In advance of the annual meetings in 2007, activist investors submitted shareholder proposals at some sixty companies seeking an advisory vote on executive pay. Targets included major corporations such as Citigroup, Wells Fargo, and Northrop Grumman.[51] In fact, some companies are ahead of the curve: Verizon and Blockbuster are among those in which nonbinding proposals to give investors a voice on executive pay have already been passed.[52]

It was toward the end of 2002, after the series of corporate scandals and the decline in investment portfolios, that things began to change. Every year since then, the number of shareholder challenges to management has risen dramatically. By now, in fact, shareholders have developed an appetite for activism. Think of the man in the chicken suit at the 2006 meeting of Home Depot, there to protest the outrageously high pay package of then CEO Robert Nardelli, who had presided over the company while its stock went down 12 percent. Not so terrible—unless you contrast it with the performance of Lowe's, Home Depot's chief competitor, whose stock during the same period rose 173 percent.

As it turned out, the man in the chicken suit was one among many thousands of Home Depot shareholders who were equally outraged by the management team technically in their employ. In fact, they were still fuming weeks after meeting, during which Nardelli had allowed neither questions nor vote counts, and which was attended by only one of the directors, Nardelli himself. As a result of all the noise, members of Home

Depot's management team decided they had better respond. They altered the rules for electing directors. They released vote tallies that made public the high percentage of shareholders who had withheld support from ten of the eleven directors. They promised at the next annual meeting to permit questions and to have in attendance more than one director. And Nardelli himself apologized for the way in which his meeting was conducted. But both he and his board were put on notice. What for the moment was a slap on the wrist threatened to become more serious. And so it did. Some months later, in January 2007, Nardelli's chicken came home to roost. His bad habit of being autocratic and ineffective all at the same time was, finally, enough to get him canned.

I should add that increasing shareholder activism is not confined only to small investors. Big holders are also behaving differently, using their investments to push for corporate change. In the 1980s challenges like these were resisted at all costs. But now corporate boards are adjusting to the new reality—to activist investors who are rich enough and powerful enough to change the face of corporate America. Billionaire financier Carl Icahn pushed Time Warner to buy back some of its shares, however reluctantly. Washington Redskins owner Daniel Snyder obliged Six Flags, the amusement park company, to put itself up for sale (after which he took over the board). Another enormously wealthy investor, Nelson Peltz, started a fund, Trian, which pursues what he calls "operational activism."[53] And two labor unions, the Indiana Electrical Workers Union and the Service Employees International Union, sued Hewlett-Packard for providing its former CEO, Carly Fiorina, with a $21.4 million severance package, which they maintained violated the company's policy on executive compensation.

The bottom line is that chief executive officers in particular are being watched as never before—by the media, by bloggers, by their own boards of directors, by shareholder activists, and by activists more generally. Gay rights activists made Bill Gates think twice about Microsoft's decision not to support a gay rights bill in Washington State. Retirees from Lucent Technologies, like retirees at other companies including Verizon Communications, General Electric, and Prudential Financial, organized to press their companies to adopt proposals that would restrict executive compensation.

In addition, there is the long arm of the law. Prosecutors, who once treated white-collar trials as "delicate affairs," have gotten tough. Backed by laws fresh on the books, such as Sarbanes-Oxley, but in the main by public opinion, still exercised by recent corporate scandals, prosecutors have transformed the way they operate in cases of white-collar crime. They handcuff defendants being brought in for booking, and they squeeze witnesses and threaten family members. Moreover, cases are no longer resolved only with a fine or a short stay in a "country club" prison. Instead, white-collar defendants face decades of real jail time, sentences that can preclude them from being considered for minimum-security prisons, and even stints in solitary confinement.[54] In fact, several former CEOs with sky-high profiles, Bernard Ebbers and Jeffrey Skilling, to take two of the most obvious examples, can look forward to little better than spending most of the rest of their lives in prison.

Bottom line: America's corporate leaders are like leaders more generally. In comparison with just a decade ago, they are easier targets—and we are readier to take aim and fire.

Government

While during the first decade of the twenty-first century there have been pockets of resistance and rebellion, such as the occasional protest on behalf of illegal aliens, in general Americans have been quiet. To be sure, there are exceptions. The genocide in Darfur, for example, has caught the attention of young people in particular, who are making something of a difference.[55] But with regard to the issue that defines the presidency of George W. Bush—the war in Iraq—there have been few public protests that were both visible and widespread. Anger over the war has been vented primarily on the Internet, through liberal activist groups such as MoveOn.org; and although various antiwar groups did finally join forces in early 2007 under an umbrella group called "Americans Against Escalation in Iraq," even it never really caught on or became very well known. (The distinction between the response to the war in Vietnam and the war in Iraq is usually attributed to the draft, which was the law of the land during the former but not the latter.)

In other parts of the world, though, things are different. There, people without obvious sources of power, authority, or influence are demanding to be heard and clamoring for change.

- In 2004 there was the "Orange Revolution," in Ukraine. The Orange Revolution was one in a sequence of peaceful democratic

upheavals, starting with the "Velvet Revolutions" in Central Europe
(after the collapse of the Soviet Union) in 1989, to the "Rose
Revolution" in Georgia in 2003. But what happened in Ukraine
was special. For the first time in its history, the country imprinted
itself, unforgettably, on the political consciousness of the world.
Vast crowds, made up in large part of young people with orange
scarves around their necks, gathered daily in subzero temperatures
in Kiev's Independence Square. They had assembled to protest the
government in general and President Leonid Kuchma in particular. This was not, though, a spontaneous outburst of public anger.
The Orange Revolution was extremely well planned. Seemingly
overnight, tents were pitched, unarmed sentries were posted, and
mounds of food and winter clothing were made available. Field
kitchens and medical aid stations were set up, instructions on civil
disobedience were provided, and an endless supply of orange posters,
banners, ribbons, flags, stickers, and badges were widely distributed. The protesters even made use of the Web—something new in
the history of East European Velvet Revolutions. In fact, as soon as
they erected their tents on Kiev's main shopping boulevard, they
announced their intentions on the Web in English. The revolu-
tionists succeeded, and brilliantly. They came to Independence
Square to demand a free and fair presidential election, and their
demand was met. In short order, Kuchma and his designated successor were gone, and a new, freely elected president was installed.[56]

- In 2005 there was the "Cedar Revolution," in Lebanon. The
  assassination of Prime Minister Rafik Hariri, a heinous act for
  which the Syrian government was thought to be at least partially
  responsible, sparked huge, daily demonstrations that signaled the
  Lebanese people were finally fed up. They were fed up with their
  Syrian-backed government and with the Syrian forces that for
  years had been parked on Lebanese soil. On the one-month anniversary of the prime minister's death, up to 1 million Lebanese,
  fully one-fourth of the population, streamed into downtown Beirut
  to demonstrate Lebanese unity and to protest Syrian intervention
  and occupation. Once again, the results were nearly immediate.
  Within weeks the Syrian-backed government fell. And the Syrian

troops, which had maintained a presence in Lebanon for nearly three decades, were finally forced out.

- In 2006 there was a "tectonic shift," in Nepal. Plans were for celebrations in Kathmandu to honor the anniversary of the democracy movement that fifteen years earlier had ushered in parliamentary rule. Instead, the city streets were filled with crowds of angry people, over three hundred thousand strong, who were protesting the monarchy. They demanded a constituent assembly that would redraft the constitution and reduce or even eliminate the king's still wide-ranging powers. It was a sea change in Nepalese politics. As one reporter put it, "What was once an untouchable reverence for the monarch seems to have vanished like clouds crossing over the mountains."[57] In fact, the dissatisfaction with the king and with the status quo he symbolized was now so great that the overwhelming majority of Nepalese, many of whom had no previous interest in politics, became invested in the process. Ordinary citizens flooded the streets and courted police beatings. Government workers staged work stoppages. And a coalition of Nepal's seven largest political parties called on teachers, bankers, transportation workers, and others to join the continuing protests. While the long-term consequences of this moment in the history of Nepal cannot yet be known, there is no question that the events of 2006 changed the political landscape. Once reverence for royalty has vanished "like clouds crossing over the mountains," it has likely vanished forever.

To be sure, the Orange and Cedar Revolutions look less "revolutionary" now than they did just a few years ago. But they were not trivial. Nor are they, along with Nepal, the only places on the planet in which people with political power and authority have been hounded by those without. A few brave souls have challenged the near-authoritarian leadership of Russian President Vladimir Putin. A few brave souls, women in particular, have marched and prayed and defied the authorities in different parts of Africa, in Zimbabwe, for example, where women fight for their rights at great personal risk to themselves. And in 2007 more than a few brave souls joined in protest against the military junta in Myanmar (Burma)—again at great personal risk to themselves—in what became known as the Saffron Revolution. But as indicated, it is China that provides the most striking example of a country in which followers—ordinary people who hold no high position—are demanding to be heard in a whole new way.

In 2005 angry villagers from a suburb of Shanghai crossed over mountains and through rice paddies to reach a pharmaceutical plant they maintained was a health hazard. As many as fifteen thousand people massed to wage a pitched battle against the authorities, overturning police cars and throwing stones, undeterred by the tear gas intended to disperse them. The point is that this particular riot was but one in the rising numbers of similar such protests. In 2004 there were approximately seventy-four thousand mass actions. While the details of each of the incidents vary, they share an accumulated anger at the corruption of local officials and at the failure of China's political system to respond to legitimate grievances.[58]

Among the most striking of the many examples are protests against China's long-standing policy of strict birth control. In 2007 there were new clashes between the police and locals in southwestern China, in which rioters smashed and burned government offices, overturned official vehicles, and clashed with the police in a series of confrontations that lasted for days. What had incited them was the government's renewed effort to control population growth by requiring mandatory health checks for women and forcing pregnant women who lacked approval to give birth to undergo abortions.[59]

All of this testifies to what must be recognized by those who pay attention to such things as a "global political awakening." To what exactly does this refer? As Zbigniew Brzezinski pointed out, this global political awakening is the newfound sense, by people nearly everywhere, that they have the right to human dignity and the right to be heard. It is, if you will, a social movement, albeit one that remains vague, ill formed, and poorly articulated. Still, it is real, fueled by the cumulative impact of literacy and mass communications. As Brzezinski further adds, the awakening is "socially massive, politically radicalizing, and geographically universal."[60] No wonder that leaders in different places and in different ways feel threatened by forces beyond their control.

China's political leaders are, for instance, doing what they can to contain the complaints. But given their interest in a rapidly growing economy, they seem to have concluded they must take the risk of political dissent. They seem also to have concluded that given their circumstance, any attempt to silence the opposition completely will be futile.

FOLLOWING FOLLOWERS

Finally, the academic marketplace is responding to the proposition I set forth at the beginning of this chapter: that this is the time of the follower. As it becomes obvious that today's leaders have less power and influence, and that today's followers have more, the literature on leadership and management is becoming slightly more expansive, to include a small body of work that focuses on subordinates, as opposed to superiors. By now there are at least two good books on followers, Robert Kelley's *The Power of Followership* and Ira Chaleff's *The Courageous Follower* (both were written to empower subordinates, especially in the workplace).[61] And the number of articles in academic literature is increasing as well. For example, "The Link Between Leadership and Followership" appeared in the *Personality and Social Psychology Bulletin*.[62] "The Role of Followers in the Charismatic Leadership Process" appeared in the *Academy of Management Review*.[63] And "Rethinking Followership: A Post-Structuralist Analysis of Follower Identities" appeared in the *Leadership Quarterly*.[64] Moreover, publications oriented toward practice, such as the Harvard Business School's newsletter, *Working Knowledge*, now regularly feature short pieces that address the question of how subordinates should relate to their superiors. Titles include "Understand What Motivates Your Boss" and "Do I Dare Say Something?"[65] Even the *Harvard Business Review*, a publication clearly targeted at superiors, as opposed to subordinates, now pays attention to the latter as well as to the former. In 2007 it featured an article titled "What Your Leader Expects of You" and subtitled "And What You Should Expect in Return."[66]

Something else is changing: more studies of leaders and leadership touch on followers and followership. For instance, although Nannerl Keohane titled an article "On Leadership," it is not leadercentric, maybe because as past president of both Wellesley College and Duke University, she understands full well the importance of those other than those at the top. Keohane does not, in any case, omit followers from her discussion. Rather, she explores the connection between leaders and followers, only to conclude correctly that given the distance between them, their connection generally is not only asymmetrical but weak.[67]

Finally, most importantly, leaders themselves are following their followers more closely now than ever before. When the CEO of JCPenney, Mike Ullman, took the helm in 2004, he was struck by the antiquated corporate culture. Employees were still expected to refer to their senior managers as Mr. and Ms. Moreover, casual attire remained unacceptable at company headquarters, even on Fridays. And decorating your office too personally or elaborately was strictly forbidden. Ullman changed all that. He especially changed those aspects of the corporate culture that divided leaders and managers from the rank and file. He emphasized the use of first names among colleagues and their superiors. He sold off the company's art collection and instead hung the walls with pictures of employees. He encouraged business-casual attire during the week and permitted jeans on Fridays. He gave employees access to every part of the headquarters campus, including the executive suite and its elevator. And to everyone he met he said, "Just call me Mike."[68]

In fact, business leaders across the board are on what has been tagged a "charm offensive." So concerned are they with their positions, now relatively precarious, that they feel a sudden urge to be, of all things, nice, especially to those in their employ. As an article in *BusinessWeek* put it, "Senior executives seem to be battling for the congeniality prize. Humility, authenticity, and responsive leadership are new buzzwords at the top. Many chief executives talk about being 'servant leaders' and team players. They care openly about everything from employees to Mother Earth. In short, they're more likable."[69]

It's clear the gap between leaders and followers is closing. The former cannot afford any longer to dismiss the latter lightly. This is not to argue that leaders are obsolete or that human nature has in some fundamental way changed. Milgram's experiments are as relevant to human nature now as they were when they were conducted. Rather, it is to point out that the "great man" theory of leadership has fallen from favor not because of political correctness, but because in the twenty-first century fewer men can wield great power, however "great" they may be.

A couple of years ago the unthinkable happened. Riccardo Muti, who for nearly two decades was the feared but widely revered conductor of the orchestra at Milan's legendary opera house, La Scala, was pushed from his perch. He was obliged to resign by La Scala's eight hundred musicians, singers, carpenters, and janitors, who, finally furious with his high-handed ways, demanded that he "Resign! Resign!" Muti's departure signaled the end of an era. Times have changed in the world of music, as they have changed everywhere else. For example, the new conductor of the New York Philharmonic, Alan Gilbert, is very different from his predecessors. He is young (forty at the time of his appointment), and he is by all accounts affable and approachable, with not a hint of the fearsome maestro about him. In sum, the imperial CEO is no more, and neither is the imperial conductor.[70] Instead, people the world over are speaking out in new and different ways, and claiming for themselves, in many cases for the first time ever, power, influence, and sometimes even authority.

CHAPTER 3

Relationships

HOW DO LEADERS AND FOLLOWERS RELATE? No less an expert on the subject than Hermann Goering had rather a simple view: leaders lead and followers follow. During his trial at Nuremberg, he told an interviewer, "It's the leaders of the country who determine the policy and it's always a simple matter to drag the people along whether it's a democracy or a fascist dictatorship . . . The people can always be brought to the bidding of the leader."[1] Goering had a point. Whatever the recent changes to which I referred in the preceding chapter, most followers follow most leaders. The question to which I now turn is why.

The rewards of leading are obvious. Power and influence, status, and access to resources including money and sex are among the benefits of being a leader. But what are the attractions of following? What's in it for us? Why do most of us go along most of the time, even with leaders of whom we do not approve?

Sometimes the benefits are readily apparent. Sometimes we follow leaders because we admire who they are and what they do. But there are other times when neither applies—and still we go along. Why? Why do we follow leaders with whom we find fault? The answer is self-interest. We calculate that the benefits of following outweigh those of not following, and we calculate that the cost of resisting is higher than the cost of going along. For example, in the workplace we (usually) comply because not to comply puts at risk the money we need and want to spend. And in the community we (usually) comply because it satisfies our need for stability and security. In any case, not to comply is often judged more trouble than it's worth. In fact, this calculus holds even when the circumstances are extreme, when we obey orders for fear that if we do not, we could be harmed or even killed.

To understand why followers generally go along voluntarily with their leaders, it's best to begin at the beginning, with one of the world's great experts on primate behavior. In his book *Our Inner Ape*, Frans de Waal explores deference in groups and finds the phenomenon ubiquitous. He begins by making the case for connection: "One can take the ape out of the jungle, but not the jungle out of the ape. This also applies to us, bipedal apes."[2] The connection between humans and other primates applies particularly in two realms: power and sex. Sex is not the primary concern here, but power obviously is. So de Waal's statements about hierarchies in general, and about the functions of followers in particular, are right on point.

Leaders are clearly advantaged—to wit the power and money to which I earlier referred. In fact, leaders are advantaged everywhere in the animal kingdom. From frogs and rats to chickens and elephants, high rank translates into food for females and mates for males. No surprise, then, that we are generally ambitious to achieve high rank—and equally no surprise that some among us will be more adept at doing so than others. But de Waal's main point is not about leaders per se, but rather about the hierarchies over which they preside. The hierarchy constitutes a whole, in which the few are superiors and the many are subordinates. As he puts it, it's hard to "name a single discovery in animal behavior that enjoys wider recognition than 'pecking order.'"[3]

Pecking orders were first observed in domestic chickens, for in certain situations the highest-ranking bird has license to peck every other bird, without retaliation. In turn, the second highest-ranking chicken accepts pecking only by the chicken one rung higher—but is free to peck all the lower-ranking chickens. And so it goes, right down the line.[4] Sound familiar?

Wolves provide another example: they too have clear hierarchies, each with a strong leader at the top. A single alpha male dominates, while all the other wolves are content to submit. This arrangement of allegiance holds the pack together and serves it well overall.[5] When wolves go after a moose, for example, they do so in a way that seems choreographed. When first approaching their prey, all the wolves fall into line behind the alpha male, the leader. Then, as soon as the leader starts to give chase, the others immediately follow suit. The lead wolf remains the most aggressive, from beginning to end, and so it is he who also decides when the hunt is over.

The thing to remember is that we, bipedal apes, have our own pecking orders. Unlike other primates, humans signal status by placing people in formal positions of power and authority, with titles and trappings to match. But, like chimpanzees, we can also determine rank by watching how people behave. For example, we can usually distinguish between leaders and followers in small groups, even when no leader is formally designated. We can tell who the leaders are by seeing which members act with confidence, which ones attract the most glances and nods of agreement, and which ones freely enter the discussion. Similarly, we can tell who the followers are by seeing which ones are shy and retiring, which ones are the most widely ignored, and which ones allow others to direct the conversation and decide the outcome.

Hierarchies contribute to our well-being: they provide social order.[6] In fact, the function of a stable hierarchy among humans is the same as it is among chimpanzees: to reduce tension so that open conflict is relatively rare. When there is harmony, as opposed to disharmony, "everybody is better off. The group can hang out together, groom each other, play and relax, because no one feels insecure."[7] This simple equation—between hierarchy and social order—makes plain why it is in the interest of followers to strike a deal with their leaders. While in a perfect world those of low rank would prefer to be higher, in this imperfect world they settle for the next best thing, which is to live in peace. I should add that hierarchies play an especially important role in times of uncertainty: when there is an outside threat. There is a reason the military hierarchy is so clearly defined and easy to read. As de Waal put it, "A chain of command beats democracy any time decisive action is needed."[8]

What seems clear is that most of the time it is important that followers follow. Not only is it theoretically impossible for everyone to be a leader, it is practically impossible as well. For all the attempts to establish Utopian democracies, in which every member of the group has a role equal to that of everyone else, they nearly never last. After a while hierarchy reasserts itself.[9]

Recall William Golding's classic novel, *Lord of the Flies*. A plane crashes on an uninhabited desert island. A group of English boys survives, only to quickly discover that all the adults on board have died. Freed from the usual constraints imposed by adults in particular and by society more generally, the boys have what appears to be a golden opportunity. With no one around to tell them what to do and when to do it, they are free to be free spirits. But it becomes apparent almost immediately that complete autonomy will never, can never, be realized. In no time flat, one of the boys—"Piggy" by name—tries to impose some order on the chaos. He suggests, of all things, holding a meeting. And so it is that in short order there is order—and in short order there is a pecking order.

Among scientists and social scientists (as well as novelists!), there is, then, widespread agreement that the Darwinian virtues of ranking include the efficient division of labor, the stability of the group or organization, and the maintenance of order. In other words, natural selection supports a propensity for hierarchical relationships. In addition, since the human animal has a protracted period of dependence in infancy and childhood, during which deference to superiors (usually parents) is essential to survival, one might even say the species depends on our capacity to defer. As Stanley Milgram put it in the wake of his experiments on obedience to authority, we are "born with a potential for obedience, which then interacts with the influence of society to produce the obedient man."[10]

Finally, there is in all this a benefit that is purely practical. Hierarchies in which the few are superiors and the many are subordinates make it feasible for the latter to get away with doing little or none of the collective work. German sociologist Robert Michels called this the "iron law of oligarchy." Michels made it plain that people in large numbers cannot govern themselves. They need some sort of structure, staffed by people who have the authority to administer our collective affairs. During the first decade of the twenty-first century, the American people ceded to President George W. Bush and the members of his administration the right to run the nation's business. In turn, whatever our opinions of how well he performed, Bush being president allowed us to turn our attention elsewhere.[11]

History confirms the obvious: it is littered with failed experiments in radical egalitarianism. Only recently, in the 1960s and 1970s, was there another effort to achieve total equality—this time in the modern women's movement. But in the end, "women's groups tended to oscillate between total formlessness at one extreme or a kind of collective authoritarianism on the other." As a result, the women's movement slowed to a crawl.[12] In other words, the movement suffered on account of its well-intentioned but nevertheless misguided attempt to fly in the face of human nature. As Michels had cautioned some decades earlier, in order for large groups to govern themselves effectively, some must be willing to be leaders, others must be willing to be followers, and the majority must be willing to go along with this arrangement.[13]

As always in these matters, there are exceptions to the general rule. In recent years one of the most frequently cited is the Orpheus Chamber Orchestra, which is one of the finest such ensembles in the world and which is self-governing, with twenty-six members and no conductor. "There is nobody other than the members themselves to decide how to weight the diversity of ideas and opinions that invariably flood the hall when a piece of music is being played."[14] But this small, highly educated, deeply motivated, and ideologically committed group is no template for more ordinary people in more ordinary circumstances. If anything, the exception proves the rule. The fact that such a rarified group is the exemplar only confirms the elusiveness of the Utopian dream.

Why We Follow—Individual Benefits

Freud was first. He was the first to provide us with a psychological explanation of why followers follow their leaders, even when they are somehow bad.[15] Freud was always interested in power relationships, including those between parents and their children and physicians and their patients. But he was never more trenchant, and poignant, on the subject of leaders and followers per se than during the years just before his death, when he was working on his last book. *Moses and Monotheism* was published in 1939, while Freud was living in England. Old and ill, he had emigrated there just a year earlier, courtesy of the Nazis, who by then had annexed Austria, obliging Freud, who was Jewish, to go immediately into exile.

It was during this period, during the waning days of his life, in which Freud decided to use a biblical theme in order to probe one of the most intriguing of questions: Why do people follow leaders? What's in it for them?

On the face of it, he was writing about how Moses did the apparently impossible: lead his people out of slavery and into the Promised Land. But the subtext was evident even then: how was Hitler, who had long made clear his militant nationalism and virulent anti-Semitism, able to command the allegiance and even adoration of the German people? "How," Freud asked, "is it possible that one single man can develop such extraordinary effectiveness, that he can create out of indifferent individuals and families one people, can stamp this people with its definite character and determine its fate for millennia to come?"[16] Here, in part, was his answer:

> *Why the great man should rise to significance at all we have no doubt whatsoever. We know that the great majority of people have a strong need for authority which they can admire, to which they can submit, and which dominates and sometimes even ill-treats them. We have learned from the psychology of the individual whence comes this need of the masses. It is the longing for the father that lives in each of us from his childhood days.*

The book *Moses and Monotheism* makes at least four important points. First, Freud claims that a strong need for authority is part of the human condition. Second, he asserts that this need is the consequence of our earliest relationship with a dominant male, usually our father. (The emphasis on the dominant male is typical of Freud, who lived in a time when men did seem, to most men anyway, more important than women.) Third, Freud made an explicit connection between our need for authority and our need for religion, for God. He implied that our (submissive) relationship to God is analogous to, and derives from, our first (submissive) relationship, the one with our parents. Finally, Freud suggested that in all power relationships there are elements of admiration and envy on the one hand, and fear and loathing on the other.

How do we think about all this today—in particular, the relationship between dominant leaders and deferential followers? On the one hand, leadership cults on the scale of great twentieth-century dictators such as Hitler and Stalin may be a thing of the past. But on the other hand, the powerful connection between superstrong leaders and their half-crazed acolytes is part of the human condition. We still see totalitarian dictators in a few countries such as North Korea. And we still see cults, in which impassioned followers respond to charismatic leaders with an adulation best described as frenzied. As Ian Buruma put it, "What has not changed is human nature, the human desires that have allowed dictators to emerge in the past. The wish to worship . . . to be mesmerized by the spectacle of power, or swept up in collective emotion, these are still with us."[17]

I should add that these "human desires" are strongest in times of uncertainty, especially in times of crisis. For example, if an election for mayor had been held in New York City on September 10, 2001, it is not at all clear that Rudolph Giuliani would have won. A poll taken earlier in the year showed that only 32 percent of New Yorkers approved of him as mayor, and his standing among African American voters was "so low as to be virtually unmeasurable."[18] But after the attacks on the World Trade Center, the situation changed dramatically: Giuliani became a hero. In good part this was because he performed admirably under impossibly difficult circumstances. In greater part this was because in that moment, a moment of crisis, his followers needed nothing so much as a leader to whom they could turn for comfort and guidance. Nine days after the towers fell, an editorial about Giuliani in the *New York Times* read in part: "He moves about the stricken city like a god. People want to be in his presence. They want to touch him. They want to praise him . . . He is not only respected, but revered. And not only revered, but loved."[19]

But there is more. In addition to providing us with stability and security, we expect leaders to provide us with the comfort of community. Who better to assuage our fear of being alone than our leaders, our ministers and managers? It is they who are the focal point of our collective attention and so it is they around whom we group. Over two thousand years ago, Plato described us as "social animals." We depend on our group to protect us from "the other," from those in different groups who might somehow do us harm. As well, we depend on our group to protect us from what Jean Lipman-Blumen has called our inner dreads: "Bolstered by the group, we become part of something. We gain meaning and worth. Banished from the group, our lives become devoid of sense and value. It is no wonder that the community reserves its severest punishment—exile— for those who violate its most cherished norms."[20]

Clearly, our needs and wants as individuals are met by our playing the part of follower, at least most of the time. We go along because we consciously or unconsciously determine it in our interest to do so. Here are only three of the reasons why: (1) leaders provide individuals with safety, security, and a sense of order; (2) leaders provide individuals with a group, a community, to which they can belong; and (3) leaders provide individuals with someone who does the collective work. Of course, some of the time, followers comply only involuntarily. Some of the time, their leader compels them to comply.[21]

We know by now that not all followers do in fact follow. For one reason or another, some subordinates resist some superiors some of the time. The larger issue of why a follower might make the usually difficult decision to defy his or her leader will be addressed later on. But I want to make one point in this general regard here: followers who resist their leaders are often at risk. To be sure, there are exceptions to this general rule: some leaders are open to dissent and some even welcome it. But in the main, leaders think of followers who defy or even dispute them as subversive. Whistle-blowers are obvious examples. Typically, they pay for their transgression by being marginalized, demoted, or even dismissed.

Up to now I have referred primarily to the relationship between leaders and followers. At this point I deviate from the conventional leadership literature to introduce another dynamic altogether: *followers follow not only because it is in their interest to conform to their leaders, but also because it is in their interest to conform to their fellow followers.* Followers provide each other with crucial reference points. The new science of siblings confirms that the impact on us of our equals (siblings) rivals that of our superiors (parents) even as early as childhood. By the time children are eleven years old, they spend approximately 33 percent of their free time with their siblings, more than they spend with their parents, teachers, friends, or even by themselves. In fact, from the time they are born, "our brothers and sisters are our collaborators and co-conspirators, our role models and cautionary tales."[22] What we can say, then, is that followers follow each other first and foremost because they model their behavior on others similar to themselves. Followers also follow other followers for some of the same reasons they follow their leaders. That is, followers go along with other followers because they (1) lend stability and security, (2) provide order and meaning, and (3) constitute the group to which they want to belong.

Of course, when followers follow other followers, as opposed to following their leaders, formal rank plays little or even no meaningful role.

No one is the designated superior—which means no one is the designated subordinate. We see this in informal groups, such as children together in a playground. We also see it virtually: participants in chat rooms, for example. Finally, we see it in groups and organizations that for one or another reason are, or are supposed to be, leaderless. The point I am making, though, is different: although it is generally in our interest as well as in our nature to organize ourselves in rank order, the pressure to conform, to go along, comes not only from leaders but from other followers as well.

WHY WE FOLLOW—GROUP BENEFITS

Freud was first here too. He was the first to provide us with a sophisticated psychological understanding of why *individuals* follow leaders. And he was the first to provide us with a sophisticated psychological understanding of why *groups* follow leaders. Nearly two decades before *Moses and Monotheism*, he wrote a book titled *Group Psychology and the Analysis of the Ego*, which was inspired in part by the work of Charles Darwin. Darwin had posited that in primitive societies groups of humans were like groups of other apes: they were despotically ruled by powerful males. This prompted Freud to dig deeper into the phenomenon he termed *primal hordes*, early human groups that bonded for safety and security.

Freud believed that we behave differently—worse—as members of groups than we do as individuals. In groups our "unconscious instinctual impulses" trump what turns out to be the fragile veneer of civilization. "By the mere fact that he forms part of an organized group," Freud wrote, "a man descends several rungs in the ladder of civilization. Isolated, he may be a cultivated individual; in a crowd he is a barbarian—that is, a creature acting by instinct," capable of committing acts in "utter contradiction with his character and habits."[23] Therefore, like Thomas Hobbes, Freud concluded that groups need leaders, strong leaders, because without them they will revert to being "barbarian."

This, though, presented Freud with a dilemma. On the one hand, groups need leaders to, among other things, protect us from ourselves. But on the other hand, bad leaders can direct groups toward danger and destruction. Finally, Freud concluded, we have no choice: bad leaders are a risk we assume, if only because by nature we have what he called "an extreme passion for authority." Put another way, well before the worst of the twentieth-century dictators—Stalin, Hitler, Mao—Freud declared that we actually want "to be governed by unrestricted force."[24]

As we have seen, Robert Michels also addressed the question of what benefits we derive from leaders. It turns out these benefits are bestowed not only on individuals but also on groups. Why the "iron law of oligarchy"? Because, as one observer put it, "Thirty people can sit around a campfire and arrive at a consensual decision; thirty million people cannot."[25] Michels went even a step further. It is, he argued, "the incompetence of the masses" that makes leaders absolutely indispensable. Thus is the common good served by having the few (the leaders) assume responsibility for the many (the followers).

Since Freud and Michels, another leadership function has emerged, one also excluded from the standard leadership literature.[26] It comes to us from the study of social movements and demonstrates that some people need leaders for the purpose of what in the late 1960s and early 1970s was called *consciousness-raising.* That is, some followers need leaders to show them the world has possibilities beyond anything they had previously conceived. This situation has been described as one in which B (the follower) finds it "impossible to conceptualize something beyond the false consensus that serves A's (the leader's) interests."[27]

Sometimes followers in need of such leaders constitute a class—in particular, one at or near the bottom of the socioeconomic ladder. Marxist thinker and writer Antonio Gramsci famously described the ascendant class (read *capitalists*) as controlling the culture in order to control everyone else (read *workers*). He called this *cultural hegemony,* claiming it enabled those in superior positions to persuade those in subordinate ones that the world they inherited was "natural, right, legitimate and appropriate."[28]

A study conducted in Appalachia in the 1970s illustrates Gramsci's point. It took place in an area in which many of the men made their living as miners. However, neither they nor their fathers before them, most of whom were miners as well, had joined what was then one of the most powerful unions in the country, the United Mine Workers of America. Put another way, this particular group of miners had never developed a collective consciousness. In comparison with other miners the world over, these men were "docile diggers."[29]

The problem was not that these miners were unaware of their plight. The problem instead was that they did not expect, nor could they even imagine, a better life. Nor for that matter could they think of taking matters into their own hands, of creating change all on their own. Of these miners, then, it could fairly be said that they needed a leader, likely one from the outside, who could transform them, change how they thought and what they did.

This kind of community organizing constituted the life's work of legendary social activist Saul Alinsky. In his most important book, *Rules for Radicals*, Alinsky described his mission: "To create mass organization to seize power and give it to the people."[30] But because Alinsky understood that people without power could scarcely imagine taking it, he developed a strategy that relied on outside "organizers" to teach the people what they needed to know. These organizers were leaders—men and women trained to rouse, to incite, if you will, precisely those who needed them most, the poor, who generally "are far too willing to acquiesce."[31] Incidentally, this brings to mind the situation in New Orleans after Katrina hit. Those who suffered damage and were wealthy or middle-class figured out what they needed to do in order to start over. "But the people stuck in the shelters, black and white, were typically not only poorer but also less demanding, less assertive, less skilled in negotiating their way through the system. Poor families in the shelters were neglected precisely because they were suffering so patiently."[32]

What other ways do leaders service followers in groups? Well, that depends, of course, on the nature of the group, on who are its members, and on what is the group's overarching purpose. In general, leaders are expected to provide their followers either with professional (task) satisfaction or with personal satisfaction. But since the nature of groups varies widely, and since the contexts within which they operate are so different, I will name three other reasons why people in groups follow their leaders: (1) leaders provide groups with a structure; (2) leaders provide groups with a goal; and (3) leaders provide groups with instruments of goal achievement.

This list is not complete. For example, in crisis situations followers in groups have needs and wants different from those in situations that are routine. Similarly, charismatic leaders provide those in their thrall with the kind of excitement and gratification that more ordinary leaders do not.

Incidentally, the thing to remember about charismatic leaders, and cult leaders for that matter, is that they lead groups that are passionate about, and even worshipful of, *them* in particular. When Mohandas Gandhi was thrown into an Indian jail by the British authorities for the first time, his followers were in shock. "They had taken it for granted that their Mahatma had super-human powers, and that if the English tried to lock him up, he would in all likelihood fly out the window."[33] And when Fidel Castro was still fighting in the sierra, going from one place to another in the middle of the forest to evade his enemies, he was reputed to have had an uncanny, almost otherworldly, sense of where the dangers lay: "Be it intuition, magic . . . or whatever, there is a quality in the man that warns him of danger."[34]

What we can conclude then is this: people go along with their leaders because leaders provide them with a range of important benefits, at the level of the individual and at the level of the group. As it turns out, while the rewards of leading are more obvious than those of following (power and money are easy to see), they are not more important. In fact, the benefits of the second are as compelling as those of the first. We are hardwired to follow because we are social creatures—and to live with others is necessarily to live in rank order. We are hardwired to follow because rank order provides us with important benefits—and only a few can be at the top. And we are hardwired to follow because following is a fair exchange: followers provide leaders with something they need and want (followers), and leaders provide followers with something they need and want (leaders). Both stand to gain from the arrangement nature intended.

A final note on following bad leaders, leaders we know full well are ineffective, or immoral, or both. In some cases, we have no choice, or imagine we have none. We go along because we are afraid that if we do not we will somehow be made to pay. But in other cases, we go along with bad leaders freely, sometimes even eagerly. This leaves us with the question of why: Why do we go along with bad leaders instead of doing them in? Why not just wrest from them the capacity to exert power, wield authority, and exercise influence, and replace them with leaders who are better?

The results of Milgram's experiments on obedience to authority go a long way toward explaining why we defer even to bad leaders. They include, in addition to the ones already mentioned, the following: the sequential nature of following, whereby small acts of going along lead gradually to a significant commitment; the social nature of following, whereby the behavior of other followers encourages people to do what they would not do otherwise; the "agentic" nature of following, whereby followers blame others, usually superiors, for acts they in fact committed; and the ideological nature of following, whereby people are persuaded the end justifies the means.[35]

But for all the rational reasons, there is in these matters something irrational, or maybe simply inexplicable. As European expert Timothy Garton Ash put it, "One question above all obsessed me: What was it [about Nazi Germany], what human strain, that made one person a dissident or resistance fighter and another a collaborator in state-organized crime, one a Claus von Stauffenberg, sacrificing his life in the attempt to assassinate Hitler, another an Albert Speer?"[36] I suppose the best way to think of this is as endemic to the human condition—remediable perhaps, to some degree, but never to be erased altogether.

FOLLOWER-LEADER RELATIONS

Now that we better understand *why* followers follow, we turn to the question of *how* they follow. What, in other words, are the different ways in which followers and leaders relate?

Of the many things to be said about relations between subordinates and their superiors, perhaps the most striking is their range. At the one end of the spectrum are leaders who are brutes, tyrants, and dictators of the cruelest sort, with followers at their mercy. And at the other end are leaders who are democrats, well-intentioned directors who consider followers to be their partners in the business of leading and managing.

For reasons that I fail to understand, leadership experts have generally avoided the one extreme: totalitarian leadership.[37] But for those who would dig deep, man's inhumanity to man, which is nothing other than one end of the spectrum, simply cannot be ignored. By now Stanley Milgram's experiments on obedience to authority have been joined by many others, all of which confirm "the banality of evil." The fact that under certain circumstances people with even momentary power crudely realized are willing, sometimes even eager, to harm those with less power than they is not, however, only a leadership issue. It is also a followership issue. For example, just as in World War II Jews were actually murdered not by Hitler but rather by his "willing executioners," and just as during the Soviet purges in the late 1930s it was not Stalin who did the actual killing but rather *his* willing executioners, so it was during the genocide in Rwanda. While Rwandans in positions of political and military authority incited the murder and mayhem, and while soldiers in the regular army did some of the killing, most of it was done by ordinary Hutus who, using low-tech agricultural instruments, attacked Tutsis who formerly were their neighbors. As Geraldine Umugwaneza has noted, the personal brutality was stunning, in part because it was exercised close up rather than from a distance. (In contrast, Hitler and his henchmen arranged for most of the killing to be done in camps outside Germany, and by "modern means" such as poison gas.) The most popular tools were machetes, locally known as a *panga*, and clubs studded with sharp nails. It was hand-to-hand combat: women were impaled, pregnant women were disemboweled, children's heads were smashed against rocks, and men's Achilles tendons were cut to ensure that they could not move and would die a slow and painful death.[38]

It turns out that man's inhumanity to man—leaders' inhumanity to followers and followers' inhumanity to other followers—is not purely a political phenomenon. It is also, albeit at levels less murderous and malevolent, the stuff of everyday life. In the workplace, for instance, problems of dominance and submission are ubiquitous, as those who have "bad bosses" or "bully bosses" can testify. The National Institute for Occupational Safety and Health, which now recognizes bullying as a form of workplace violence, reported that nearly one-fourth of companies surveyed had some sort of bullying problem.[39] As the Badbossology.com Web site demonstrates (other sites do the same), the abuse of power in the workplace is widespread and manifests itself in many ways. In addition to bullying there are discrimination, harassment, poor pay, violations of legal rights, and the invasion of privacy. Such behavior is not trivial. It is the more acceptable—psychological abuse being more acceptable in corporate America than physical abuse—manifestation of how miserable can be the relationship between superiors and their subordinates.

Would you have wanted to work for UN ambassador John Bolton, who was said in the past to have threatened his underlings, throwing things at them and behaving sometimes like "a madman"? Would you have wanted to work for air force procurement officer Darleen Druyun, who was said to have bullied subordinates, skewered industry executives, and sought personal advantage at government expense? Would you have wanted to work for Josh Emett, a tall, thin chef from New Zealand, who was reputed to have established his authority in the kitchen by making the cooks "realize that they were sniveling, loathsome insects who deserved to be degraded and publicly humiliated"? Or, for that matter, would you have wanted to work for Joe Allbritton, the widely feared chairman of Riggs Bank, who was famous for yelling even at high-ranking managers, for publicly humiliating his subordinates, and for firing people over the phone?[40]

Exactly how superiors justify their abusive behavior, and exactly how subordinates who have any choice at all explain their willingness to be so abused, remains something of a mystery. This is not for lack of trying to grasp what seems beyond the pale. Only recently, another professor of psychology, Albert Bandura, concluded that executioners working in American prisons are able to do what they are paid to do by morally disengaging. "Moral disengagement," says Bandura, "is where all the action is. It's in our ability to selectively engage and disengage our moral standards, and it helps explain how people can be barbarically cruel in one moment and compassionate in the next."[41] Still, again, for all the explanations, the wellspring of evil continues to elude us, as do the real reasons for being nasty when being nice would seem just as easy.

Man's inhumanity to man explains why, for all the academic discussions about the semantic differences among the words *power, authority,* and *influence,* in common parlance it is the word *power* that matters most. Most people judge most leader-follower relationships by one all-important measure: by how much power the former exercises over the latter. *Power,* though, is a highly flexible and fungible word, one that means different things to different people in different situations. A well-known article published nearly fifty years ago described different kinds of "social power" on which leaders can draw, including reward power (the capacity to reward), coercive power (the capacity to punish), legitimate power (consequence of title or position), and expert power (consequence of knowledge).[42] More recently, Joseph Nye made what by now has become a familiar distinction, between "hard power" and "soft power." Nye grants that "power is the ability to influence the behavior of others to get the outcomes one wants." But he goes on to point out that there are several ways to affect such behavior. "You can coerce [others] with threats," he writes. Or you can "induce them with payments." And, he continues, there is a third way as well: you can "attract and co-opt them to want what you want."[43] These differences, especially the one between coercion (hard power) on the one hand and attraction (soft power) on the other, matter, not only, as Nye emphasizes, in world politics but in everyday life as well. How the relatively powerless experience the relatively powerful depends on what is the nature of their power—and on how it is exercised.

Still, while these differences and distinctions are important, it is also the case that ordinarily the word *power* is equated with dominance and submission, with the idea that some people, leaders, can get other people, followers, to do what they want them to do. As we know by now, this can get complicated, for we want to be free of powerful people, first our parents. But at the same time, we need them to be strong so they can take care of us when the situation requires. In short, we don't want our leaders to control us; but we do want them to protect us.[44]

In any case, we learn early on to accommodate ourselves to those who have more power than we do. In fact, the most faithful of followers are extolled for their good behavior. As children, we are rewarded for toeing the line, for going along with those more powerful than we, usually parents and teachers. And later in life, in the workplace, we are similarly rewarded, for being, in general, compliant.[45] Recall the long saga of succession at General Electric, when CEO Jack Welch was preparing to retire. For many months he made it clear that one of his three lieutenants, all of whom had long been under his thumb, would be anointed as his heir. The nod would go to Jeff Immelt, to James McNerney, or to Robert Nardelli. How did each get to be a heartbeat away from replacing the legendary Welch? *By being superior at being subordinate.* In fact, superior subordinacy paid off in all three cases. While it was Immelt who became CEO at General Electric, McNerney became CEO at Boeing, and Nardelli at Home Depot.[46]

Of course, our interest in power, in matters of dominance and deference, is as old as human history, and traditionally is in the realm of governance. Virtually every great political theorist has grappled with the question of what is the proper relationship between the ruler and the ruled. The liberal ideal has been constant: equality. No one is superior and no one is inferior; ergo, no one should dominate and no one should defer. The standard utilitarian formula makes this plain: "Every man to count for one and no one to count for more than one."[47] But the virtue of equality is not self-evident, nor has it ever been universally accepted, with some of history's greatest political thinkers going in the other direction entirely. Recall that Thomas Hobbes proposed we maintain the social order by establishing a system in which the rights of followers be severely constrained—and the rights of leaders nearly unconstrained.

But complete equality is, of course, no more than, and no less than, an ideal, a fantasy. Among the most intractable of our problems are those situations in which there is an extreme imbalance of power. In families, think child abuse or spousal abuse or even elder abuse. At work, think leaders and managers callously indifferent to the well-being of those on rungs lower than theirs. And at the level of the state, think of Zimbabwe, which for so many years suffered a brutal dictator, Robert Mugabe, who was ready, willing, and able to suppress every challenge to his authority. The imbalance of power runs the gamut, from slavery and serfdom at the extreme, to the much more subtle forms of control and intimidation that are the stuff of everyday life. But they have this in common: they deny subordinates "the ordinary luxury of negative reciprocity: trading a slap for a slap, an insult for an insult."[48]

Of course, not all followers are content to follow—which in a book such as this one inevitably is a recurring theme. Some are so angry, upset, or unhappy at having to surrender control that they resist. Such resistance can be organized, premeditated, and preplanned. Or it can be spontaneous, erupting all of a sudden, without previous forethought. Similarly, such resistance can be a solitary act, or it can be in concert with others, who are similarly disgruntled. Finally, resistance to power can be covert, hidden from view; or it can be overt, in which case open confrontation is usually the result.

In his book *Domination and the Arts of Resistance*, James C. Scott makes this point: people who resist, who speak "truth to power," are rare, really rare. Scott does not claim that speaking truth to power is impossible, that subordinates can never speak freely and frankly to their superiors. But he does argue that when there is a high degree of control by the latter over the former, resistance is unlikely to be open. It's just too dangerous. What, then, is the alternative? Does this mean there is no resistance at all? Or do followers find other ways of opposing leaders who give them no way to say their piece?

Scott argues that what you see is *not* necessarily what you get. What you see in such situations is usually no more than a public performance of some sort, in which followers' feelings are concealed, as opposed to being revealed. In fact, Scott writes, "the more menacing the power, the thicker the mask."[49] However, the importance of what lies behind the mask—of what subordinates really think and feel—should not be underestimated. These truths are contained in what Scott calls "hidden transcripts," which can be found in every situation in which one individual or group dominates another.[50] Hidden transcripts tell us what is being said privately, behind closed doors. And they manifest themselves in secret acts of rebellion, such as sabotage, poaching, pilfering, and tax evasion. In short, hidden transcripts are "written" by the powerless in order to resist the powerful, without risking their lives in the process.

Scott's message is far-reaching in its consequences, for these private forms of resistance pave the way for public resistance later on. "The first public declaration of the hidden transcript, then, has a prehistory that explains its capacity to produce political breakthroughs." Of course, if this first act of defiance by subordinates against their superiors is decisively defeated, it is unlikely to be repeated. But if it succeeds, its capacity to beat back oppression "is potentially awesome."[51]

At the other end of the spectrum from totalitarian leadership is, of course, democratic leadership, leadership in keeping with a social contract, in which power between leaders and followers is shared. Democratic leaders are presumed to be credible, caring, considerate, consultative, consensual, and concerned. And democratic followers—that is, followers in democratic systems—are presumed to be prepared to participate. They are expected to cooperate with the group, and to collaborate with their leaders, at least if they so deserve.[52] Conversely, if this presumption does not pertain, if leaders do not "so deserve," then it's up to democratic followers to fix what's broke and to make their leaders pay the price.

The terms *transactional* and *transformational leadership*, as described by groundbreaking political scientist James MacGregor Burns, generally presume both democratic leadership and democratic followership. That is, they presume followers who know where their interests lie, and who are ready, willing, and able to act accordingly. According to Burns, transactional leadership is based on an economic model in which leaders and followers have an exchange of some kind, from which both parties stand to benefit.[53] Transforming leadership, in turn, "occurs when one or more persons *engage* with others in such a way that leaders and followers raise one another to higher levels of motivation and morality."[54] Clearly, Burns intended for the two types of leadership to be quite different. But the differences notwithstanding, transactional and transformational leadership are in the most important way similar: they take into account not only the needs and wants of leaders but those of followers as well.

Burns's work has focused almost entirely on leadership in the public sector. Yet it is the private sector on which his ideas on democratic leadership have had their greatest impact. In particular, his ideas about transformational leadership have been of interest to corporate leaders and managers who thought to apply his theories to their practices. No wonder, for the picture Burns paints of leaders and followers as collaborators is in keeping with a corporate culture now increasingly convinced of the virtues of the flattened hierarchy. As well as anyone else—and nearly inadvertently, for his interest was in politics, not business—Burns captured the slowly changing sensibility. "'One-man leadership' is a contradiction in terms," he writes. "Leaders, in responding to their own motives, appeal to the [motives] of potential followers. As followers respond, a symbiotic relationship develops that binds leader and follower together."[55]

Contexts and Characteristics

The ways in which followers and leaders relate depend on the contexts within which they are embedded. This in any case we know: context is critical. As the great sociologist George Homans put it, "The relationship between superior and subordinate is to some degree the same in every group." But, he added, "It varies greatly in intensity from group to group according to various circumstances, including the relationship of the group to its environment, the ability of the subordinate to escape from authority, and the extent to which the superior is chosen by the members of the group."[56]

But exactly which context matters most is not always obvious, for contexts are concentric circles in which one, the smaller, is situated within the larger. Say, for example, you worked as a salesperson in Saks Fifth Avenue's flagship store, in New York City. Your closest context would be the department in which you worked—for example, men's shoes. But this particular department is just one among many such at Saks, which together make up the whole, that large store in midtown Manhattan. It is the store that would constitute the larger context that was your primary point of professional reference.

But Saks Fifth Avenue's midtown store would itself be embedded within another context, since it is only one out of over fifty stores in the Saks Fifth Avenue chain, which itself is a subsidiary of Saks Incorporated. To carry the point even further, Saks Incorporated is located in the American fashion industry more generally, which in turn is part of the larger American economy and, for that matter, of the fashion industry worldwide. The point is that every one of these contexts, from those that are up close and personal to those that are somewhere in the distance, can have an impact on the leader-follower relationship. If Saks Incorporated suffers a downturn, your superior in the men's shoe department in the Fifth Avenue flagship store might have no choice but to send you packing.

The contexts within which groups are embedded are not only spatial, related to size; they are also temporal, related to time. How, for example, to understand the relationship between Russia's president, Vladimir Putin, and the Russian people, without understanding at least something about the history and culture of Russia more generally? The past matters to the present. It matters that Russia has a tradition of autocracy and dictatorship, going all the way back to the czars and continuing through Stalin and even up to Gorbachev. It matters that Russia has never known democracy, at least not as we understand it in the West. It matters that Putin, however much of an autocrat he seems to Americans, is acting in perfect accord with what many Russians have come to expect and even want in their national leaders. As the martyred, muckraking Russian journalist Anna Politkovskaya remarked about her people, "They expect everything to come down to them from above, and if what comes down from above is repression, they resign themselves to it."[57]

How leaders and followers interact is determined also by key characteristics such as group relations and group size. As I use the term, *group relations* refers to the ways in which followers interact. Recall that followers follow their leaders—and that in coherent groups they follow each other as well. Members mirror each other in their beliefs, attitudes, values, and behaviors. "The members of an adolescent gang are readily identified by their distinctive style of dress. Work groups engaged in some specialized task develop a jargon that seems esoteric to outsiders. Marital partners tend to become more alike over the course of their marriage. And participants of a group engaged in social reform come to share an ideology about the nature of the social world that they aspire to change. Even among dedicated nonconformists one finds a monotonous similarity of hairstyles."[58] The initial shock of what was at the time the Beatles' very long hair quickly wore off, because so many men "rebelled" by wearing long hair as well.

The reasons for the similarities include shared exposures and experiences, and shared values. But in the main the mirroring manifests the pressure to conform, which virtually every group exerts on virtually every member. All groups want their members to behave in ways that are in keeping with what the entire group needs and prefers. Why, for instance, would you want anyone in your bible club who was not willing to follow, at least in a general way, the dictates of your church? Why would you want anyone in your bridge club who would not play according to the rules of the game?[59] Put simply, we are rewarded for conforming: we get the benefits that community life provides. Conversely, at least some of the time, we are punished for refusing to conform by being marginalized or even banished.

There are, though, some downsides to conforming, among them *groupthink*. The term was coined by psychologist Irving Janis, who analyzed several U.S. foreign policy fiascos, beginning with the Bay of Pigs. "How," Janis asked, "could bright, shrewd men like John F. Kennedy and his advisers be taken by the CIA's stupid, patchwork plan" to invade Cuba?[60] After studying several such policy failures, including the Vietnam War, every one of which was planned and executed by small groups of smart decision makers, and then comparing these with policy successes, such as the Cuban Missile Crisis, Janis reached a conclusion. The problem was groupthink: faulty decision making as a result of the pressure to conform.

It was this pressure that precluded nearly all of the small group members from thinking independently and from carefully appraising different courses of action. Incidentally, by nearly all accounts Iraq should now be added to this list. For example, in his book *Fiasco: The American Military Adventure in Iraq*, Thomas Ricks blames the Bush administration for decision-making processes in which alternatives other than first going in and then "staying the course" were excluded from the discussion.[61]

Typically, leaders are blamed for decision-making fiascos of this kind— in this case, one or another American president. But followers play their part as well. They do have a voice—and they could choose to use it.

Finally, the leader-follower relationship is determined by group size. Are we, for example, looking at leaders and followers in small groups or in large organizations? Or are we, for that matter, looking at leaders and followers in large collectives, such as, to take an entirely random example, Brazil, the largest and most populous country in South America? Above all, size determines distance: the greater the size of the group or organization, the greater the distance between the leader on the one hand and the followers on the other. CEOs of companies that number only a hundred can get to know every one of their employees. But CEOs of companies that number a thousand or more, not to speak of leaders of countries with populations of a million or more, can connect personally to only a small or even a tiny fraction of those in their employ or under their jurisdiction.

Size also determines distance in more subtle, less obvious ways. Larger size is "ordinarily accompanied by the greater need for structural complexity, more filtered and delayed information, geometric increases in the number of dyadic and group relationships, greater social distance, and additional constraints on change."[62] In addition, large groups and organizations are characterized by large differences in earnings between those at the top and those at the bottom. In 2005 the CEOs of America's five hundred largest companies received an average of $11.75 million in total compensation—more than four hundred times the salaries of their poorest-paid workers. The compensation of CEOs even vastly outstrips those immediately beneath them: in executive suites the earnings discrepancy between those at the top and those immediately below them has swollen to 260 percent.

The distance between leaders and followers is the most apparent in large nation-states, nearly all of which bestow on those in charge great power, symbolized by a great residence. Buckingham Palace—with its 19 state rooms, its 52 principal bedrooms, its 188 staff bedrooms, its 92 offices, and its 78 bathrooms—is a vestige of the day and age when England's kings and queens still mattered. The tradition continues. To this day splendid homes separate the rulers from the ruled, even in liberal democracies. For example, in spite of the Founders' aversion to monarchy, nearly from the start American presidents have lived in a large white house on Pennsylvania Avenue, which in itself signals distance between them and everyone else.

Nannerl Keohane, who, as earlier mentioned, was president both of Wellesley College and Duke University, has aptly described the impact of distance on the relationship between leaders and followers. She concludes that the word *relationship*, as in *leader-follower relationship*, is typically misused. To have a relationship, she writes, is to have a close, affectionate, and enduring affiliation with a parent, lover, husband, sibling, colleague, or friend. But while followers may feel they "know" their leaders, in part because they watch them so closely, and while the importance of this connection is not to be underestimated, it is generally one-way. "No leader," Keohane writes, "can have a direct, personal connection with large numbers of followers; this is possible only for those with whom [he or she] works most immediately." Thus, with the possible exception of leaders and followers in small groups, the connection between them is simply not symmetrical. Bottom line: size matters. In large groups and organizations, "the connection between the leader and her followers must be more abstract, detached, and impersonal than the term 'relationship' can usefully be expected to describe."[63]

FOLLOWERS TO THE FOREFRONT

Cult members are among the few followers actually to have been studied. In part this reflects the numbers—polls taken in the 1980s estimated that in the United States more than 50 percent of teenagers had some interest in cults. And in part this reflects the nature of the sample—cult members are clearly contained, easily identified, and in thrall to their leaders. They also behave as followers are expected to behave. That is, they follow.[64] Followers of charismatic leaders are similar. An article in the *Academy of*

Management Review reported that while followers of charismatic leaders are not identical to followers of cult leaders, they have important things in common, such as their willingness to make personal sacrifices in the interest of the mission and their strong emotional attachment to their leaders.[65]

All of which raises this question: what happens when we ratchet down the level of engagement, when instead of looking at followers of cult leaders or of charismatic leaders, we look at followers of more ordinary leaders, leaders who are transactional, say, rather than transformational? The findings are predictable: the leader's capacity to motivate followers—or, if you will, the followers' readiness to be so motivated—depends on the leader's ability to "behave in a way that exemplifies the values and ideals that are shared by the groups they lead."[66]

Now the next question: what do we know about followers in those circumstances in which the leader is not a cult leader, or a charismatic leader, or even a leader who exemplifies shared values and ideals? In short, what do we know about most followers in most situations—situations in which leaders are other than, less than, inspirational or exemplary? The fact is, we know very little. Moreover, what we do know is not very heartening. By this I mean that much, if not most, of the time followers disengage. They go along with their leaders not because they are captivated, either by the messenger or by the message, but because the alternative, not going along, is less attractive. In the workplace we behave as we are expected to because such behavior feels to us to be good enough; or because we don't much care; or because for us to do otherwise, somehow to resist, would be costly. Similarly, we go with the flow in political life because we calculate that to fight the system is in some way too costly, just not worth it. As I earlier wrote, for all the widespread anger and disenchantment over the way George W. Bush handled the war in Iraq, only a very few Americans bothered to make their views known. As a general rule, we went along silently, if sulkily, with a president of whom we strongly disapproved and whom we heartily disliked. (Near the end of his two terms in office, Bush's approval ratings were usually no better than in the high twenties or low thirties.)

This brings us to the matter of values. There is an enormous literature on how to be a good leader. But there is only a meager literature—a very meager literature—on how to be a good follower.[67] Moreover, this literature, such as it is, is recent. Nevertheless, we should be aware of the pre-vailing view: leaders are responsible for what happens—*and followers are as well.* There is the presumption that leaders in all groups and organizations should be as ethical as they are effective. And there is now the further pre-sumption that if they are not, it is up to their followers to set them right.

On one level this message is familiar. We've heard it before, at different times and in different places, at least since the American Revolution. Each of the following lines, or slogans, is in the same spirit, and each says more or less the same thing: dominance and deference are out and self-determination is in.

- "Government of the People, by the People, and for the People."

- "Workers of the World, Unite! You Have Nothing to Lose but Your Chains!"

- "Power to the People!"

Curiously, though, so far as the leadership literature is concerned, such sentiments are only of more recent vintage, for only now is it beginning to address what is the followers' role and what are the followers' rights and responsibilities.

Ira Chaleff's book *The Courageous Follower* captures this change—which is all about bringing followers "into parity" with leaders. Well, maybe not quite; for Chaleff is no revolutionary. In fact, he wants followers to support their leaders and to "contribute to leadership development." But he does address the importance of speaking truth to power; and he does encour-age subordinates to "sustain the courage it requires to be honest" with their superiors.[68] I should add, though, that the possible, if not probable, consequences of such courage are downplayed. What are we to do when speaking truth to power is risky, or even dangerous? What are we to do when the going gets rough—when the leader is unreachable or unrecep-tive, and the follower has little or no real leverage?

These are, of course, questions without easy answers. But let me be clear: subordinates who in any serious way challenge their superiors should count on doing some heavy lifting. As I said, this is not to argue that all leaders and managers are difficult to deal with or resistant to change. Some welcome honest feedback, and some embrace the new and different. Rather, it is to get real—to remind us that those who have more power, authority, and influence than we do generally are in a position to resist even the most heartfelt of our entreaties and to punish us if we continue to press on.

Having said this, I would also argue that the very fact that we are starting to ask not only what leaders should do, but also what followers should do, is a sign of change in the right direction. It indicates we are aware that leadership is a relationship that involves at least two people, one leader and one follower. And it indicates we are aware that followership is a relationship that involves at least two people, one follower and one leader.

CHAPTER 4

Types

WE FIXATE ON OUR LEADERS and on the similarities and differences among them. But followers are different. We do not bother even to distinguish one from the other, either because we assume they make no difference or because we assume they are all one and the same. As we will see, there are a few exceptions to this general rule. But by and large we scarcely notice that, for example, followers who mindlessly tag along are altogether different from followers who are deeply devoted; and we scarcely notice that the distinctions among followers are every bit as consequential as those among leaders.

Curiously, outside the leadership field and outside what I here call the "leadership industry," people seem quite clear that there are differences between, for example, American voters who vote in every election, federal, state, and local, and American voters who, while eligible to cast a ballot, never do. People seem similarly to understand that those in Motorola's employ for a decade or longer are more likely to be loyal to the company than those who joined the company only recently. And nearly everyone in the Western world knows perfectly well that Jesus's disciples were different in their dedication from all but the most pious of modern Christians. Still, most of us are stuck, stuck in a place where leaders are scrutinized at every turn, while followers are ignored so completely that differences among them are neither noticed nor understood.

The first prominent exception to this general rule seems to have been English philosopher and statesman Francis Bacon, who in the sixteenth century wrote an essay titled "Of Followers and Friends." Bacon determined that followers were different from one another—and that some were trouble. He cautioned against "Costly Followers"—followers who were literally costly by draining "the Purse," and metaphorically costly by being demanding and wearisome. Bacon was similarly leery of "Factious Followers," malcontents not to be trusted; and of "Glorious Followers," who roused envy by trumpeting their triumphs. Finally, he warned against "Dangerous Followers," who "enquire the Secrets of the House, and beare Tales of them to Others."[1]

But only in more recent years have a handful of experts on leadership and management developed more formal typologies, in which followers of one sort were distinguished from followers of other sorts. Each of the following typologies was based on work conducted primarily in corporate America; and each divided followers into several different groups.

PAST TYPES

Harvard Business School Professor Abraham Zaleznik was the pioneer. For more than a decade, during the 1960s and 1970s, he focused in part at least on followers.

Abraham Zaleznik

In 1965 the *Harvard Business Review* published an article by Zaleznik titled "The Dynamics of Subordinacy." The piece focused on subordinates rather than on superiors, with Zaleznik arguing that "individuals on both sides of the vertical authority relationship" were important to how well organizations perform. To distinguish among the different kinds of followers, he placed them along two axes: dominance and submission was one, and activity and passivity was the other. The first axis ranged from subordinates who want to control their superiors to those who want to be controlled by them. The second axis ranged from subordinates who "initiate and intrude" to those who do little or nothing. When the two axes intersected, followers were divided into four groups: (1) impulsive subordinates, (2) compulsive subordinates, (3) masochistic subordinates, and (4) withdrawn subordinates.

- *Impulsive subordinates* are rebellious. They challenge people in positions of authority. However, they can be constructive, even "spontaneous and courageous," and they have an "urge to create and achieve." In fact, some impulsive subordinates "influence events." That is, they lead.

- *Compulsive subordinates* seek similarly to control people in positions of authority, but through "*passive* means." They have strong guilt feelings that derive from their wish to dominate— which, in turn, derives from what Zaleznik, a Freudian, considered the universal wish to usurp our very first figure of authority, our father.

- *Masochistic subordinates* actually want to be in pain; they want to submit to the "control and assertiveness of the authority figure." Masochism manifests itself when subordinates invite criticism by deliberately, if unconsciously, performing poorly.

- *Withdrawn subordinates* care little or even not at all about what happens at work, and they behave accordingly. At the extreme, withdrawn subordinates see the world as malevolent and unforgiving, so they pull back entirely. But withdrawn subordinates present a problem even in cases that are less extreme, for their "lack of trust, interest, and involvement makes [them] unsusceptible to influence."[2]

Zaleznik's four types now seem somewhat dated. Moreover, his typology is more about subordinates who are dysfunctional rather than functional. Nevertheless, he was a pioneer. He was first among the experts in leadership and management to point out that followers were important, that there were distinctions to be made among them, and that these distinctions mattered both in theory and in practice.

Abraham Zaleznik and Manfred F. R. Kets de Vries

Ten years after "The Dynamics of Subordinacy" appeared in the *Harvard Business Review*, Zaleznik returned to the subject, this time in collaboration with Manfred F. R. Kets de Vries. In a book titled *Power and the Corporate Mind*, which, as its title suggests, was primarily about leadership, not followership, they nevertheless included a chapter that further explored what Zaleznik continued to call "subordinacy."[3]

The template was the same: subordinates were divided into the same four groups along the same two axes: dominance and submission, and activity and passivity. But the book made even clearer than did the original article the importance of those other than the man in charge. One of the tales tells about General Douglas MacArthur, who was fired for insubordination by President Harry Truman. It makes for a gripping story, in part because the extraordinary subordinate (MacArthur) thought himself every bit the equal of his extraordinary superior (Truman), and in part because the stakes were so high. The two men had fierce disagreements, mainly about whether the Korean War should be negotiated to an early end or expanded, with the American military giving chase to the Chinese. Truman was in favor of the former; MacArthur in favor of the latter. For some time Truman tolerated MacArthur's resistance and rebelliousness. Finally, though, the president had enough. When MacArthur went around his commander in chief one more time, he was summarily dismissed.

Zaleznik and Kets de Vries argued that under the circumstances, the general should have either submitted or resigned. Still, the standoff between the general and his commander in chief raises some key questions: What does it mean to be a good follower? What does it mean to be "loyal yet independent"? And what does it mean to be, simultaneously, a team player and a freethinker?[4]

Power and the Corporate Mind provides another example of a president who was badly served by his underlings. This time, though, the disservice was done not by followers who were rude and resistant, but by followers who were cooperative and compliant. The Watergate cover-up of Richard Nixon's administration was the consequence of a president determined at all costs not to be found out. It was also the consequence of trusted advisers who made the mistake of colluding in the wrongdoing. According to Zaleznik and Kets de Vries, "What fortified the misjudgments and immoral behavior of both the president and his subordinates was a psychological collusion fed by ambition and the desire to maintain supremacy against real and imagined rivals."[5]

Who was the target audience for all this psychological theorizing? More particularly, to whom exactly was Zaleznik speaking, even as he described the superior-subordinate relationship in Freudian terms? In the main, he wrote for leaders and managers in America's largest and most successful corporations. His article on the dynamics of subordinacy was published by the *Harvard Business Review*, and his book with Kets de Vries referred in its title to "the corporate mind." It seems clear, then, that Zaleznik was motivated by the conviction that if superiors better understood their subordinates, it would be to the advantage of the former and likely to the latter as well.

Robert Kelley

In the modern literature on leadership and management, Robert Kelley's 1992 book, *The Power of Followership*, is the first written for followers, as opposed to leaders. The book seems genuinely motivated by an interest in, and concern for, "what it feels like to be a follower."[6] Moreover, it seems genuinely intended to encourage followers—the workers of the world, if you will—to act in their own interest. In this sense Kelley's book is a manifesto, urging followers *not* to follow their leaders, or, more precisely, not to do so blindly and without deliberate forethought.

Kelley's interest was in "exemplary" followers. Unlike Zaleznik, whose focus was on failed followers, Kelley's was on those who acted with "intelligence, independence, courage, and a strong sense of ethics."[7] So, first thing, he debunked what he called the "the myth of leadership," the leader-centrism joined in recent years by teachers, scholars, consultants, coaches, and even the media, all of whom he considered had a vested interest in fixating on leaders at the expense of followers. Kelley claimed that the leadership myth was "debilitating," that it damaged followers. And he warned that it "enticed people to let down their defenses in the presence of leaders," and set them up for "potential abuse."

To find the followership he most admired, Kelley turned to Hermann Hesse, who in *Journey to the East* portrayed a group on a mythical journey. The main character, Leo, is a servant and is seen as such by the others. He does the cooking and the cleaning, and all the rest of the menial chores. But in spite of his lowly status, it is Leo who buoys the group with his good spirits and who keeps it on track. But when Leo unexpectedly vanishes, everything falls apart. "The group, it turns out, cannot continue on its own without their servant and supposed follower, Leo. The journey is abandoned."[8]

Most people interpret this story to mean that in spite of his low rank, Leo was the leader. But Kelley saw it differently. He saw Leo not as a leader but as an "exemplary follower, the kind of person that no leader or group can succeed without." Clearly, Kelley considers followers to be every bit as important as leaders. Great followers, exemplary followers, have an innate sense of dignity, as well as pride in what they do and in who they are. As one software developer told Kelley, "I've been a follower all my life. It is simply the role I prefer to play. I'm considered one of the best computer jocks in this company. But I have no desire to lead people . . . I simply turn out great software that people want to buy. So do all the computer hackers sitting along this corridor. Now you tell me: Who is more important to this company? Those of us who create and make the products or the bosses who do the razzle-dazzle?"[9]

Like the handful of others who have studied followers, Kelley recognized that followers were different from one another. As a result, he too divided them into several groups, first according to their motivation. Why "did Aristotle choose to follow Plato?" he asked. "How did Carl Jung find his way to Sigmund Freud?" And, "What led Ellen Gates-Starr to follow Jane Addams and make Hull House an international achievement in providing a settlement center for Chicago's poor immigrants?"

Kelley's interest was in *voluntary* compliance, in those who freely follow for one, or maybe more than one, good reason. For example, "apprentices" follow because by attaching themselves to leaders, they are more likely to become leaders themselves. "Disciples" follow because they want to bond with leaders they deeply admire. "Mentees" follow because they are likely to benefit from establishing close relationships with people higher positioned than they. "Comrades" follow because they seek the intimacy and social support that groups typically provide. "Loyalists" follow because of an obligation or personal commitment. "Dreamers" follow because their leaders embody an idea, or a cause, in which they deeply believe. And then there are those like that software developer referred to above—people who are followers simply because, for whatever reason, they prefer it to being leaders.[10]

Kelley also distinguished among followers according to their "followership style." Like Zaleznik, Kelley placed followers along two axes (see figure 4-1). The first was independent thinking; the second was (also) level of activity. At the one end of the first axis are followers who are innovative

FIGURE 4-1

Robert Kelley's followership styles

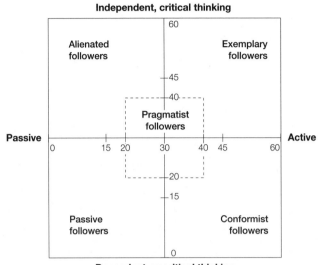

Independent, critical thinking

Alienated followers	Exemplary followers
Passive	Pragmatist followers	Active
Passive followers	Conformist followers

Dependent, uncritical thinking

Source: From *The Power of Followership* by Robert E. Kelley, copyright © 1992 by Consultants to Executives and Organizations, Ltd. Used by permission of Doubleday, a division of Random House, Inc.

and independent; and at the other end are followers who "don't think." At the one end of the second axis are followers who take initiative; and at the other end are those who are lazy and passive.

According to Kelley, there are, then, five different styles of followership.

- *Alienated followers* think freely and critically; but they do not participate in the groups and organizations of which they are members. They score high in independent thinking and low in active engagement.

- *Exemplary followers* perform well in every aspect. They exercise "independent, critical thinking, separate from the leader or the group," and they also are actively engaged.[11] They score high across the board.

- *Conformist followers* are content to take orders, to defer to their leaders. They score high in active engagement and low in independent thinking.

- *Passive followers* let their leaders do the thinking for them, which means they require constant supervision. They score low in independent thinking and in level of engagement.

- *Pragmatist followers* "hug the middle of the road." They question their leader's decisions, but not very often and not too critically. They score "middling" in independent thinking and "middling" in terms of engagement.

Kelley's crusade was to turn all followers—especially those in the workplace—into exemplary followers. In a short essay written years after the publication of his book, Kelley's ambition and idealism were still in evidence. In fact, he made even plainer then than he did earlier that the very best followers were anything but "passive sheep." They were actively engaged in helping their organizations succeed while at the same time they were independent operators who could, if necessary and appropriate, "exhibit courageous conscience."[12]

Ira Chaleff

The virtues of "courageous" followers were trumpeted even more loudly by Ira Chaleff in *The Courageous Follower*.[13] It too is a pioneering work in the study of followership, particularly because Chaleff's primary purpose is to promote not leadership development but followership development. This is more of a self-help book than is Kelley's. It is pragmatic and practical, intended to embolden, at least slightly, subordinates in their interactions with their superiors.

The titles of the different chapters—for example, The Courage to Assume Responsibility, The Courage to Serve, and The Courage to Challenge—signal the point. Followers, Chaleff argues, have "far more power" than they generally understand. But what they do not usually have, he continues, is courage, which is "so antithetical to the prevailing image of followers and so crucial to balancing the relationship with leaders."[14] Note the similarities between Chaleff and Kelley in their ideology and intentions. Both are dismayed by the leadership myth and try to counteract it. And both describe follower power and how it might actually be used.

Chaleff also divided followers into several different groups. Once again there are two different axes, and once again they intersect (see figure 4-2). The result is four different "followership styles." The first continuum is the

FIGURE 4-2

Ira Chaleff's followership styles

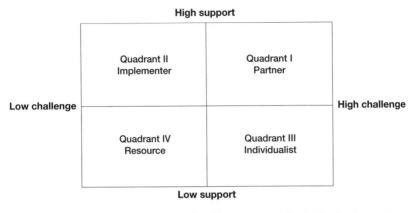

degree of support the follower provides the leader: high or low. And the second, which in effect is the obverse of the first, is the degree to which the follower challenges the leader: high or low.

According to Chaleff, the four different followership styles are:

- *Implementer*—These followers are the most common, especially in large organizations in which superiors depend on subordinates to get the work done.

- *Partner*—These followers fully support their leaders; but they are also ready and willing to challenge, if necessary.

- *Individualist*—These followers tell their leaders and, for that matter, everyone else, just what they think and how they feel. But because they regularly withhold their support from people in positions of authority, they are marginalized.

- *Resource*—These followers "do an honest day's work for a few days' pay but don't go beyond the minimum expected of them."[15]

Chaleff describes the four different followership styles. Implementers are dependable, supportive, and considerate. Partners are goal-oriented risk takers. Individualists are independent, self-assured, and forthright. And resources are available to their leaders—but not committed to them. Again, Chaleff writes mainly about followers in the workplace, especially in large organizations. Nevertheless, the message of *The Courageous Follower* is intended to be overarching. Chaleff describes at the outset how "since becoming aware as a child of the systematic destruction of six million European Jews," he understood the importance of followers. So his original motivation goes all the way back to Hitler. "Never again," he writes, should followers follow "a vicious leader to the logical conclusions of his psychosis."[16]

PRESENT TYPES

Of course, my own work on followership reflects my own vantage point: that of a political scientist. Nevertheless, I have long been struck not by the differences between, for example, leadership in government and leadership in business, but by the similarities.[17] And so it is with followership—I am struck by the similarities among followers, independent of the situation in which they are embedded.

This is not to say that context does not matter. As I earlier made clear, it does. To be a follower in Asia is different from being a follower in South America. To be a follower in a small group is different from being a follower in a large organization. To be a follower in a moment of crisis is different from being a follower when the situation is stable. To be a follower who is high on the organizational ladder is different from being a follower who is lower down. To be a follower of a leader who is benevolent and benign is different from being a follower of a leader who is mean and malevolent. To be a follower in a large multinational corporation is different from being a follower in a small family business. And to be a follower in the twenty-first century is different from being a follower in the eleventh. Still, the underlying dynamic between those who have power, authority, and influence and those who do not is not nearly as variable as appearances would suggest. For whatever the differences, to consider followership is to consider dominance on the one hand and deference on the other.

This work differs from that of my predecessors first because of the ground I cover—all the way from Merck to the American military, from Nazi Germany to the Catholic Church. Second, the stories are deeply detailed—four are told in full. Third, the picture I paint is complex—each type of follower is traced not only in relation to the leader but also in relation to the other followers. Fourth, the distinction I made at the beginning of this book, between followers as defined by rank and followers as defined by behavior, permeates the whole. Finally, this work is more descriptive than prescriptive. I do want to change the way people behave, to embolden subordinates in relation to their superiors, and to encourage superiors to relate to their subordinates. But at the same time, I presume that such a change requires a readiness to act. This is why the stories I tell are intended primarily as parables, more intended to illuminate than to instruct.

Like the few who tilled this soil before me, I came to conclude that followers are different one from the other, and that they can and should be divided into at least a few different groups. The question was how to distinguish among them? I could have differentiated among followers according to the size of the group in which they were embedded. We know, for example, that followers in small groups behave differently from followers in large organizations. Or I could have differentiated among them by how exceptional they were. Some followers are, fundamentally, ordinary. And others behave in ways that are extraordinary, heroic even. Or I could have distinguished followers by rank, by their distance from the top. Were these particular followers high up, close to the leader? Or were they way down the organizational hierarchy, near a lower-level manager, perhaps, but far from the main man, or woman, nevertheless?[18]

I settled finally on a typology based on a single, simple metric. It aligns followers along only one—the all-important one—axis. It is *level of engagement*. That is, I divide all followers into five different types, according to where they fall along a continuum that ranges from feeling and doing absolutely nothing on the one end to being passionately committed and deeply involved on the other. The five types are:

- Isolate

- Bystander

- Participant

- Activist

- Diehard

Rank is presumed. That is, each type presumes that followers are by definition in subordinate roles in which they have less power, authority, and influence than do their superiors. Each of these five types also presumes behavior of one kind or another, the range running from doing absolutely nothing to going full tilt. What cannot be determined only from the typology is disposition: how followers feel about their leaders. As we will see below, Isolates are completely detached and so constitute a special case. But Bystanders who would appear on the surface to be similarly detached, can and do have opinions and attitudes, on which, however, they choose not to act. As to the rest—Participants, Activists, and Diehards— we cannot tell from knowing only their level of engagement whether they are devoted and submissive, or antagonistic and adversarial. Do these followers follow their leaders? Or do they instead, their rank notwithstanding, resist them?

Because they are completely withdrawn, Isolates are discussed immediately below. The other four types are, in contrast, somehow involved. At a minimum they know what's going on around them, which is why they are discussed in detail, later on.

Isolates

Isolates are completely detached. They do not care about their leaders, or know anything about them, or respond to them in any way. Their alienation is, nevertheless, of consequence. By default—by knowing nothing and doing nothing—Isolates strengthen still further leaders who already have the upper hand.

Consider the case of the American voter or, more precisely, the case of Americans who are eligible to vote but never do. I became interested in this particular type of follower through a student in one of my classes, who had served for eight years as councilwoman in a good-sized city in the American Midwest. She enjoyed public service, campaigning gladly twice over to be elected and then reelected to political office. But one day she calculated the time and money she had spent to win the votes that were cast in her favor. The results were dismaying, so dismaying she began to wonder whether her investment in vote getting was worth it. Among other things, out of the approximately ten thousand registered voters in her county, fewer than six hundred actually voted in every election, including primaries and special elections.

Who were the other ninety-four hundred, and why did they fail to get out and vote when it would have been easy enough for most of them to do so? And what about the tens of thousands of others who were eligible to vote but did not bother to even register? Since these numbers are so large, we can safely assume that there is more than one reason why so few Americans, especially in comparison with eligible voters in other Western democracies, take the trouble to go to the polls.

Some people do not vote because they decide for one reason or another not to participate or, at least, not to participate on a regular basis. They consciously opt out, deliberately disengaging both from the political process and from those who people it. These nonvoters are Bystanders. They are aware of the political context within which they are necessarily embedded, but they choose to stand by and watch rather than to step up and participate.

However, there is another type of nonvoter who is so completely detached from the political system, and from those in positions of political authority, that they pay nothing and no one the slightest mind. These are Isolates: they stand separate and apart.

Some 15 million Americans reported that they did not vote in 2004 because they "were not interested in the election or were not involved in politics."[19] In 2005 the municipality in which my student served as councilwoman was run, in effect, by fewer than 25 percent of eligible voters, by those relatively few who went to the polls. In other words, followers who are Isolates leave it to leaders, *and to followers of other types*, to make their political decisions for them. (I should add that some would consider this perfectly rational behavior. As Anthony Downs put it a half century ago, "It is irrational to be politically well-informed because the low returns from data simply do not justify their cost in time and other resources." In other words, since my vote doesn't count anyway, why take the time and the trouble to be politically informed?[20])

The level of citizen engagement has been of interest to observers of the American polity especially since the 1960s and 1970s, since Vietnam and Watergate, and since the assassinations of John and Robert Kennedy and Martin Luther King, when the decline in trust of American government began to accelerate. Of course, the term *citizen engagement* refers to a range of activities that include more than just voting. Still, the numbers of people who are eligible to vote, and who actually do, has long been considered perhaps the most important indicator of citizen engagement. This explains why books that carry titles such as *Why Americans Don't Vote* and *Political Alienation and Voting Turnout in the United States, 1960–1988* began to appear in the 1980s—they reflected the growing concern about the growing gap between political leaders and their disengaged followers.[21]

The findings explain why Isolates in particular know so little and care even less. Again, I emphasize the distinction between nonvoting Isolates and nonvoting Bystanders. Bystanders make a deliberate decision not to go to the polls. They do *not* so decide because they are uninterested or uninformed, but because they consciously conclude that "all candidates in the campaign, or even all politicians, are dishonest, crooked, and not worth voting for"; or because they deliberately determine that none of the "candidates could represent their interests or meet their expectations."[22]

Isolates, in contrast, do not vote because they *are* uninterested and uninformed. They think themselves powerless and are, therefore, unmotivated to pay attention. Further, so far as they are concerned, politics is meaningless—meaningless as in so uncertain and so unpredictable that the only response they can even imagine is none, to refrain even from being informed.[23]

For those who believe that political participation matters, the decline in the numbers of voters among the young in particular is bad news. As experts have noted, "fewer Baby Boomers are registered or habitually vote than the generation that came before them, and there is an even larger fall-off from Boomers to the succeeding generations."[24] While this trend is not unusual or irreversible, the decline has accelerated in recent years. Surveys show that in the 1972 presidential election some 52 percent of those between the ages of eighteen and twenty-four went to the polls; by 2002 this figure had dropped to only 36 percent.

Once more, these nonvoters are not simply Bystanders. They are Isolates as measured by, for example, their level of cognitive engagement, which turns out to be a good predictor of political engagement.[25] Of all Americans born between 1965 and 1976, the so-called Generation X, only 37 percent said they followed government and public affairs "most of the time." Less than one-third reported regularly reading newspapers or news magazines; and for that matter, less than one-third regularly read the news on the Internet. In other words, there is no question that young people today pay less attention to political life than do their elders. But let me not be misunderstood: the problem of the political Isolate—presuming that it is a problem—is not confined only to the young. National surveys of the general public indicate that the "percentage of people who are completely inattentive to politics has been rising over the past 16 years, even as the percentage who are *very* attentive has remained about the same."[26]

When eligible voters were asked after the 2002 elections why they did not go to the polls, some of their reasons were practical—for example, "I recently moved and haven't yet registered at my new address." But if you add up the number of "good" reasons for not voting and then compare these with the number of reasons that reflect nothing more than voter detachment, it is easy to see that the large majority of people who did not vote just tuned out and dropped out. Consider this: over 80 percent of nonvoters in the 2002 election claimed it was for one of the following reasons.

- "I'm not interested in politics."

- "It's too hard to get information about who to vote for."

- "My vote wouldn't make any difference in what happens in my life."

- "I really dislike politics and government."

- "There's no difference between the two parties."

- "Voting is too much trouble."[27]

Since the subject here is followership, I should point out that the disenchantment that underlies each of these excuses is less with government as it is broadly conceived than it is with public officials, with leaders. "The vast majority of Americans find the playing field of politics to be tilted. Fifty-six percent agree that politics is a means for the already powerful to maintain advantage; just one third believe that politics is a way for the powerless to acquire equal footing."[28] Among the youngest nonvoters (those born after 1976), there was an especially high degree of negativity and widespread alienation. More than half of this group associated political leaders with words such as *lying* and *corrupt*, and well over a third think of politics as being only "for the rich" and for "white guys in suits." Having reached these dismal conclusions, some Americans simply step away altogether. They pay politics no mind.

Few experts take the position that the growing gap between the American electorate and their political leaders is not a problem, or is a problem we should lightly dismiss. Nor is it confined to the United States. Declining rates of political participation among younger citizens in particular have attracted attention in many other countries—for example, in Canada.[29] The reason is simple: democratic theory is based on the proposition that government is not only for the people but of and by them as well. Therefore, too great a divide between those who rule and those who are ruled is a sign generally seen as ominous. As Tocqueville cautioned, "Democracy has a tendency to slide into nihilistic mediocrity if its citizens are not inspired by some larger national goal."[30]

The divide between leaders and followers is most disconcerting when the latter find the former badly wanting. In mid-2006 a CBS poll found that 71 percent of respondents said that America was heading in the wrong direction. But this astonishingly high level of dissatisfaction did not in any obvious way translate into political engagement.[31] In fact, in a key Democratic primary that took place in Connecticut just a few months later, and that received widespread national attention, turnout was only 43 percent. While on the one hand this number was far higher than the average for a primary election in Connecticut, on the other hand not even half of registered Democrats, at least some of whom were Isolates, bothered to vote. Moreover, this group made up barely 15 percent of the state's total voting-age population.[32]

So far, the frustratingly low level of citizen engagement as measured by the level of voter participation has proved a problem as intractable as it is alarming. This is not just about political theory; it is also about political practice. For the effect of ceding control to a relatively small number of voters who tend to be at the extremes of both the Democratic and Republican parties is ever greater polarization, which leads in turn to more rancor and less progress. To demonstrate just how concerned are many of the experts, consider this rather radical solution, proposed by veteran political observer Norman Ornstein. Australia provides the model: registered voters who do not go to the polls must either provide a reason for not voting or pay a modest fine that increases each time there is another offense. The result is a turnout rate of more than 95 percent. The fine is obviously a disincentive to stay home and not vote. But the system is about more than penalizing political truants. It instills the idea that voting is a social obligation and that it elevates the political dialogue. "Australian politicians know that all their fellow citizens, including their own partisans, their adversaries' partisans and nonpartisans, will be at the polls."[33]

But there is just one small problem, to which Ornstein himself admits: in the United States "compulsory voting would be a tough sell." However modest the loss of freedom, it seems to Americans too high a price to pay, even for democracy in practice rather than only in theory. What, then, is to be done? I am obviously arguing that step one is to make a distinction between the nonvoter who is a Bystander and the nonvoter who is an Isolate. As it stands now, there are countless "get out and vote" efforts, most of which are one-size-fits-all. The same pitch is being made to entirely different kinds of people (followers) who have entirely different kinds of reasons for not going to the polls. It makes no sense. It makes no sense to target nonvoters who know nothing and care less just as you would those who know a lot and care even more. Therefore, any voting drive aimed at Isolates in particular must begin at square one, by persuading those who are completely detached from the political system that they should take notice. I might add that the best way of persuading Isolates that *they* should take notice would be by telling them that *others* are taking notice, especially others to whom they relate. Once again, getting people to do this or to do that is often less about leaders than it is about other followers. We tend to conform to what others are doing, especially others like us.[34]

This discussion of Isolates is illustrative—a short story about a large group that, for all the hand-wringing, continues to frustrate and even alarm those who believe that democratic government means participatory government.[35] However, the problem of the Isolate is scarcely confined to the political realm. We know full well that the workplace similarly has a considerable contingent of subordinates who are totally detached, there to do what they must to get by and no more. Isolates in the workplace are uninformed, uninterested, and unmotivated. They have no relationship with their leaders or managers. They are alienated from the system, from the group or organization that constitutes the whole. Finally, they are silent because they are detached—and because they are silent, they are ignored. Isolates have a problem. Isolates *are* a problem.

Bystanders, Participants, Activists, and Diehards

The four other types of followers are all in some way engaged. They are engaged with their leaders, and with other followers, and with the group or organization in which they are embedded. Recall that they each presume subordinate rank, and they are ordered according to the level of their engagement.

- *Bystanders observe but do not participate. They make a deliberate decision to stand aside, to disengage from their leaders and from whatever is the group dynamic. This withdrawal is, in effect, a declaration of neutrality that amounts to tacit support for whoever and whatever constitutes the status quo.*

- *Participants are in some way engaged. They clearly favor their leaders and the groups and organizations of which they are members—or they are clearly opposed. In either case, they care enough to put their money where their mouths are—that is, to invest some of what they have (time, for example) to try to have an impact.*

- *Activists feel strongly about their leaders and they act accordingly. They are eager, energetic, and engaged. Because they are heavily invested in people and process, they work hard either on behalf of their leaders or to undermine and even unseat them.*

- *Diehards are as their name implies—prepared to die if necessary for their cause, whether an individual, or an idea, or both. Diehards are deeply devoted to their leaders; or, in contrast, they are ready to remove them from positions of power, authority, and influence by any means necessary. In either case, Diehards are defined by their dedication, including their willingness to risk life and limb. Being a Diehard is all-consuming. It is who you are. It determines what you do.*

I have elsewhere made the point that to posit a typology of any kind is to invite argument.[36] This caution notwithstanding, dividing followers into several different types, in particular according to a criterion as obviously critical as level of engagement, serves at least two purposes. The first is theoretical. The typology allows us to make simple but significant distinctions among different sorts of followers, and to impose an order on the whole that up to now has been largely lacking. The typology also serves a practical purpose. It enables both parties to the relationship, leaders as well as followers, to translate what they know into what they do. This is not to suggest that this typology is a template for radical change. As I earlier observed, getting subordinates, and for that matter their superiors, to conduct themselves in any way differently from what have been their past patterns is no mean task. But to provide another lens, another way of seeing things that is from the bottom up rather than from the top down, is likely over time to make a difference in how people with less power, authority, and influence respond to those who have more, and vice versa.

The next four chapters, which constitute part II of the book, are, in turn, about Bystanders, Participants, Activists, and Diehards. In each case, I tell only one story. I tell it at some length and in some detail to provide a strong sense of how followers behave—and why. Three of the four stories are about followers who followed their leaders; the fourth is about followers who, in spite of their subordinate rank, resisted.

My primary point is this: we are followers. Followers are us. This does not, of course, mean that all of us follow all of the time—sometimes we lead. But all of us follow some of the time. It's the human condition.

PART II

Being a Follower

Nothing appears more surprising to those who consider human affairs with a philosophical eye than the easiness with which the many are governed by the few, and the implicit submission with which men resign their own sentiments and passions to those of their rulers.

—DAVID HUME

CHAPTER 5

Bystanders

Nazi Germany

Bystanders observe but do not participate. They make a deliberate decision to stand aside, to disengage from their leaders and from whatever is the group dynamic. This withdrawal is, in effect, a declaration of neutrality, which amounts to tacit support for whoever and whatever constitutes the status quo.

FORETHOUGHT

Let me make clear even now my bias—against followers who stand by and do nothing. My bias is particularly pronounced against followers who stand by and do nothing when lives are at risk, which was, of course, the case in Nazi Germany.

The thing to remember, though, is that Bystanders matter to every group and organization of which they are members. And they matter in situations far less onerous than the one described here. Maybe the main problem with Bystanders is that they do nothing even when doing something is not especially costly or especially risky. Think of Bystanders as free riders, content to let others make the group's decisions and do the group's work.

To be fair, most of us are busy. We have many things we need to do and many other things we want to do. In other words, most of us don't have a lot of time on our hands, which does explain to some extent why so many of us spend so much of our lives disengaged from the communities to which inevitably we belong. It also explains why we cannot, simply cannot, support every worthy cause or step in every time someone somewhere ought to be doing something.

But the usual litany of excuses for doing nothing—including lack of time, lack of interest, lack of concern, and lack of courage—just doesn't cut it. The fact of the matter is that followers who stand by and do nothing give other followers a bad name. By doing no more than going along with their leaders, and with other followers as well, it is they who come to mind when we make the mistake of thinking all followers sheep.

BACKGROUND

In a letter she wrote to her teacher, famed philosopher Karl Jaspers, dated August 17, 1946, equally famed philosopher Hannah Arendt railed against him for writing in a recent book that high-level Nazis should be dealt with in court. "Your definition of Nazi policy as a crime strikes me as questionable," she wrote. "For these crimes, no punishment is severe enough."[1]

The debate over how exactly to categorize the Holocaust in particular, or even to think about Germany's crimes against humanity during the Second World War, continues to this day. On the one hand, genocide seems the simplest of crimes in that it is the most blatantly heinous. But on the other hand, the case of Nazi Germany seems even now elusive, as in beyond our capacity to understand. Not only was Germany perhaps the most cultured country in Europe, a land conspicuously proud of its poets and thinkers, and of musicians as great as any as the world has ever known. But Jews were also a part of this tradition, threaded for hundreds of years through German culture and consciousness. In fact, pointing out similarities between Germans and Jews had become nearly commonplace, at least among intellectuals, some of whom thought it was precisely Germany's preeminence in European learning and higher education that "provided the chosen ground for the unfolding of Judaism within a Gentile and even nationalist matrix."[2]

Wanting to make sense of what happened in Germany during the Nazi period has led nearly always to one man, Adolph Hitler. As discussed in chapter 1, leaders simplify. We are leadercentric at least in part because leaders help us to order a world that is otherwise confusing, daunting, nearly overwhelming. Leaders enable us to perceive and to process, which is why in this particular drama, the drama of Nazi Germany, Hitler, the formidable führer, remains, more than sixty years after his death, front and center.

It has been said of Adolph Hitler that the key to his rise to power was his strength as a speaker.[3] He knew early on he had a gift. In his autobiography, *Mein Kampf*, written in the 1920s, when he was in his midthirties, Hitler recalled the very moment he discovered that as an orator he was so effective, so mesmerizing, that, like a religious evangelist, he could convert crowds. This reaction to Hitler at the podium by an early Nazi sympathizer, Kurt Luedecke, was typical: "My critical faculty was swept away . . . I experienced an exaltation that could only be likened to a religious conversion . . . I had found myself, my leader, and my cause." And so was this reaction, by actress and later legendary filmmaker Leni Riefenstahl. She recalled being in Hitler's thrall after hearing him speak in Berlin in 1932: "It seemed as if the earth's surface was . . . spewing out an enormous jet of water, so powerful that it touched the sky and shook the earth. I felt quite paralyzed."[4] Above all, there was Hitler's charismatic appeal to the many, to the enormous crowds who in his presence were transfixed and transformed. The American journalist William Shirer remembered how women responded to Hitler at a Nazi rally in Nuremberg in 1934: "They looked up at him as if he were the Messiah, their faces transformed into something positively inhuman. If he had remained in sight for more than a few moments, I think many of the women would have swooned from excitement."[5]

Hitler's hypnotic appeal—an admirer once called him a "virtuoso on the keyboard of the mass psyche"—explains his grip on the few who were Nazi Diehards from the start. It also explains the millions of German followers who took part in Nazi politics and policies in other, slightly lesser ways, Participants and Activists.[6] Finally, and by extension, Hitler's grasp says something about the millions of other Germans who played no real role in perpetrating either anti-Semitism before the war or genocide once the war began, but who, nevertheless, by standing by and doing nothing while the Nazis did their dirty work, gave tacit support. These were the Bystanders, whose handiwork was in evidence from day one, when they said nothing and did nothing about small humiliations, such as signs that read, "Jews are no longer allowed to buy groceries except between 4:00 and 5:00 P.M."[7]

DIEHARDS, ACTIVISTS, AND PARTICIPANTS

But before we turn to these Bystanders, some further information about the context within which they operated, and about their leader and their fellow followers, is in order. In a situation such as the one in Nazi Germany, as seemingly crazy as it is complex, it would be impossible to understand the role of the Bystander without knowing at least something about each of these other parts of the whole.

In Support of Hitler

Ian Kershaw, arguably Hitler's best biographer, writes that the idea of heroic leadership was associated with Europe's right wing even before the First World War. "The rebirth of the nation was promised through the subordination to a 'great leader,' who would invoke the values of a 'heroic' (and mythical) past."[8] The great leader would be "a man of destiny, born not elected to leadership, not bound by conventional rules and laws." His followers, in turn, were similarly idealized. They were to be devoted and dutiful, loyal and obedient.[9]

So the soil was prepared for the cult of the great leader to become the cult of Adolph Hitler. In other words, the führer phenomenon was the consequence of two things: Hitler's desire to *be* a heroic leader and his disciples' desire *for* a heroic leader. By Hitler's thirty-fourth birthday (1923), he was already being referred to by one of his chief lieutenants, Hermann Goering, as the "beloved leader of the German freedom-movement." In other words, even by then, a decade before he became head of the German state, Hitler worship was "unmistakable."[10]

By and large, those of Hitler's followers who were the most slavishly devoted, Diehards, were with him from the beginning to the bitter end. For reasons that even now are difficult to fathom, they invested their lives in this man who was, after all, not to the manner born, not well educated, not physically prepossessing, and not even one of their own—Hitler was Austrian, not German. This, though, was presumably part of his appeal. Hitler came out of nowhere, a vessel into which each of his most ardent disciples could pour the fantasy of their own transformation.

Members of Hitler's inner circle—the above-mentioned Goering, Heinrich Himmler, and Rudolph Hess, among others—anticipated his every wish and whim, hung on his every word, expressed their passion for the man and his movement at every turn, and followed his every order. They were the true believers, not only in Hitler but also in the anti-Semitic ideology he trumpeted from day one. Even in *Mein Kampf* he made plain that Jews should be, somehow, removed.[11] Kershaw writes that what exactly was meant by "removal" was suggested at the start: "The bacterial imagery implied that Jews should be treated in the way germs were dealt with: by extermination."

The Diehards closest to Hitler were a curious crew. Albert Speer, for example, was a cultured and handsome architect. Yet for all his education and bearing, after hearing Hitler speak just once, Speer signed on, quickly becoming a member of Hitler's inner circle. During the glory years, 1933–1939, Speer played the part of "official architect." He was ultimately responsible for the great surge of buildings and performances that testified to the glory of the Third Reich. And during the war, Speer was promoted yet again, first to Reich minister for armaments and munitions and then to a position that put him in charge of all German production, civilian and military.[12]

Speer lived to write his autobiography (in prison), in which he recalled being enraptured by Hitler from the first moment he saw him. Hitler's greatest gift, Speer thought, was to convey through a kind of mass "hypnosis" that he "cared about each of us," even "that he loved us."[13] Whatever the connection, there is no doubt that Hitler and Speer forged a special relationship, considered by some even to have "traces of an erotic motif." Nor is there any doubt that Hitler ultimately bestowed on Speer all the benefits of great prestige and all the benefits of great power.[14]

On the surface, the contrast between the good-looking and prepossessing Speer, who went with Hitler nearly to the grave, and the small, ferretlike Joseph Goebbels, who with his weak left leg went with Hitler literally to the grave, was striking. But the similarities between them are more to the point. Goebbels and Speer had in common not only the benefits of a good education (Goebbels had a doctorate in literature and philosophy) but also an unwavering, nearly slavish dedication to the führer. Moreover, Goebbels, like all the other members of Hitler's inner circle, benefited mightily from the connection: he became a powerful leader as well as a worshipful follower. In ten years, Goebbels went from being an editor and journalist to being head of the newly created National Ministry for Public Enlightenment, and then head of the newly created Chamber of Culture. In other words, in exchange for his fealty to Hitler, Goebbels had complete control over Germany's press, radio, theater, films, literature, music, and all the other fine arts during the entire Nazi era.

Goebbels's adoration of, and dedication to, Hitler was boundless. "Hitler is great," he would say. Or "Hitler is brilliant." Or, "I love him."[15] But nothing Goebbels ever did testifies as vividly to his obsession with Hitler as what he did at the very end. Just before Hitler committed suicide in his bunker on the afternoon of April 30, 1945, he drafted a will in which he appointed Goebbels chancellor of Germany. But soon after Hitler died, Goebbels summoned Hitler's trusted secretary and dictated to her the following: "For the first time in my life I must categorically refuse to obey a command of the Fuehrer." Not only could he not and would he not replace Hitler, he would join him. And so it was that within hours of the führer's death, Goebbels and his wife committed first murder and then suicide. Magda Goebbels arranged for each of their six children—they ranged from ages four to twelve—to be poisoned in their sleep. And then, because life without Hitler was life apparently not worth living, she and her husband each killed themselves.

While the most visible of Hitler's followers were the Diehards in his inner circle, many ordinary Germans were also dedicated to the man and to his party. Some similarly were Diehards, completely committed to the cause. Others—more ordinary Germans, if you will—were less fully engaged but nevertheless were critical to the Nazi juggernaut. Some were Activists, followers who were heavily invested first in the Nazi party and then in Germany's winning the Second World War. Others were Participants, less involved but nevertheless part of public life in Germany from 1933, when Hitler was first appointed chancellor, to 1945, when the war was lost and Hitler was dead.

The big debate has been about the nature of these followers, of Activists and Participants in particular. Were they malicious and malevolent nationalists, interested above all in German supremacy? Were they virulent anti-Semites, wanting nothing so much as to exterminate Jews or, at least, somehow get rid of them? Or were they instead ordinary people trapped in a vise from which they could not escape?

When Hitler became chancellor, times were tough. Germans were still suffering from their humiliating defeat in the First World War and from the deprivations of the Depression. Moreover, German politics were in disarray: the parliament was divided into more than a dozen political parties, and the chancellor increasingly had to rely on emergency powers to pass legislation.[16] Germans were therefore especially vulnerable to, and receptive to, a strongman such as Hitler, who promised to restore their national honor while also employing them at a level to which they had earlier been accustomed.

As a result of Hitler's appeal in an election that was held less than a year after he came to power, he and his party received more than 90 percent of the vote. Moreover, the turnout was extremely high, 95.2 percent of those eligible. To be sure, by then all political parties other than the Nazis had been banned. But still, there was strong support for Hitler and the Nazi party, and this "in spite of what people could read in the press and hear by word of mouth about the secret police, the concentration camps, official anti-Semitism, and so on."[17]

There were many opportunities for followers to engage. For example, Activists could enlist in the military or join the police. (By the end of 1933, more than half a million men were Nazi storm troopers.) Or they could participate in one or another of the countless demonstrations, such as the one in Osnabrück in 1935, against Jewish businesses. It took Activists to slap crude signs and slogans on Jewish-owned shops and take pictures of their customers (later to be displayed in public). And it took Activists to take part in "the high point of the struggle against the Jews," a gathering of some twenty-five thousand locals who assembled to listen to Nazi leaders speak on the topic "Osnabrück and the Jewish Question."[18]

April 20, 1939, was just a few months before the start of the Second World War. It was also Hitler's fiftieth birthday. The "lavish outpourings of adulation and sycophancy" surpassed those on any previous such occasions.[19] "The Fuehrer is feted like no mortal has ever been," proclaimed

Goebbels. While the organizers of the event obviously pulled out all the stops, there was also, as Kershaw notes, "no denying Hitler's genuine popularity—even near deification by many—among the masses." In other words, even though war was imminent, many Germans remained besotted. In honor of his birthday, tens of thousands sent Hitler letters and poems expressing their undying devotion, testifying to the fact that "although there was much fear of war, belief in the Fuehrer was extensive."[20]

There is a great debate between those who believe that once the war started, most of Hitler's followers were "ordinary men"—that is, Participants obliged by the circumstance they were in to carry out the führer's orders; and those who believe that they were "willing executioners"—that is, Activists and Diehards perfectly prepared and in some cases even eager to murder a people they despised. Wherever the truth lies on this particular question, here is the important point: in cases of mass murder, leaders rely "on others to do the killing and to administer the torture."[21] Hitler, then, like every genocidal leader before him and after, got his *followers* to do the dirty work.

Making distinctions among Hitler's followers is critical, and never more so than with regard to the annihilation of some 6 million Jews. We have seen that before the war there was strong support for Hitler and his party, and we have also seen that among the German people there was a strong streak of anti-Semitism. But there is a difference between disliking Jews and despising them. As Benjamin Valentino has pointed out, "even apparently high levels of political support for murderous regimes and leaders should not automatically be equated with support for mass killing itself."[22] In this case we need to separate widespread German indifference to Hitler's hatred of Jews, which was apparent, from widespread German support for Hitler's plan to exterminate Jews, which was not. In fact, most scholars have rejected the idea that German public opinion favored violent measures against the Jews. Rather, anti-Jewish attitudes are considered to have been in the realm of "tacit acquiescence or varying degrees of compliance." Moreover, anti-Jewish behavior generally "shied away from widespread violence against them, urging neither their expulsion from the Reich nor their physical annihilation."[23]

This brings us to the following question: if widespread public approval of genocide against the Jews was lacking, how was the genocide carried out? The answer in the case of Nazi Germany is the same as in most cases of mass killing: "The majority of the actual violence is carried out by a relatively small segment of society." Valentino writes, "These killers are almost always young men, typically members of an organized military group, militia or police organization. A tiny minority of such men, well armed and well organized, can generate an appalling amount of bloodshed when unleashed upon unarmed and unorganized victims."[24]

Daniel Jonah Goldhagen has estimated that the number of Germans who "knowingly contributed in some intimate way to the mass slaughter of the Jews" was over one hundred thousand—a number that, however, constituted less than 1 percent of the adult male population of Germany in 1938.[25] This brings us back to the question of what drove these followers in particular to commit mass murder. In his book *Hitler's Willing Executioners: Ordinary Germans and the Holocaust*, Goldhagen makes the argument that the case of Germany is singular: German anti-Semitism was of such long standing, and was so deeply ingrained, and was so virulent that it alone accounts for the mass murder. Goldhagen's claim, in other words, is that anti-Semitism was a sufficient and necessary cause for German participation in "the persecution and mass slaughter of Jews *and* for Germans to have treated Jews in all the heartless, harsh, and cruel ways that they did."[26] Goldhagen is especially focused on the cruelties, on the gratuitous pain inflicted on Jews by those of Hitler's subordinates who were Activists and Diehards. He is struck, for example, by the so-called death marches that took place at the very end of the war—precisely because they had no apparent motivation other than to inflict pain. "Why," Goldhagen asks, did German soldiers "stay with Jews and continue until the final moments to kill and torture them, even though the war was clearly lost?"[27]

Christopher Browning has famously taken on Goldhagen, airing their dispute in his book *Ordinary Men: Reserve Police Battalion 101 and the Final Solution in Poland*.[28] In contrast to Goldhagen, Browning argues that most Germans who killed Jews were, merely, Participants—that is, that they had no singular, all-consuming hatred of those who ended up their victims. Rather, these agents of the state were as the title of his book suggests: ordinary men who were taught to obey authority and who as a consequence did no more and no less than follow orders. After closely studying one battalion in particular, which consisted largely of middle-aged, working-class men from the port city of Hamburg, Browning did not deny they were imbued with a "sense of their own superiority and racial kinship as well as Jewish inferiority and otherness." But he went on to argue this did not amount to bloodlust.[29] Rather, it was that Germany's genocide, like other genocides, took place in a context that sanctioned and even encouraged mass murder.

What is clear, in any case, is the degree to which the obsession with Hitler is to a degree misguided. His entire political program, including war and genocide, depended on his having a large cadre of followers ready, willing, and able to do his bidding.

In Opposition to Hitler

Most astonishing in hindsight is "not how much, but how little" Hitler had to do to consolidate his power. By and large he simply enabled others, "now rushing to implement what they took to be his wishes."[30] As a result, it took only months for the Nazis to establish a system of governance in which resistance was increasingly dangerous—and increasingly infrequent. Of course, some Germans still refused to defer. For example, Lutheran philosopher-theologian Paul Tillich was the first "Aryan" to be dismissed from his post for speaking out against the Nazis (in 1933). But he was in the minority, the very small minority. In general, the overall political climate, the various laws that were passed, and the secret police gave the government "a veneer of legality." This made it easy for the overwhelming majority of Germans to support Nazi rule and difficult for the relatively few who were opposed to resist it. In fact, as time went on, even verbal criticism of the government was criminalized.[31] This meant that Germans openly critical of Hitler were vulnerable to punishment up to and including incarceration in one of the newly established concentration camps, intended to lock away, in addition to Jews and other undesirables, real or perceived enemies of the state.

Given all this, it is no wonder that while some Germans did resist the regime in ways both big and small—among them, other theologians, such as Rudolph Bultmann and Dietrich Bonhoeffer, who dedicated their lives to undermining the regime—most Germans stood by and did nothing.[32] Even the elites fell into line, although in the early days at least, they could have dissented with only minimal risk to themselves. As noted by historian Fritz Stern, "the German professoriate, for example, shamefully betrayed both the hallowed principle of academic autonomy and their own colleagues, accepting the dismissal of Jews and 'non-Aryans' from academic posts and all other public offices."[33]

Of course, one of the most important questions in all this is, What did the German people know and when did they know it? More specifically, after the war started, what did they know about the mass murders and when did they find out?

The familiar refrain even all these years later is that most Germans knew little or nothing about the Holocaust in particular until after the war was over. But there is evidence to the contrary, evidence that information about what was happening to Jews and, in smaller numbers, to other groups of people, such as Communists, gypsies, and homosexuals, did get out in bits and pieces. For example, in the summer of 1942, a group of exceedingly brave if foolhardy students in Munich who called themselves "White Rose" wrote, printed, and distributed leaflets containing scathing criticisms of the Third Reich, in particular its treatment of Jews. White Rose claimed that since the beginning of the war, some three hundred thousand Jews had been murdered in Poland (a figure far too low), and described the killings as "the most frightful crime against human dignity, a crime that is unparalleled in the whole of history."[34]

Predictably White Rose came to a grim end. The group had six student leaders, all from conservative, middle-class backgrounds and all "fired by Christian beliefs and humanistic idealism." Three were quickly arrested and put on trial. Four days later they were sentenced to death in the morning and guillotined in the afternoon. The remaining three soon suffered the same fate. Others, less directly involved, were sentenced to long terms in prison.[35]

Another group provides a more heartening example of what can happen when followers refuse to stand by and do nothing, when they refuse to follow a bad leader or, at least, when they refuse to follow without raising their voices in protest. In February 1943 the Gestapo arrested some ten thousand Jews who remained in Berlin. While most were sent directly to Auschwitz, approximately two thousand were locked instead in a detention center on a street named Rosenstrasse—because their wives (most of the detainees were men) were non-Jews. As soon as news of the arrests traveled through the city, hundreds of women hurried to the site to protest. "Give us our husbands back," they chanted.[36] The subsequent demonstrations capped ten years of a less public struggle with the Gestapo, in which non-Jews fought to save loved ones who were Jewish from deportation and disappearance. As a direct consequence of this public display, the Nazis did what they nearly never did otherwise: they pulled back. Little more than a week after the protests in the Rosenstrasse began, Goebbels himself issued an order calling for the immediate release of intermarried Jews and *Mischlinge*, offspring of marriages between Jews and Gentiles.

It is difficult to overestimate the importance of this generally overlooked episode in the history of Nazi Germany—*if only because the demonstrations in the Rosenstrasse were the single "incident of mass protest against the deportation of German Jews."*[37] To be sure, all along there were pockets of resistance to Hitler. In 1941 Catholics in Bavaria protested a decree by the local minister of education that crucifixes should be removed from the schools and that school prayers should be replaced by the singing of Nazi slogans. During the same year resistance to "euthanasia" (this term was used, but these were not mercy killings) came to a head, when people in the village of Asberg gathered to show their sympathy as mentally deficient patients were rounded up, loaded on buses, and taken to near-certain death.[38] And by 1943 thousands of women throughout Germany were quietly disobeying Hitler's decree that ordered them to work. But the demonstrations of a thousand or more in the Rosenstrasse were unique.[39] They constituted the only instance in which large groups of Germans persistently intervened on behalf of Hitler's most obvious victims.

The Nazis retreated in this instance for purely political reasons. The protests made them look bad—and they were afraid they would spread. Of the decision to release intermarried Jews and *Mischlinge*, one of Goebbels's chief aides said years later, "That was the simplest solution—to eradicate completely the reason for the protest. That it wouldn't make sense to protest anymore. So that others . . . didn't begin to do the same."[40] This raises the question: if, in fact, Hitler and his henchmen were not oblivious to public opinion—there is other evidence to suggest that public approval was important to Hitler—is it possible that more widespread public resistance to the führer would have obliged him to cease and desist, at least from genocide?

Those who have studied the Rosenstrasse demonstrations most closely are careful in their claims. They recognize that Berlin was a particularly fortuitous venue, that women were more difficult to target than men, and that this particular protest, which was, after all, about a matter of the heart, made it hard for the government to respond in its usual way. Nevertheless, this story teaches a lesson worth always remembering: the importance of numbers. "Regardless of when they occurred and whether they opposed fundamentally important or lesser programs, effective acts of opposition [to Hitler] were also collective, or at least aggregate."[41]

Notwithstanding the virtues of resisting authority in large numbers, the history of Nazi Germany is also the history of a few followers who on their own dared to stand up and do what they believed to be right. In other words, not every soldier did what he was told. And not every civilian turned a blind eye.

Browning tells of one Major Wilhelm Trapp, who was so distressed by the order to shoot on the spot some fifteen hundred Jewish women, children, and elderly that he gave his men, and himself, an out. He did not insist that every soldier under his command participate in the operation—in fact, he went so far to tell his men that if they did not feel up to the task, they did not have to execute it. As it turned out, though, out of about five hundred men, only twelve "instinctively seized the moment to step out, turn in their rifles, and then excuse themselves from the subsequent killing."[42] Later in the day, when actually faced with the task of giving a "neck shot" to their Jewish victims, a few other soldiers begged to be reassigned. And still others—but only a handful—made similar requests after they began actually shooting and then found it too painful to continue.[43]

In spite of being explicitly told they were free to leave the killing field, the number of those who opted out was obviously small, woefully small. Still, the number was sufficient for Browning to make this point: not *all* men are ordinary. Some are extraordinary, which means those who killed "cannot be absolved by the notion that anyone in the same situation would have done as they did. For even among them, some refused to kill and others stopped killing. Human responsibility is ultimately an individual matter."[44]

A few of those at the top of the military chain of command were as conflicted about the Nazi regime as were a few of those lower down.

Even before the war, some army officers, disgusted with the man and his party, had explored the possibility of overthrowing Hitler. But with the stunning successes of the German armed forces after the invasion of Poland, the opportunities even to think about planning his downfall diminished nearly to zero. It was not until 1942, when it became obvious that Hitler was not invincible, and when "the magnitude of the calamity towards which Hitler was steering Germany" became obvious as well, that the German opposition began to "flicker back to life."[45]

Once Hitler's assassination began to be considered more seriously, the few who were in on the plot were transformed. They became Diehards, subordinates at the highest level of the German military who had once sworn their fealty to Hitler, but who nevertheless were now committed to eliminating him. The difficulties and dangers of their position were obvious. There was the "existential fear of the awesome consequences—for the families as well as for the individuals themselves—of discovery of any complicity in a plot to remove the head of state and instigate a *coup d'etat.*"[46] And there was the shared understanding among the conspirators that they were acting alone. Popular support for the overthrow of Hitler was still lacking, while his fanatical backers continued to dominate German politics and policies.

Those who were in on the plot against Hitler were by no means of one mind. Some, for example, were conservatives who wanted nothing so much as to restore Germany to a traditional government with traditional German values; others were simply appalled by the mounting barbarity of the Nazi regime. In any case, their efforts came to center largely on one man, Colonel Claus Schenk Graf von Stauffenberg, who, while initially attracted to the Nazis, came in time to be repelled by them and ultimately to conclude that Hitler had to be eliminated.

Stauffenberg brought to the opposition a new momentum. But Hitler was a moving target—it was difficult to know where he would rest his head from one night to the next—and the number of those willing to risk doing the deed of doing him in was obviously very small. Finally, in July 1944, an opportunity presented itself. Stauffenberg had recently received a promotion that provided him with what up to then he had lacked: access. His newly acquired proximity to Hitler at military briefings meant he no longer needed to look for someone else to do the deed. Stauffenberg could and would do it himself—he would plant the bomb in his own briefcase.[47]

Kershaw describes the scene: "Hitler had been bent over the heavy oaken table, propped up on his elbow, chin in hand, studying air reconnaissance positions on a map, when the bomb went off—with a flash of blue and yellow flame and an ear-splitting explosion. Windows and doors blew out. Clouds of thick smoke billowed up . . . Parts of the wrecked hut were aflame. For a time there was pandemonium." Eleven of the badly injured were rushed to the nearest hospital, where several died. But for all the destruction and damage, both to people and to things, Hitler himself had "the luck of the devil." He survived the assassination attempt with no more than a few superficial wounds.[48] Meanwhile, less than twenty-four hours after the bomb went off, Stauffenberg and his closest conspirators were arrested, sentenced to death, and summarily shot.

Finally, there were the rescuers: the few, the very few Germans who by saving Jews, refused to follow not only Hitler but also the overwhelming majority of their fellow followers. These people were Activists, who at great risk to themselves nevertheless did what they thought was right. Unlike Bystanders who bore witness and did nothing, rescuers bore witness and did something.

In her book *The Hand of Compassion: Portraits of Moral Choice During the Holocaust*, political philosopher Kristen Renwick Monroe grappled with the question of what distinguished the rescuers from everyone else. "What drove these particular individuals?" she asks. "What caused them to engage in their moral acts?"[49] To get at these questions, she focused on five individuals, men and women—two were German, one Dutch, one Polish, and one Danish—all of whom went out of their way, far out of their way, to save Jews. By and large, the rescuers speak for themselves: they try to explain what motivated them to do right when most others did not.

Margot was a wealthy German woman, born in 1909. But she was different from the start. Her father was head of General Motors for Europe, and she was highly educated and spoke many languages. She had lived abroad, in England and Switzerland, and had married a Jew, a banker, with whom she had two children. By the late 1930s, Margot had left Germany for the Netherlands, had divorced or perhaps only separated from her husband, and on a trip to Czechoslovakia, just before the war, had agreed to carry out her first secret mission against the Nazis.

Margot was not especially articulate with regard to what she did or why. We know that while living in Holland, which had been occupied by the Nazis since 1940, she saved Jewish lives. We also know that she was sent to prison for her troubles. But when she was asked how exactly all this came about, Margot made it sound as if it was not much more than happenstance. Monroe asked her, "How did you decide whom to help then?" Margot replied, "Well, I didn't decide. There's no decision . . . You either help or you don't."[50] Later on Monroe asked, "So how did you get into the Resistance?" Margot replied, "I don't know how I came. Somebody asked me to help because I knew all these languages and so forth. It's not like you have a particular job with the Resistance. You don't get a job. You just do what you think is right. Somebody comes and says, 'Can you hide me?' I know a woman who came and said, 'Oh, God, I'm so scared.' I said, 'Come on the couch.' I made a bed for her. Things like that. You help."[51]

Monroe made meaning of answers like these by reaching two conclusions: first, "the complexity of moral life." As it turned out, there was no single explanation—not religion or family, for example—for why these particular people intervened while nearly everyone else did not. Second, as Margot's replies suggest, there is the impact of identity: "The rescuers' sense of who they were, and how they saw themselves in relation to others, so limited the range of actions the rescuers perceived as available that they literally did not believe they had any other choice than to help Jews."[52]

Do these findings pertain to Bystanders? Do they tell us anything about Germans who, while they did not actively support the Nazis, nevertheless did nothing to stop them, either before the war or even during it, when mass murder became the norm? Not much, I'm afraid. For the scarcity of those who in any way intervened to spare Jews or save them confirms what by now we already know: followers usually follow.

BYSTANDERS

As we will soon see, not all those who were Bystanders were Germans. But most, of course, were. I am reminded of the famed German novelist,

Günter Grass, who in his recent memoir *Peeling the Onion* recalled his mother saying, "I can't understand why they've got it in for the Jews. We used to have a haberdashery sales rep by the name of Zuckermann. As nice as he could be, and always gave a discount."[53]

Germans

"All that is necessary for the triumph of evil is for good men to do nothing." So famously said British statesman and political philosopher Edmund Burke, as if he had a crystal ball, as if he knew in the mid-eighteenth century what would happen in the mid-twentieth. For above all, the story of Nazi Germany, the story of the Holocaust in particular, is about presumably good men, and women, who did nothing in the face of evil.

Assuming that culpability is at issue, every discussion of Bystanders must begin and end with the question earlier raised: Who knew what when? In this case, though, while the question is important, it is not all-important. Why? Because there is overwhelming evidence that before the war virtually all Germans knew perfectly well the state was taking increasingly onerous measures against the Jews. And there is good, albeit not overwhelming, evidence that during the war many, if not most, Germans knew perfectly well that, at a minimum, Jews were being removed and never returned.

This raises another issue. It was one thing to have known there was discrimination against Jews, and even that Jews were being forcibly removed. But it would have been another thing altogether to have known that Jews were being slaughtered en masse. Yet even here we have sufficient evidence to be terribly troubled by followers who were "good men" but who did nothing. Take as an example the Rosenstrasse protests earlier described. Of these events, Walter Laqueur, a distinguished expert on the Nazi period, wrote, "The Rosenstrasse protest also shows that, contrary to a belief persisting to this day, the fate of those deported was no longer a secret at this time. If it had been believed that those arrested were merely being enlisted for work away from their homes, it is doubtful whether the women would have been willing to risk arrest—and worse—by defying the Gestapo. They must have known that if their husbands, fathers, and sons were deported, they would never be seen again."[54]

In 1933, 525,000 Jews lived in Germany.[55] During the next six years, this number dropped by more than half. In other words, in response to government-sponsored anti-Semitism, up to 300,000 Jews decided to leave before things got worse.[56]

Obviously, not all of those who quit Germany left at once. Rather, they left in stages, in response to the growing severity of measures taken against them. The first stage was the first half year of Hitler's rule, from early 1933 to mid-1933. Among those who suffered at the hands of the Nazis during this initial period were, of course, Jews as well as other enemies of the state, including Communists and Socialists. Torture, beatings, and gangsterlike killings took place even then, "in a highly charged atmosphere of street demonstrations, marches, elections, the take-over of state and local governments and the dissolution of the political parties, workers' associations and trade unions."[57]

The second stage began during the summer of 1933. Police brutality was institutionalized in newly established detention (concentration) camps. And legislative activity against Jews continued, affecting "primarily professionals, students, foreign Jews, Jewish employees and workers, the legal position of Jews, the theatre and Jewish business."[58]

The year 1935 constituted the third stage. During the early months, attacks against Jews were stepped up, and anti-Jewish propaganda became increasingly virulent. Later in the year, the notorious Nuremberg Laws were passed, which "deprived Jews of German citizenship rights and led to the exclusion of all remaining Jewish civil servants, artists, university teachers, judges and other public servants."[59] In addition, the activities of other Jewish professionals, such as lawyers and doctors, were further curbed; and there was strong pressure on Jews who owned businesses to sell quickly.

Phases four and five, roughly the years 1936 through 1939, were more of the same. Jewish physicians and lawyers lost their remaining practices. Licenses were withdrawn from Jewish salesmen and agents. Jewish communal institutions endured a change in their legal status and other privations. Synagogues in the great cities of Munich, Düsseldorf, and Nuremberg were torn down, for obvious, if not for officially sanctioned reasons. And in late 1938, subsequent to the infamous *Kristallnacht*, which was in effect a state-sponsored pogrom, all Jewish activities in the German economy were prohibited. The final phase of the emigration lasted until October 1941, after which Jews were flat-out forbidden to leave. It was at this point that the deportations and exterminations began in earnest.[60]

Victor Klemperer was a Jew who lived in Germany throughout the entire Nazi era, able to survive because he was married to a non-Jew. Late in his life the former professor of Romance languages published a remarkable two-volume "diary of the Nazi years," in which he described what it was like for him, living in Germany during the Hitler era, before and during the war. Here is an excerpt from December 1938:

> *Today is the Day of German Solidarity. Curfew for Jews from 12 noon until eight. When at exactly half past eleven I went to the mailbox and to the grocer, where I had to wait, I really felt as if I could not breathe. I cannot bear it anymore. Yesterday evening an order from the Minister of the Interior: local authorities are henceforth at liberty to restrict the movement of Jewish drivers both as to time and place . . . Every day brings new restrictions. Only today, Saturday, December 3, the newspaper reports ghettoization and limitations on the free movement of Jews in Berlin. Further stringent measures are promised. What for? Pure madness?*[61]

I include this brief chronicle of emigration and experience to demonstrate that it would have been virtually impossible for non-Jewish Germans to be ignorant of what befell Jewish Germans during the years 1933–1939. Nazi measures against Jews were simply too many and too harsh not to be widely known. Of course, we have already seen that large numbers of Germans, including Participants, Activists, and Diehards, openly supported Hitler and the anti-Semitism that was his public policy. Now we know more: that nearly all the rest—that is, those Germans who were discomforted by, or who disapproved of, what was happening to their former friends, neighbors, and associates—said little or nothing about their mistreatment and did little or nothing to help them. It was a moral outrage—and it was stupid to boot. Bystanders in Nazi Germany were not only morally bankrupt and pusillanimous, they were remarkably unimaginative as well. It appears they could not, or would not, conceive of anything they might do to stop bad things from happening. Of course, any such initiative would have been more difficult and dangerous as time went on, which makes the question of why so little was done early on especially troubling.

Once the war started, the consequences of people standing by and doing nothing were catastrophic. An extreme example is what happened—or, if you prefer, what did not happen—in the rural Austrian village of

Mauthausen. (Germany annexed Austria in 1938.) Until the Nazis decided to build a concentration camp alongside the stone quarries nearby
(1938), Mauthausen was far removed from the politics of the day. But during the years that followed, both the village and the surrounding country-
side "became a center of murder."[62]

At first residents of the area viewed the camp as an intrusion. But over
the months and years, the lives of those living in the camp and those living
in the village became entwined. Locals, including day laborers, suppliers, assis-
tants, and secretaries, were hired to service Mauthausen, as well as the "euthanasia" center that was set up nearby. They could not help but soon be
aware that those in the camp were suffering. To be clear: Mauthausen was
not a small or insignificant operation. Even in the early years, camp inmates
were often tortured and shot. And before it was all over, almost 119,000
people died there, including Jews, political prisoners, and Russian prisoners
of war. The final months, before the camp was liberated in May 1945, were
especially bad. "Prisoners were often murdered 'within sight of, and often
with the active complicity of, wide sections of the civilian population.'"[63]

Before further exploring how it happens that "good men" stand by
and do nothing in the face of mass murder, I want to return to the issue of
who exactly is a Bystander. The legal definition accords with my own. That
is, I define Bystanders as followers who are aware of their surroundings
but who make a deliberate decision to disengage. The legal definition
reads in part, "One present but not taking part . . . a spectator, beholder,
observer." The point is that Bystanders are distinguished from those who
are ignorant—that is, from Isolates. And they are distinguished as well
from those who are actively involved. They are not protagonists—nor are
they the objects of the action. Bystanders are, in fact, those who stand by.[64]

Of course, since we are talking here about people and not things, the
lines between the various types of followers are fungible, as opposed to
being precisely delineated. So, for example, Germans who voted once or
even twice for the Nazis but then, as things deteriorated, made a decision
to disengage may be considered Bystanders, as opposed to Participants.
The point is that Hitler had many hundreds of thousands of followers
who to all appearances were neutral. That is, by standing by and doing
nothing, they in no way supported the Nazi regime, and they in no way
resisted it. But as I made clear in my original definition of the Bystander,

this disengagement, which would appear at first glance to be neutral in its impact, is misleading. The truth is that being a Bystander amounts to providing tacit support "for whoever and whatever constitutes the status quo." The bottom line is that Bystanders matter—they matter a great deal. In fact, if their numbers are large, we can go so far as to say that Bystanders "shape the course of events."[65]

And there is more. For to call someone a Bystander, at least in the case of Nazi Germany, tells us something in addition to simply the status of the person. It tells us that the individual's decision to disengage was not only cognitively deliberate, it was morally questionable.

Bystanders during the Nazi era can be seen as operating at three levels: individual, institutional, and international.[66] Individuals acting alone made the decision to observe rather than participate for any one of several different reasons—likely first among them the overweening power of Hitler, the Nazi party, and Nazi ideology, which together dominated public life. Second, there was the element of fear. As we have seen, nearly from the start the Nazis "dealt decisively with the few cases of protest or resistance they encountered."[67] Third, individuals learned to distance themselves psychologically from what was happening politically. Even in the case of Mauthausen, the townspeople, "although cognizant of the terror in the camp . . . learned to walk a narrow line between unavoidable awareness and prudent disregard."[68] Fourth, as we saw in the Milgram experiments, it is easy enough to deny personal responsibility for what happens, even if what happens is dreadful. Even killers can placate any qualms they might have by reminding themselves that they are only following orders. Fifth, there was the larger context within which Bystanders were operating, one in which forces such as industrialization, modernization, and urbanization "eradicated the social fabric necessary for a traditional sense of individual ethical responsibility to survive."[69] Sixth, there was the social setting. As I like to point out, essentially we are social creatures, affected not only by what our leaders are doing but by what our fellow followers are doing. So it was that Bystanders, "eager to abandon individual uncertainty for the sake of collective identity," were content to conform.[70] Finally, there was an overwhelming sense of powerlessness, whether real or imagined. Most Bystanders in Nazi Germany insisted they were helpless to do anything more than they did, which was, of course, nothing.

German institutions played their part as well. Churches, universities, and governmental bureaucracies such as the judiciary and the civil service all accommodated themselves, and quickly, to the Nazi regime. As mentioned, there were some pockets of opposition and even resistance—for example, in the Confessing Church, a group within the German Evangelical Church that committed itself to remaining independent of the Nazi regime. But even in the Confessing Church "the majority of church leaders never protested the state racial laws." Some went so far as to support certain measures against Jews, while others simply advised the church against openly criticizing Hitler or the Nazi party. In other words, even in this case those who ostensibly were well intentioned "offered neither protest nor resistance, for example, when millions of Germans had to obtain proof of their 'Aryan' heritage from church records."[71]

Among the most notorious examples of institutional conformity was the medical profession. While one might have supposed that those in the healing arts would have been at the forefront of those who were opposed first to the persecutions and then to the exterminations, quite the opposite was the case. Many doctors were Diehards, Activists, and Participants, who freely cooperated with the Nazis, in some instances even volunteering to conduct gruesome experiments on the most helpless of their victims.[72] In other cases, doctors, and those in the medical profession more generally, simply conformed to the prevailing norms, doing what they were told to do during the entire Nazi period, without resisting. This pattern held even when there were personal misgivings—for example, with regard to state-sponsored "euthanasia" intended to eliminate the mentally defective. It was this kind of blanket endorsement—bestowed by institutions on individuals—that further explains why so many of Hitler's followers chose to conform rather than to resist or in any way intervene.

Others

Germans were by no means the only Bystanders. For example, less well known than what happened in Germany is what happened in the Netherlands. Suffice it to say here that during the Nazi occupation, "71 percent of all Jews in the Netherlands ended up in death camps, the highest percentage in Europe outside Poland."[73] This is not to say that all Dutch stood by and did nothing while Jews were being taken forcibly away. But it is to point out that in the Netherlands as in Germany, "only a small number of people were active resisters." As Ian Buruma put it, while there were, of course, some Dutch who in some way refused to go along, the larger history of the Netherlands during the Second World War is one of "indifference, cowardice, and in some cases active complicity."[74]

What, meanwhile, did the rest of the world do in the face of Nazi genocide? What was done by those *not* living in Germany or under Nazi occupation to stop the mass killing? Non-Germans were not, of course, Hitler's followers in the conventional sense of this word. Still, if Hitler was murdering Jews by the hundreds of thousands and finally by the millions, and people living elsewhere in the world knew what was happening but did little or nothing to intervene, were they complicit? Were they for all practical purposes among the führer's followers?

Over the last several decades there has been considerable soul-searching over precisely these questions, especially as they pertain to Americans and to Europeans not living under the Nazi boot—for example, the British and the Swiss. As a result, the word *Bystander* is often applied now not only to those within Nazi Germany who stood by and did nothing, but also to those without. Among other reasons, it is assumed that many of these people, statesmen and citizens alike, could somehow have intervened, and at little or no personal risk.

Incidentally, I should note that this question is not only of historical interest, if only because dictators and genocides are not only historical artifacts. Since the end of the Second World War, there have been genocides in Cambodia and Rwanda and more recently in Darfur. In each of these cases, the world community did little, or in any case too little, to stop the mass murder.

So far as the Holocaust is concerned, scholars have moved beyond blanket indictment, beyond simply pointing the finger of blame, in particular at the United Sates and England, for not saving more Jews while there was still time. Some point to the different circumstances in the different countries, arguing that the "category of bystanders cannot be used in a uniform or unproblematic sense" to describe the response of democratic nations to the persecution of the Jews during the Nazi era.[75] Others suggest that only a nuanced approach to so complex a matter does the subject justice: "Liberal ambivalence within the state and the public enabled both restrictionism and generous rescue policies to succeed within bystander nations at different times and different places."[76]

Still, most studies of so-called bystander nations have found some fault. Among other things, we now know that information about the Holocaust was available earlier and more widely than initially thought. By 1941 the International Committee of the Red Cross had received reports that concentration camps were killing centers in which European Jews were being murdered in large numbers. (Although the Red Cross shared the information, it "never issued any public statement during the Holocaust" about the Holocaust.)[77] And by 1942 there was conclusive evidence, available both in the United States and in Europe, that hundreds of thousands of Jews were being murdered. Although this figure would turn out to be wrong—it was an underestimate—it should have received widespread attention, but it did not. For example, in the early 1940s some American church leaders tried to mobilize their constituencies against Nazism but found the response to their appeals was negligible.

Essentially, the complaint against the United States, especially Franklin Roosevelt, and against England, especially Winston Churchill, was twofold: first, neither did enough to take in Jews or arrange for them to be removed from harm's way. Second, neither did anything directly to destroy the killing centers, in particular the deadliest of all, Auschwitz.

Charges of indifference against Roosevelt and other members of his administration were leveled most memorably, because they were so shocking at the time, by David Wyman. In his 1984 book, *The Abandonment of the Jews: America and the Holocaust, 1941–1945,*Wyman offered a devastating critique of Americans as Bystanders.[78] Essentially, he charged that information about Nazis systematically annihilating European Jews was available in the United States in November 1942, but that no one did much of anything about it, not the State Department, not the War Department, not the president himself.[79] Wyman's critique of Roosevelt was especially harsh. He wrote in his concluding chapter that "America's response to the Holocaust was the result of action and inaction on the part of many people. At the forefront was Franklin D. Roosevelt, whose steps to aid Europe's Jews were very limited. If he had wanted to, he could have aroused substantial public backing for a vital rescue effort by speaking out on the issue. If nothing else, a few forceful statements by the president would have brought the extermination news out of obscurity and into the headlines. But he had little to say about the problem and gave no priority at all to rescue."[80]

Nor have the British been exempt from similar charges—for example, against Churchill for refusing to bomb Auschwitz in 1944, when at least some experts have claimed it would have been relatively easy for him to give the order to do so. We know that in the summer of 1944, the proposal to attack Auschwitz and the rail lines leading up to it was the subject of intense debate within the British government. However, in retrospect it has seemed that so far as the prime minister was concerned, this was not a priority. Had Churchill considered the destruction of Auschwitz to be all-important, it likely could have and would have been done.[81] But at the most opportune moment, the prime minister's attention was elsewhere, on what was happening in Warsaw. As British historian and Churchill biographer Martin Gilbert put it, "It was the agony of Warsaw, not the agony of the Jews that had come to dominate the telegraphic exchanges of the Allied leaders."[82]

Again, these views, implicating Roosevelt and Churchill in particular, are by no means universally held. Holocaust scholars are divided on the question of who among the Allies were Bystanders, if any.[83] But the debate itself signifies.[84] It signifies that the issue of the Bystander is not, nor should it be, only about Germans. It is about anyone anywhere who knew about the extermination of the Jews but did little or nothing to stop it.

To all this I must add one last note: some have questioned whether Jews themselves were somehow Bystanders, complicit in their own destruction. How can this be? Because while some Jews resisted—in Germany and elsewhere—most did not. Most of the murdered millions, many of whom, of course, were women, children, and elderly, did not take on those who were doing them in. (Nor, for that matter, did most of the millions of Jews far from the killing fields scream and yell on their behalf.)

This explains why it was not uncommon for Zionist pioneers to be humiliated by the "lack of widespread rebellion against the Nazis among European Jews." It further explains why survivors were received in Israel "not only with relief but also, at times, with suspicion and bureaucratic indifference."[85]

Where, then, does this leave us, those of us coming to grips with followership? Can it fairly be claimed that by being too passive too long, European

Jews contributed to their own demise? Can it fairly be claimed that by being too passive too long, Jews outside Nazi-occupied Europe were complicit?

I end with these questions because of this question: is being a Bystander part of the human condition? We know by now that even in the case of Hitler's Germany, there were exceptions to the general rule that followers follow. To start, whatever the indictments against them, the war against the Nazis could never have been won without the unwavering commitment and dedication of leaders like Roosevelt and Churchill, and the men and women who soldiered at their command. Next there were the German exceptions, those who dared to protest, or to rescue, or to in some other way be heroic under impossibly difficult circumstances. In fact, as earlier mentioned, names like Dietrich Bonhoeffer, the anti-Nazi theologian who was arrested and finally hung by Hitler, and Oskar Schindler, the German industrialist who risked all to save some one thousand Jews who worked in his factory, have become the stuff of legend. And there were Jewish Participants, Activists, and Diehards as well, in Europe and elsewhere around the world, some of whom did everything they humanly could to stop Hitler and his henchmen.

Still, there is this: powerful leaders exert strong pressure on groups and organizations to conform. In turn, groups and organizations exert strong pressure on their individual members to conform, both in their beliefs and in their behaviors. This explains at least in part why rescuers who believed that "all human beings were entitled to decent treatment merely by virtue of being human" were deviants who, if discovered, were nearly certain to pay heavily for doing what was right.[86] In short, Bystander behavior is normal behavior. As Fritz Stern put it, "The wars and revolutions of our time have been made possible not so much by a few leaders or sects as by the multitudes of passive citizens who smugly thought that politics was the responsibility of statesmen."[87]

In early 1933 Sonderburg was a small, peaceful German town, with some four thousand inhabitants, one hundred fifty of whom were Jews. There were no noticeable tensions of any kind, including between Jews and Gentiles. In fact, even at the height of Hitler's power, Sonderburg never become a Nazi stronghold. Only six hundred townspeople joined the Nazi party, and of those, only about one hundred were hard-core members.[88]

Nonetheless, within days after Hitler became chancellor, "the Jewish residents of Sonderburg were feeling the cold wind of Nazism—and much of it came from the actions of their neighbors."To take just a single example, a man by the name of Joshua Abraham was in the habit of playing cards twice a week with his friends. But as soon as the Nazis came to power, he was no longer told when or where they planned to play. "Everything stopped," he remembered. "I would see them on the street and we pretended we didn't see each other. Not one of them spoke to me."[89]

The situation in Sonderburg deteriorated quickly. Most amazing of all was not the behavior of hard-core Nazis but rather the "immediate and spontaneous accommodation" of ordinary Germans to the new order. "With striking suddenness, the non-Jewish citizens of Sonderburg began treating their Jewish neighbors and co-workers differently." As a result, nearly overnight, Jews became "a nonentity, invisible, irrelevant."[90]

From everything we know, it seems likely that under ordinary circumstances the residents of Sonderburg would have continued to get along, to live and let live. But under the Nazis, non-Jews became Bystanders who did what sometimes happens in these cases: they slid down a slippery slope. First they stood by while Jews were being excluded. Then they stood by while Jews were being persecuted. Finally, they stood by while Jews were being exterminated. The bottom line is that they remained throughout the Nazi period essentially uninvolved, as if the fate of others was no concern of theirs.

AFTERTHOUGHT

I said at the outset that I had a bias—a general bias against those who stand by and do nothing and a particular bias against those who stand by and do nothing when human lives are at stake. The story here told is extraordinary. But the lessons to be learned extend to the ordinary, to everyday life. Which raises the question of what specifically can we extrapolate from the extreme circumstance that was Hitler's Germany to apply to circumstances more mundane?

First and foremost is individual responsibility for what happens, whether up close and personal or in the distance. We are our brother's keeper—and to abnegate this responsibility at the level of the individual is to abnegate it at the level of the group. Second, once the habit of standing by and doing nothing is developed, it is difficult to break. Better, then, to get engaged early on. Finally, to withdraw is to cede to those who have more power, authority, and influence than do we the right to decide. Sometimes we're lucky: our leaders and managers are good. But sometimes we're not so lucky: our leaders and managers are bad. When that happens, to stand by and do nothing is to risk going from bad to worse.

CHAPTER 6

Participants

Merck

Participants are in some way engaged. They clearly favor their leaders and the groups and organizations of which they are members—or they are clearly opposed. In either case, they care enough to put their money where their mouths are—that is, to invest some of what they have (time, for example) to try to have an impact.

FORETHOUGHT

By and large, leaders *want* followers who are Participants. Assuming they are in support, rather than in opposition, Participants are the fuel that drives the engine. They provide the everyday energy that makes for a good group or organization, which in turn enables leaders to do what they want and intend. The opposite is true as well. There are Participants who, because they were distanced or became dissatisfied, undermine their leaders, in small but potentially significant ways. Finally, there are Participants such as those described here who, while generally supportive of their leader and of the organization of which they are members, nevertheless go their own way. At Merck the Participants who mattered most were those Peter Drucker called "knowledge workers."[1] They were experts who, as a result of their expertise, worked independently and, ultimately, without sufficient oversight from the man supposedly in charge.

To read about Bystanders in Nazi Germany is to discover how much followers matter even when they do nothing. To read about Participants at Merck is to discover something else altogether: how much followers do matter, can matter, when they are part of the process. It is also to be reminded of how misleading is what was earlier called the "leader attribution error." For if the story told here does not demonstrate the potential importance of those *other* than those at the top, it demonstrates nothing at all.

BACKGROUND

On April 5, 2006, a New Jersey jury found that Merck's arthritis drug, Vioxx, had caused John McDarby, a seventy-seven-year-old retired insurance agent, to suffer a heart attack. The jury further found Merck guilty of consumer fraud for failing to warn the public of the drug's cardiovascular risks. The court ordered Merck to pay McDarby and his wife $4.5 million, plus another $9 million in punitive damages for misleading, presumably deliberately, the U.S. Food and Drug Administration (FDA).[2]

The defeat was a loss not just for Merck but for the pharmaceutical industry more generally, whose reputation in recent years has, in any case, plummeted. Once among the most admired of American businesses, drug companies are now near the bottom of the list, ranked slightly higher than those in tobacco and oil, but lower than, for example, those in airlines, banking, and insurance.[3] Of course, the reasons for this are many, including, for example, consumer anger over constantly escalating drug prices. But the problems associated with this single drug, Vioxx, are singular. More than anything else, the saga of Vioxx accounts for the fact that Merck, which a decade earlier was an exemplar of corporate virtue, became an exemplar of corporate greed. For failing to carefully caution its customers—its patients if you will—that Vioxx could be deadly, Merck lost in every way.

How did this happen? How did a company that was held in such high esteem fall so far so fast? The most conventional of several explanations is leadership—and no doubt it played a role. Roy Vagelos, who was Merck's chief executive officer from 1985 to 1994, was credited with its strong ascent. Similarly, Raymond V. Gilmartin, chief executive officer from 1995 to 2004, was blamed for presiding over the company's decline.

Vagelos was outstanding, "the undisputed king of the pharmaceutical industry."[4] Under his leadership and for years running, Merck was anointed by *Fortune* the "most admired company in America." And Vagelos personally was honored by the National Management Association as American Manager of the Year (1990), and by his peers as Chief Executive of the Year (1992). He had a long string of successes that included a revamped research organization and expanded global marketing, and a leadership style that was enormously appealing. A highly accomplished scientist as well as a much-heralded chief executive, he nevertheless drove his own Honda to work, ate regularly in the company cafeteria, and solicited feedback from anyone at Merck who would give it, including those down the corporate ladder. Vagelos retired when he had to, at the mandatory retirement age of sixty-five. But even then it was considered a loss, for under his leadership Merck had thrived, in the economic marketplace as well as in the court of public opinion.

Vagelos's immediate successor, Gilmartin, thus had the unenviable task of filling some very big shoes. To be sure, he had background and experience that Vagelos lacked. Above all, he understood the increasingly important role of managed care, which was considered by the board that selected him to be a major asset. But he was not a scientist, nor did he have experience in the pharmaceutical industry, nor was he familiar with Merck's corporate culture. Again, this was in direct contrast to Vagelos, whose own long years as a medical researcher had made him an expert in pharmaceuticals in his own right. And so it was that under Vagelos's leadership, his followers, his fellow researchers, produced a veritable string of lifesaving drugs, and this "in large part because of the inspiration" they drew from his "passion and sense of purpose."[5]

The first five years with Gilmartin at the helm went well enough. Although never as highly respected as his predecessor, he had his own successes, including new drugs to replace those whose patents were expiring, and a steady rise in the company's annual sales and net income. But by the new millennium, the good times were over. In 2001 Merck's shares went down fully 38 percent. Moreover, the company that only recently was the largest drug producer in the world fell behind its two largest competitors, Pfizer and GlaxoSmithKline.[6]

Gilmartin never really recovered his footing. Several of Merck's most profitable products became vulnerable to competition. Late-stage testing on some promising new drugs had to be stopped. And in 2003 the company was obliged to announce that because of a critical drop in earnings, thousands of jobs had to be cut. Of course, the blame for Merck's misfortunes fell primarily on Gilmartin. Industry analysts charged that under his leadership Merck had developed problems it had never had before—for example, a misplaced rise in the number of middle managers and a drop in the number of new drugs, especially "blockbuster" drugs that work wonders for the bottom line. Under Gilmartin, turnover had doubled and morale had sagged.[7]

Gilmartin did not take the criticisms lying down. At Merck's 2004 annual business meeting, he defended his leadership and outlined his plans for the future. He insisted that despite some recent setbacks, the company was pursuing the strategy that was right for Merck and in the best interest of its shareholders.[8] Still, his protestations notwithstanding, it's clear that during the first few years of the twenty-first century, neither Merck nor its chief executive were in the best of health.

This languishing could in and of itself explain the sad story of Vioxx. Merck badly needed a best-selling drug, and so did Gilmartin. The possibility that anything could be really wrong with Vioxx—first one of Merck's most promising products and then one of its most profitable ones—was apparently too painful to consider carefully. And so it was that Gilmartin presided over a situation that in the end got out of hand.

This, though, is not in the main a tale about a leader. Rather, it is about his followers. From day one Gilmartin was focused on strategic decision making, leaving day-to-day management issues, including those pertaining to research, in the hands of his subordinates.[9] As a result, whatever the mistakes and misjudgments with regard to Vioxx, they were made mainly by those who were not at the top of the corporate ladder.

This is not to say that Merck's chief executive officer abdicated responsibility. He did not. Instead, it is to point out that it was those who worked under him—especially the knowledge workers, the experts, the scientists and physicians—who developed the drug and then ran with it until they were permitted to do so no longer. When Merck finally decided in September 2004 that it had no choice but to take Vioxx off the market, Gilmartin was left holding the bag. No surprise. Leaders are accountable for what happens on their watch. But it was the Participants working under him who drove the drug from day one—and so it was they who were directly responsible for one of the great fiascos in the history of American business.

THE PRODUCT

Before 1980 the pharmaceutical industry was successful; after 1980 it was "stupendously" successful.[10] For reasons that ranged from Ronald Reagan's business-friendly public policies to a growing sense of entitlement more generally, for the last two decades of the twentieth century, drug companies were among the most profitable of all American businesses. This was the bullish context within which Merck first developed Vioxx and then began to test it.

Among the most promising of all classes of drugs in the late 1990s were COX-2 inhibitors: nonsteroidal anti-inflammatory agents that relieved aches of all kinds, but above all, those from arthritis. So promising were these drugs that several major drug companies rushed to the marketplace with their own COX-2 inhibitors, among them obviously Merck. In November 1998, on the basis of clinical trials involving fifty-four hundred patients, Merck submitted to the FDA an application seeking approval for Vioxx as a treatment for osteoarthritis. In the process, Merck claimed among other things that the rates of cardiovascular risk were "similar" among patients taking Vioxx, a placebo, or other pain relievers. In part as a result of this assurance, the FDA gave Vioxx its stamp of approval. In May 1999 Vioxx was made available for sale.

However, less than a year later Merck received the preliminary results of a trial, which suggested that patients taking Vioxx were at higher risk of cardiovascular problems than those taking an older pain reliever, naproxen (sold under the name of Aleve). In fact, in this particular trial, patients taking Vioxx suffered five times as many heart attacks as their Aleve-taking counterparts. While this was the first clear indication that taking Vioxx might be dangerous to your health, no warnings were sounded or, at least, no warnings the public could hear.[11]

Shortly thereafter, in November 2000, a study of Vioxx was published by the most prestigious, most-cited medical publication in the world, the *New England Journal of Medicine (NEJM)*. The article touted the benefits of taking the drug—it effectively alleviated pain caused by inflammation—while seeming to downplay its risks. As a result, large numbers of doctors began prescribing Vioxx, and large numbers of patients began taking it.

One more year passed—to February 2001—before evidence that something might really be wrong made the FDA visibly nervous. In fact, by then the FDA had become so uneasy, it established an advisory committee charged with holding hearings on Vioxx per se and on how the drug was being marketed. As a consequence of these deliberations, the FDA sent Gilmartin a strongly worded letter—a *very* strongly worded letter. It stated that it considered Merck's promotional campaign to be misleading. It "minimizes the potentially serious cardiovascular findings," the FDA claimed, and "thus misrepresents the safety profile of Vioxx."[12] The FDA further cautioned that it considered Merck's claim that Vioxx had a "favorable cardiovascular safety profile" to be "incomprehensible." Finally, the FDA charged that the comparison Merck was making between Vioxx and naproxen was "inaccurate," and that the rate of patient heart attacks was higher if they were taking the first rather than the second.[13]

The strong tone of the FDA's missive notwithstanding, more than another year passed before Merck revised the label on Vioxx to include a warning about the increased risk of heart attacks and strokes. But by then it was too little, too late. One month later, in May 2002, Merck was sued over Vioxx—for the first but definitely not for the last time. A woman by the name of Carol Ernst alleged that her fifty-nine-year-old husband, Robert Ernst, a Wal-Mart manager who ran marathons, died as a result of taking the drug.

It took two more years for Merck to stanch the bleeding. In 2004 the company finally stopped its long-term study of Vioxx, publicly acknowledging that the drug could double the risk of having a heart attack if taken for longer than eighteen months. Given that in 2003 Vioxx had earned for Merck a cool $2.5 billion, which accounted for fully 11 percent of the company's total sales, making this admission was a difficult pill to swallow.

In September 2004 Vioxx was pulled from the market altogether. Gilmartin made the announcement: "We are taking this action because we believe it best serves the interests of patients. Although we believe it would have been possible to continue to market Vioxx with labeling that would incorporate these new data . . . we concluded that a voluntary withdrawal is the responsible course to take."[14] Of course, by this time some 20 million Americans had already taken the drug, many only for short periods of time, but many for longer than a year and a half.

Whatever the company's transgressions or lack thereof, Merck has since paid dearly for putting Vioxx on the market in the first place and then for keeping it there as long as it did. In addition, it would continue to pay for some time, both in the court of public opinion and in the court of law. A vigorous ad campaign intended to defend the company notwithstanding—Merck claimed its actions on Vioxx were "consistent with putting the interests of patients first"—slings and arrows have been fired from every direction, transforming at least for a time this once venerated bastion of corporate integrity into what I earlier called an exemplar of corporate greed.[15] Moreover, this was considered greed of an especially onerous sort, for as industry critic Marcia Angell put it, "Drugs are different. People depend on them for their health and even their lives."[16]

Within months after Vioxx was pulled from the market, people began to pile on. Physician Robert Burton charged in *Salon* that the "pharmaceutical giant" Merck knew there were heart risks associated with Vioxx—but that "its own studies were designed to avoid finding out how serious they were." Burton called the whole thing "a tragedy."[17] Similarly, the *New York Times* made plain its view in an editorial: "Internal e-mail messages and documents showed that Merck scientists had been concerned about cardiovascular risks even before Vioxx went on the market and continued to be concerned thereafter, even while resisting regulatory efforts to add warnings to the drug's label and devising strategies to dodge any concerns from doctors."[18] And the *Chicago Tribune* did the same. In December 2005 it ran an editorial titled "A Sin of Omission." The piece charged that Merck's conduct in the case of Vioxx tarnished "the company's once-shiny reputation" and made it nearly impossible to believe that it "never misled users about the risks of Vioxx. What else would you call the omission of data that may hurt rather than help a drug's prospects?"[19]

The legal ramifications were potentially the most threatening. Soon after Vioxx was pulled from the shelves, plaintiffs all across America were lining up to file suit against a company they claimed was guilty of deliberately misleading them (or their loved ones) into thinking that Vioxx was safe. It started slowly—just a few hundred lawsuits and then a few thousand and then tens of thousands of product liability lawsuits were filed against Merck for failing to warn the public adequately of the cardiac risks associated with taking Vioxx. (Another study that came out a few years later added more fuel to the fire: it suggested that, like other drugs in its class, Vioxx could have posed a risk for "renal events," including kidney dysfunction.[20])

Merck's legal strategy was (is) simple: it vowed to defend itself on a case-by-case basis, setting aside some $675 million (later upped to $1 billion) to cover legal fees alone. Still, the results of the first federal Vioxx trial, in which a jury found Merck liable for the death of the aforementioned Robert Ernst, were stunning: Ernst's widow was awarded a whopping $253.5 million in damages. While the state of Texas capped the final figure at $26.1 million, members of the jury had made their point. However thin the evidence that Vioxx was directly responsible for Ernst's death, they clearly had no sympathy whatsoever for a pharmaceutical giant they believed had put at risk the health and welfare of an ordinary American.

Not every plaintiff was as brilliantly successful as the first. Throughout 2005, 2006, and most of 2007, some won their cases against Merck, others lost, other claims ended in a mistrial, and still others were pending.[21] Moreover, as of late 2007, none of the people who sued Merck had received payments from the company, since every verdict against it was being appealed. But whatever was the outcome of the individual trials, in every case in which Merck was forced to defend itself, there was bad publicity. For example, various news organizations reported that in a Los Angeles courtroom, a plaintiff's lawyer, Thomas Girardi, had accused Merck of showing "careless disregard" for its patients. Speaking on behalf of his client, a seventy-one-year-old widower who had taken more than two hundred Vioxx pills over a period of two years before suffering a heart attack, Girardi charged that Merck knew that Vioxx could cause "massive, terrible side effects and they didn't tell anybody."[22]

The years since Vioxx was pulled from the market were difficult for Merck—some forty-five thousand product liability cases were finally filed— but not in the end deadly. Gilmartin staunchly defended his company— for instance, in testimony before the Senate Committee on Finance. The problem with Vioxx, he assured the committee, was "unexpected." He went on to say that Merck's clinical data had shown "no difference between Vioxx and a placebo," and that he personally had believed so "whole-heartedly" in Vioxx that his wife used it "until the day we withdrew it from the marketplace."[23] Still, Gilmartin's days as CEO of Merck were numbered. He left the company in 2005.

Prognostications of Merck's imminent demise were, in any case, wrong. The company brought in a new CEO, new drugs entered the pipeline, and there was early evidence that the stock price would be more resilient than originally feared. In addition, Merck's legal strategy, to defend itself one case at a time, paid off. While Merck agreed to pay merely $5 billion to settle the Vioxx-related lawsuits, it had successfully extricated itself from the litigation and bad publicity that had threatened to distract it for years. Still it will take a while for Merck to regain the trust of the American consumer and to shed completely its reputation as a company that put the interests of its shareholders before those of its patients.[24]

The Participants

Since September 2004, when the risks associated with Vioxx were made public, everyone at Merck, from the president on down, defended themselves and the company by insisting that whatever the problems, they were, to use Gilmartin's word, *unexpected*. The evidence, however, suggests otherwise.

As Angell points out, for years there were "signs of trouble." She refers particularly to the previously mentioned and now infamous November 2000 study published by *NEJM*, in which it was reported that Vioxx was easier on the stomach than Aleve. "Unfortunately," Angell adds, "the study also showed [although it downplayed] at least a fourfold increase in the risk of heart attacks." In fact, an FDA analysis revealed the drug was more likely to cause heart attacks or strokes than to prevent stomach ulcers. At least some of the evidence was confirmed the next year, when there were still further findings that taking Vioxx increased cardiovascular risk. Angell continues: "What Merck should have done after it got the results of [the second study] was immediately launch a large enough clinical trial to investigate the cardiovascular risk as quickly as possible. Instead, a few months later, it signed Dorothy Hamill to skate its problems away. The company reportedly spent $160 million on direct-to-consumer ads for Vioxx in 2000, and continued to spend approximately $100 million a year during the next four years."[25]

In his 2004 book, *Overdo$ed America: The Broken Promise of American Medicine*, John Abramson, a family doctor and clinical instructor at the Harvard Medical School, reached similar conclusions. Referring to the November 2000 article in *NEJM*, he reports suspecting even then that something was wrong. No mention was made, he noted, of the single most important result, which in fact was damning evidence: "Overall, including GI, cardiovascular, and all other serious complications, the people who took Vioxx had 21 percent more 'serious adverse events,' complications that usually lead to hospitalization or death, than did the people who took naproxen."[26]

Again the question is, How did this happen? How did it happen that one of America's most respected, long-established, and largest pharmaceuticals came out with a drug that raised at least some questions right from the start—and then continued to sell the drug until it was morally, if not legally, obliged to withdraw it from the market? Of course, the overarching motivation was money. The pharmaceutical industry is different from what it was; in fact, the general effects of commercialization on health care are everywhere apparent.[27] But money does not in and of itself explain the fact that for several years Merck pushed a drug that turned out to be, potentially at least, devastatingly dangerous. For a fuller understanding of the Vioxx debacle, we need to look elsewhere.

Inevitably, Gilmartin was one of the leading actors in this drama—he was, after all, Merck's chief executive officer for the duration. But as we have seen, he was not a scientist or a physician, nor had he had long years of experience in the pharmaceutical industry. This lack of expertise dictated that Gilmartin had no choice: to run the company, he had to depend absolutely on his subordinates for guidance and even instruction, especially on the benefits and deficits of particular drugs, such as Vioxx. Which subordinates mattered most? The answer is clear: Participants who were knowledge workers, researchers who wanted badly for Vioxx to be a runaway success. It was they who did what they could to persuade people inside the company and out that the drug was safe.

Who, more specifically, were these Participants, these subordinates who had such an impact on their superiors? I focus on four in particular: Edward Scolnick, Alise Reicin, Louis Sherwood, and Nancy Santanello.

Arguably, the first among them was Edward Scolnick, an MD from Harvard, who from 1982 to 2003 worked at Merck in a range of research capacities, including finally as president of Merck Research Laboratories. Scolnick was a man of high reputation, who reputedly influenced a generation of so-called laboratory sleuths, and whose influence within Merck, especially as a holdover from the still-venerated Vagelos era, remained high. What is clear with the benefit of hindsight is that Scolnick played a major role in the aggressive development and marketing of Vioxx, one that was not ultimately salutary.

We know that so far as Vioxx was concerned, Scolnick was hot to trot from day one. As far back as 1998, after reading a report by a Wall Street analyst that suggested that Merck badly needed a new blockbuster drug, Scolnick e-mailed colleagues to the effect that "essential to Merck" was the development of a painkiller that could be marketed as more effective than any other.[28] But as it turned out, Scolnick had some doubts about Vioxx in particular early on: in 2000 he considered combining Vioxx with an anticlotting agent to mitigate the potential cardiovascular risks.[29] In a videotaped deposition provided to a jury in Houston, he admitted e-mailing some colleagues in 2000 to caution that the danger of taking Vioxx was "clearly there." He called it a "shame," and went on to compare Vioxx to other drugs with known side effects, adding, "There is always a hazard."[30]

Shortly after Scolnick wrote the above-mentioned e-mail, he was given new information that suggested Vioxx was safe. Still, there is evidence that his doubts about the drug were never put fully to rest. Around the time that Merck issued a press release to tout the virtues of Vioxx, Scolnick wrote several of his colleagues that his "worry quotient" remained high. In other words, by his own testimony he remained from start to finish in "minor agony" over the possibility that taking Vioxx might be dangerous to at least some who ingested it.[31]

This did not, though, stop Scolnick from aggressively defending the drug against all comers. In another e-mail to his colleagues, this one sent in 2001, he urged them to hang tough. However strongly the FDA suggested that warnings be placed on all Vioxx products, Scolnick insisted Merck should "not accept this label."[32] In fact, during the several years that Vioxx was on the market, Scolnick continued to play the role of Vioxx watchdog, generally defending the drug within the company and attacking those outside who questioned its safety. He was especially angry at the FDA, which he called "devious" in its attempts to monitor Vioxx, and at certain FDA officials, whom he called "bastards" for daring to suggest that if Vioxx was going to continue to be sold, Merck should make clear to consumers the attendant risks.[33]

The gap between Scolnick's private reservations about Vioxx, shared with only a few of his associates, and his public performance as unrelenting pitchman became apparent only several years later. Only after the fact did we learn that Scolnick's doubts were trumped by his will to protect a drug that he knew could become, as indeed it did, a blockbuster. So Scolnick was nothing if not a Participant, a follower who failed to warn his leader adequately about dangers that could lie ahead. In fact, not only did he not stop the train, he did nothing whatsoever even to slow it.

Scolnick's efforts on behalf of Vioxx were joined by those of another Participant, Merck's vice president for clinical research. Alise Reicin was another knowledge worker, a top researcher who became invested in Vioxx early on, promoted the drug both within the company and without, and defended it to the end, even after its safety became an open question. Reicin joined Merck in 1996. She worked on the compound that developed into Vioxx in 1997. She helped design the clinical trials that led to FDA approval in 1998. And later, when things turned nasty, when Merck was obliged to defend itself in a courtroom, Reicin was Merck's "star witness."[34] Described by her bosses as a "tenacious defender of the Vioxx franchise," Reicin was the one who spoke frequently on behalf of the defense.[35] She was poised as well as "authoritative and firm about her conviction that [Merck] acted appropriately."[36] No wonder jurors liked her and found her in particular to be a credible witness.[37]

Still, Reicin's defense of Vioxx remains suspect. However skilled her performance in a courtroom, there is evidence that what she said on the stand was other than the whole truth and nothing but. In public, she "consistently provided the scientific underpinning to Merck's claim it acted in good faith before pulling [Vioxx] from the market."[38] However, company e-mails reveal that as far back as 1997 Reicin, like Scolnick, had doubts about the drug, admitting even then that "the possibility of increased CV [cardiovascular] events is of great concern." In fact, in order to protect Vioxx from being revealed to the FDA as potentially unsafe, she went so far as to propose that people with a high risk of heart problems be kept out of the clinical trials so that the difference in the rate of cardiovascular problems between patients taking Vioxx and those who were not "would not be evident."[39]

Moreover, Reicin's coauthorship of that November 2000 article in *NEJM* turned out to be an embarrassing, if not disreputable, contribution to the literature on COX-2 inhibitor drugs. To be sure, Reicin subsequently attempted to explain away some of the discrepancies, particularly as they relate to timing. However, in 2005 the *NEJM* editors were themselves obliged to admit (this was not the highpoint of their professional lives either) that the Merck-funded study on which the article was based was missing critical data. "Information about three heart attacks suffered by patients taking Vioxx in a clinical trial wasn't sent to the journal's editors before the article was published, in November of 2000."[40]

The question, of course, is why Reicin and her coauthors did not update the piece before publication, especially since the total number of heart attacks was raised by three to twenty out of four thousand patients. This was no small matter, for despite the small increase (to 0.5 percent), the implications were "potentially big," especially "when multiplied times the estimated 20 million people" who were taking Vioxx before it was removed from the market.[41]

The main charge against Reicin and her coauthors was that they gave incomplete and therefore misleading information. Reicin responded by pointing out that when the article was first submitted for publication (in May 2000), the data on the additional heart attacks was not yet available—and that besides, the study had a cutoff date. But since the information was in fact available by July, and since the article in question was published in November, it seemed to at least some experts that the authors (and editors) had had ample time to amend their piece. Had they done so, the message to readers, especially to physicians considering pre-scribing Vioxx, would have been different. With regard to the risks of taking Vioxx, it would have been considerably more forthcoming.

The degree to which science might have bent to commerce in this instance is suggested in an early e-mail exchange between Reicin and Briggs Morrison. Morrison was another Merck researcher who worked on Vioxx during the first stages of its development. In 1997 he sent his colleagues an e-mail that read in part, "I know this has been discussed to death but [in the] real world everyone is on it, so why exclude" aspirin?[42] He added that without aspirin's blood-thinning effects, "you will get more thrombotic events"—that is, blood clots—and "kill [the] drug."[43] This was the e-mail to which Reicin replied when she wrote that the company was in a "no-win situation," and when she proposed that people at high risk of cardiovascular problems be excluded from the study so that the difference between the rate of risk associated with Vioxx and other drugs "would not be evident." (For the record, one of Merck's lawyers, Ted Mayer, said the internal e-mails and marketing materials were "taken out of context" and did not "accurately reflect the conduct of Merck and its employees.")[44]

Reicin, not surprisingly, held her ground at every turn. Regarding the piece in *NEJM*, she provided a brief written statement: "Ensuring the integrity of scientific data is of utmost concern to me as a doctor and scientist, and I would never do anything to compromise that principle. I have been honest and consistent in my testimony regarding the availability of the Vioxx data and its disclosure to *NEJM* and the Food and Drug Administration."[45]

Nancy Santanello, head epidemiologist at Merck and responsible for the Vioxx project, was yet another Participant. She also helped to make Vioxx one of the biggest-selling drugs in America; and she also defended it even after its risks became known. For example, Santanello was called to the stand in the case brought by Carol Ernst. She was questioned by Ernst's superb attorney, Mark Lanier, who confronted Santanello with that 2001 letter from the FDA, which had warned Merck it was misleading the public by minimizing the risks of taking Vioxx. Lanier also questioned Santanello about a Merck marketing technique called "dodge ball," which he charged taught Merck's sales force to avoid tough questions—in particular, those pertaining to Vioxx. Finally, Lanier asked Santanello about an internal document that said Vioxx's salespeople were supposed to "neutralize" and "discredit" doctors who didn't prescribe Vioxx.[46]

During her six days on the stand, Santanello defended herself and her company against Lanier's charges, insisting, among other things, that "neutralize" meant providing doctors with information about the drug's safety; that "discredit" meant getting a pro-Vioxx doctor to speak at a medical conference; and that "dodge ball" was a teaching technique rather than an attempt to avoid answering a question. But as it turned out, her defense seemed to the jurors to be lame. When Santanello refused to reply directly to a question put to her by Lanier, he accused her of "dodging" it. And so it was that Ernst won against Merck and won big.[47]

Finally, there was Dr. Louis Sherwood, another Participant in the Vioxx story. Sherwood retired from Merck in 2002, after ten years as senior vice president for medical and scientific affairs in the company's U.S. Human Health Division. For a decade Sherwood was responsible for all Merck's medical activities in the U.S. market, including clinical development, outcomes research and management, medical services, and academic and professional affairs.[48]

Sherwood's role in the rise and fall of Vioxx happens to have been vividly told on June 9, 2005, on National Public Radio's (NPR) daily news show *All Things Considered*. The focus of the piece was on how Sherwood exerted his influence, or tried to, on some of the world's most prominent individuals and institutions. Above all, there was Sherwood's effort to "fix" Dr. Gurkirpal Singh, who, as a result of new information, had switched from being one of Vioxx's most prominent (and well-paid) defenders to being one of its most prominent critics. In light of Singh's metamorphosis, Merck ditched him as company pitchman. But still Merck did not trust him. The pressure on Singh to hold his tongue continued.

On a Saturday morning in October 2000, Sherwood called the home of Dr. James Fries, a professor of medicine at Stanford University, who happened also to be Singh's superior. Fries described the incident as follows: "I received a call from a medical director at Merck [Sherwood], stating that someone on my staff had been making wild and irresponsible public statements about the cardiovascular side effects of Vioxx."[49] Sherwood's specific complaint was that Singh was "irresponsibly anti-Merck and specifically anti-Vioxx."[50] Fries went on to say that Sherwood had hinted there would be repercussions for him and for Stanford (likely cut-backs in funding) if Singh did not cease and desist.

As NPR reported the story, at this point Fries made some calls of his own, only to discover that researchers at seven other institutions, including the University of Minnesota, the University of Texas Southwestern, and a Harvard teaching hospital, had also raised doubts about the safety of Vioxx—and that Sherwood had placed vaguely threatening calls to each of these institutions as well. "A number of investigators who had spoken publicly [against Vioxx] had been called or the chairs of their departments had been called," said Fries. "A variety of veiled and not so veiled threats had been made—that they were saying bad things about the drug company, and that the people to whom they reported should take steps to see that this stopped." M. Thomas Stillman, for example, a professor at the University of Minnesota, also received a call from Dr. Sherwood. Stillman told of having had a "direct conversation that I wouldn't call friendly. It had a tone to me of, 'You better be careful of what you're saying' . . . I thought that was inappropriate."[51]

NPR obtained a copy of an e-mail that Sherwood sent to Merck's marketing department in November 2000. It seemed to support the suggestion that Sherwood's calls were part of a larger campaign by Merck to try to intimidate the critics of Vioxx into being silent. Sherwood's message read, "Fries and I discussed getting Singh to stop making the outrageous comments he has in the past few months . . . I will keep the pressure on and get others to help." Sherwood goes on to advise one of the marketing executives how to proceed: "Tell Singh that we've told his boss about his Merck-bashing. And tell him, should it continue, further actions will be necessary (don't define it)."[52]

Finally, the effort to "get" Singh, to punish him for being a turncoat, amounted to a full-court press. In addition to Sherwood, some twenty-three other local, regional, and national Merck executives became involved in Singh's case. A dossier on him was compiled, containing among other things some eighty e-mails exchanged between Merck and Singh, from March 1999 to October 2000. Years later (2005) the material was reviewed by a top administrator at Columbia University's College of Physicians and Surgeons, whose comment on the file was as follows: "One can't help but almost frame it in terms of an FBI dossier, except here Dr. Singh is not cavorting with possible communists, or possible gangsters. Here the dossier is filled with Dr. Singh's take on Vioxx . . ." For his part, Singh heard from a friend inside Merck that "Dr. Louis Sherwood, who was then vice president at Merck, had become 'very interested,' in quotes, in what I was doing, and that Dr. Sherwood is 'very powerful, and he's going to crush you and he's going to fix you.'"[53]

Sherwood subsequently denied trying to get anyone to do anything, insisting that he "never made any threats to withdraw funding or hamper anyone's faculty appointment." A lawyer representing Merck similarly claimed that "Merck was not trying to silence its critics." Still, in an internal memo intended to justify his behavior, Sherwood clearly indicated that on several occasions he had used his influence to lean on critics of Vioxx and on the institutions for which they worked. Sherwood: "I will only get involved when our representatives . . . have felt frustrated by their inability to reach out or to 'balance' selected individuals. Without trying to appear immodest, I believe I am the most respected physician in the pharmaceutical industry among academic chairs and deans . . . Therefore, when I call them on a matter of urgent concern, they generally take it seriously . . . This has been a source of strength . . . as I have been able to exert balanced leverage in some difficult situations."[54]

A final word about Merck Participants—who included not only the four on which I focused but others as well, including, of course, nonscientists.

Merck's main mantra during the Vioxx years was how safe it was to ingest and how salutary were its effects. Of course, everyone in the company was expected to chant in unison, high among them those responsible for selling the product. Marketing manager Susan Baumgartner was another Participant who got on the bandwagon, for example, regarding Gurkirpal Singh. In 2000 she wrote in an e-mail, "Dr. Singh continues to play up the cardiovascular adverse events associated with Vioxx . . . I think there are many other speakers who deliver good messages, and we should not risk supporting the negative messages that he continues to deliver." Along similar lines, an e-mail sent by Terry Strombom, senior business director for the San Francisco region, shows Strombom wanted to silence Singh but worried about alienating him: "The one thing I am pretty sure of is that Dr. Singh could impact on us negatively if he chose to do so . . . I would recommend we handle this very carefully."

But if in theory everyone at Merck was expected to chant in unison, in practice not everyone toed the company line. Heather Robertson,

Merck's coordinator of health education liaisons for the San Francisco region, was, for example, an exception to the general rule. She was a follower who did not follow. She dared to put her opinion in an e-mail. Singh, she said, was on to something: "[It appears] that no amount of work would change Dr. Singh's [newly critical] position, and although we may not like to hear about it, his information is scientifically accurate."[55]

THE CHALLENGERS

The story of Vioxx played out as it did because Participants within Merck were invested in the drug, even as there were signs it could be hazardous. But they were not alone: other people in other places played other parts that illuminate the whole. Here are three of Merck's leading opponents, each of them a David who took on Goliath.

Gurkirpal Singh

As things turned out, Louis Sherwood never did silence Gurkirpal Singh. In fact, several years later, when Senator Charles Grassley, chair of the Senate Finance Committee, decided to hold hearings on Vioxx—it had, after all, been ingested by some 20 million Americans—Singh stepped forward to testify to his experience. His testimony was damning. Singh said that "we know" that in November 1996 "Merck scientists were seriously discussing a potential risk of Vioxx—association with heart attacks." Singh further said that we also knew, from internal Merck e-mails, "that in early 1997, Merck scientists were exploring study designs that would exclude people who may have a weak heart so that the heart attack problem would not be evident." Singh testified that when he saw the results of a November 2000 study (presumably the earlier-mentioned article in *NEJM*), which showed a large "increase in the risk of heart attacks with Vioxx," he was "stunned." It would have been "unethical" for him, he claimed, not to discuss his concerns in public at the time, even though, as we have seen, Singh was warned that if he continued to do so, he would suffer "serious consequences." In particular, Singh said that he was told that Sherwood would make life "very difficult" for him, both "at Stanford and outside." Before his congressional testimony came to an end, Singh fired his final volley:

"Most importantly, [Merck made] no attempts to design and carry out large safety studies to prove or disprove the link of Vioxx to heart attacks . . . It is regrettable that scientific decisions on patient safety are influenced by perceived marketing and public relations concerns. In my opinion, it is better to kill a drug than kill a patient."[56]

It seems clear that Merck tried to control Singh. It seems equally clear that Singh refused to be so controlled. In fact, he went in the other direction. In response to Sherwood's attempts to get him to go along, Singh dug in his heels. He spoke out just when Merck wanted him to shut up.

Eric Topol

There were others who warned of the dangers, other experts who questioned the safety of Vioxx early on and who made it a point to do so out loud. One of the most visible of these was Dr. Eric Topol, a cardiologist at the Cleveland Clinic who coauthored an article on Vioxx published back in 2001, in the *Journal of the American Medical Association*. The article claimed that Merck's own study, the same one published in *NEJM* in 2000, which Alise Reicin had coauthored, "most likely showed that Vioxx raised the risk of heart attacks."[57]

Like Singh, Topol told of being hounded by Merck so that he would cease and desist—and like Singh, he refused. Topol testified in a federal trial involving Vioxx that after it became known that he planned to publish a paper that questioned its safety, he received a personal visit from Alise Reicin. She told him that his work was in error and that he would be "embarrassed" if it was published. Internal Merck e-mails reveal that Reicin tried to rework Topol's manuscript to "tone down" its recommendation that Vioxx be avoided in patients with heart problems. Her revisions were not in Topol's paper as it was finally published—which is what likely so infuriated Raymond Gilmartin that he personally complained about Topol to the chair of the Cleveland Clinic's board of trustees, Malachi Mixon. "What has Merck ever done to the Cleveland Clinic to warrant this?" Gilmartin demanded to know.[58]

For his part, Topol made his own position abundantly clear: in the matter of Vioxx, he found certain aspects of Merck's behavior to be "repulsive" and "appalling."[59] It appears the feeling was likewise. Less than a week after giving the videotaped testimony that lambasted Merck, Topol lost his title as chief academic officer of the Cleveland Clinic's medical college. He believed his demotion was not mere coincidence—he believed it was related to his testifying against Merck. "The hardest thing in this world," Topol was quoted as saying, "is just trying to tell the truth, to do the right thing for patients and you get vilified. No wonder nobody stands up to the industry."[60] A spokeswoman for the Cleveland Clinic nevertheless denied any connection. Topol's demotion was just part of a broader administrative reorganization, she insisted, stating for the record that the "organization made the decision that [his] position was no longer needed."[61]

David J. Graham

While they were worried about Vioxx early on, it can reasonably be claimed that officials at the Food and Drug Administration did not do enough fast enough. At a minimum the FDA failed to send an early warning, both to health-care professionals and to the public more generally, that Vioxx could pose cardiovascular risk.

After Merck withdrew Vioxx from the market, a whistle-blower emerged (albeit somewhat belatedly). Dr. David Graham, who had been with the FDA for twenty years, claimed on the air that since 2000 the agency had evidence the drug should be pulled. On ABC's *Nightline*, Graham, who was described as a "Boy Scout leader" and "devout Christian," charged that "we have a system that is biased toward approving drugs almost regardless of the safety risks."[62]

Graham told his superiors in August 2004 (one month before Merck withdrew Vioxx) that his research indicated that high-dose prescriptions of the drug tripled the rate of heart attacks and that therefore it should be banned. But he was silenced. Dr. John Jenkins, the FDA director of new drugs, turned his back. Another supervisor, Anne Trontrell, called Graham's recommendation "particularly problematic since FDA funded this study." Dr. Steven Galson, acting director of the FDA's drug-evaluation division, said his research was "junk science." And the FDA's acting commissioner, Dr. Lester Crawford, criticized Graham for violating the FDA's "long-established peer review and clearance process."[63]

But the FDA subordinate triumphed over his FDA superiors: Graham had his day in court, at least in the court of public opinion. He too testified before the Senate Finance Committee, and he too gave testimony that was damning. In an interview held with Graham about a month after his congressional appearance, he described the FDA's efforts—in particular, "those above me in the 'food chain'"—to intimidate him. "They contacted Senator Grassley's office, to try to convince Senator Grassley that I wasn't worth his support, that I was a liar, that I was a cheat, a bully, a demagogue, and untrustworthy."[64] Still, Graham, who previously had a strong track record of warning about potentially dangerous drugs, went ahead and testified, in part as follows: "The problem you are confronting today is immense in scope. Vioxx is a terrible tragedy, and a profound regulatory failure. I would argue that the FDA, as currently configured, is incapable of protecting America against another Vioxx. We are virtually defenseless. It is important that this Committee and the American people understand that what has happened with Vioxx is really a symptom of something far more dangerous to the safety of the American people. Simply put, FDA and its Center for Drug Evaluation and Research are broken."[65]

David Graham was not exactly alone in his assessment of what happened in the case of Vioxx—and indeed in his judgment of the FDA more generally.[66] Nevertheless his decision to come forward cost him dearly. For sending his message, Graham was marginalized. Already skinny, he stopped eating and became painfully thin. He felt, he confessed, like a marked man. "I'm hoping things will calm down," he said, "but I don't think the FDA will let that happen."[67]

VIOXX REDUX

The story of Vioxx did not take place in a vacuum. While the pharmaceutical industry continues to boast of its investment in research and development, it is also a colossus, "used to doing pretty much what it wants to do."[68] In fact, critics consider large pharmaceuticals to be as much (if not more) profit driven as research driven.[69] Similarly, the FDA, which since the early 1990s has been depending on drug companies for some of its funding, is not entirely an independent federal agency. David Kessler, once the FDA's commissioner, now says there is "no doubt that user fees give the industry leverage on setting the agency's priorities."[70] Finally, Merck is hardly the only health-care company that has run into trouble. The Guidant Corporation, for example, a leading manufacturer of medical devices including defibrillators, was cited by an expert panel for having "systematically failed to fully assess patient safety in deciding whether to publicize product failures."[71] And GlaxoSmithKline, which in 2006 rang up more than $3 billion in worldwide sales of its diabetes drug Avandia, suffered a serious blow in 2007, when *NEJM* released the results of an analysis that linked Avandia to a higher risk of heart attacks. (Not incidentally, the research, which of course is being contested, was conducted by prominent cardiologist Dr. Steven Nissen, also at the Cleveland Clinic and also involved in raising early safety concerns about Vioxx.)[72]

Moreover, there are, in theory at least, good and sound reasons why Merck was forced to defend itself against product liability lawsuits numbering in the tens of thousands. For instance, a 2006 article in the *Harvard Business Review* describes how, without realizing it, corporate "decision makers ignore certain critical information." In fact, the article cites this case: "It is quite possible that some members of Merck's top management team did not fully understand how harmful the drug was"; adding that since CEO Raymond Gilmartin was reportedly a man of ethics, he presumably "would have pulled Vioxx from the market earlier if he had believed that it was killing people."[73]

I though would not explain away the ineffectiveness of Merck's chief executive officer or absolve him of responsibility. In fact, it was Gilmartin to whom the FDA directed that letter, which warned, first, that comparisons between Vioxx and naproxen were "inaccurate," and, second, that Merck's marketing campaign "minimizes the potentially serious cardiovascular findings." Yet in spite of this clear caution, Gilmartin was in no apparent hurry to act. It took another year for Merck finally, grudgingly, to revise the Vioxx label, and three more years for the company to pull Vioxx from the market altogether.

Still, to look closely and carefully at the facts of this case is to conclude that the main lessons learned are *not* about the chief executive officer— Gilmartin does *not* explain the Vioxx juggernaut. Rather, this is a story about subordinates, about how those who formally worked under Gilmartin were, as knowledge workers, positioned to take the ball and run with it. Participants such as Scolnick, Reicin, Santanello, and Sherwood were so invested in pushing the drug that they lost perspective. They were unable or perhaps simply unwilling to take adequate account of the cardiovascular risk that had been a source of serious concern all along. Moreover, a cadre of other Participants, such as Baumgartner and Strombom, were content to stand guard: they did what they could to protect Vioxx from harm, knowing all the while that it might harm at least some who ingested it.

Gilmartin deferred in this matter to his subordinates—partly, but not entirely, because he himself was not a scientist or a physician. If Vioxx was good enough for them, Vioxx was good enough for Gilmartin to defend and for Merck to market. Which of course raises another question: why did the experts stay with Vioxx as long as they did, in spite of the problems or, at least, the potential problems? I already noted their history with Vioxx, in effect from day one. But there was something else going on, a dynamic that was not, in contrast to the conventional wisdom, about followers in thrall or even in lockstep with their leader. Remember, we are talking here about Raymond Gilmartin, not Roy Vagelos. No, the story of Vioxx is less a story about the tie between leaders and followers than it is about the tie between followers and other followers, all persuaded and emboldened by each other, and all too heavily invested in the company that employed them.

From all the available evidence, dissent within Merck was muted; in any case, it was ineffectual. No one from inside the company rang the alarm long enough and loud enough, and no one resigned in protest. Moreover, Merck's research team showed signs of faulty decision making, of groupthink. Among other things, there was no one who played the part of devil's advocate, who regularly reminded the group that the questions being raised about Vioxx were of the utmost importance, not only to the company but also obviously to those who took it.

In addition, everyone at Merck had an overarching mandate: to help those who needed it *and* to fill company coffers. So to the extent that they misjudged and made mistakes, Participants did so not because they were following particular orders issued by particular superiors, but because they themselves were determined that Merck finish first. Scolnick, Reicin, and Santanello were committed to Vioxx per se—because it was a fruit of their labor and because it promised to be, and then was, a blockbuster. For his part, Louis Sherwood went after the likes of Gurkirpal Singh to protect his own operation, as well as the company for which he had worked for fifteen years. None of these individuals were strongly committed to Gilmartin per se. Instead, they were committed to each other, to the work they shared, and to Merck.

The saga of Vioxx would end only when the last of the lawsuits claiming damages was disposed of. Merck, meantime, professed to rest easy. In September 2006 the investigator hired by Merck's board to examine the company's conduct rendered his verdict: Merck had "behaved more or less perfectly."[74] While not everyone agreed—lawyers for plaintiffs against the company charged that the investigator's report was a "whitewash"—Merck was determined at all times to move on.[75] To bolster its own morale as well as its public image, it created a new slogan: "Merck—Where Patients Come First."

AFTERTHOUGHT

Not every chief executive who joins a company from the outside, and who is not fully familiar with the product the company produces, runs into trouble. Louis Gerstner, for example, came to IBM from Nabisco and managed brilliantly to transform his skills at running a company that makes cookies into running a company that makes computers. But what happened to Gilmartin at Merck is a caution: when inexpert leaders lead expert followers, the former must closely monitor the latter. For knowledge workers are decision makers. While formally subordinate to the chief executive, their expertise bestows on them power and influence. As Drucker put it, "Every knowledge worker in modern organization is an 'executive' if, by virtue of his position or knowledge, he is responsible for a contribution that materially affects the capacity of the organization to perform and to obtain results."[76] Moreover, when knowledge workers join forces, to push a particular idea or a particular product, the person in charge has to be hypervigilant, again, especially when he or she has no more than modest knowledge about the matter at hand.

Knowledge workers, in turn, do not benefit from having leaders who are weak, or from developing a fortress mentality that pits them against others who are critical. Nor should they ever benefit from putting the health and welfare of themselves or their organizations ahead of the health and welfare of those on the outside.

A final note, one that repeats a theme that runs through this book: experts everywhere and at every level of every organization are more vulnerable now than they used to be. However brilliant the research team at Merck, the product they developed was bound to be closely scrutinized by other researchers based in other organizations. And in fact, Vioxx was brought down rather rapidly. Why? Because outsiders were ready, willing, and able to challenge Merck in ways to which it was not yet accustomed. As the *Wall Street Journal* put it with regard to drugs in particular, "Outside critics have been empowered to challenge big-selling drugs."[77] The parallels between what happened to Merck because of Vioxx and what happened to Glaxo because of Avandia (at least initially) are, in fact, striking.[78] In both cases individuals and institutions were accused of being too committed to a best-selling drug. In both cases the Food and Drug Administration was charged with falling down on the job. And in both cases there were a few who challenged the system—and were in turn punished for doing so.[79] I need hardly add that the lessons learned extend far beyond the pharmaceutical industry. They extend to followers and leaders in organizations of different kinds in different places.

CHAPTER 7

Activists

Voice of the Faithful

Activists feel strongly about their leaders and they act accordingly. They are eager, energetic, and engaged. Because they are heavily invested in people and process, they work hard either on behalf of their leaders or to undermine and even unseat them.

FORETHOUGHT

To those of you who have Activists in your groups or organizations, I say—great! Or, depending on the circumstance, I say—beware! Activists are followers who, their subordinate positions notwithstanding, are determined somehow and in some way to create change. They care—they care a great deal. Activists care about their leaders, pro or con. Activists care about each other, presumably pro. And Activists care about the whole of which they are a part.

If their determination to have an impact is channeled in the right direction at the right time, Activists are an asset, to their fellow followers most of the time and to their leaders some of the time. The resources they

151

invest, including their own time and energy, constitute capital not easily come by. If, on the other hand, their determination to have an impact is ill considered or wrongheaded, Activists can be dangerous. So, they should be watched and they should be judged. If your group or organization has Activists whom you support, consider joining their ranks. If, on the other hand, your group or organization has Activists to whom you are opposed, consider taking them on. For if the size of their group is large enough, and if they work hard enough and long enough, the chances are good that the means they use will secure the ends they want—as did Voice of the Faithful (VOTF) and others who joined their cause.

BACKGROUND

The headline in the *Boston Globe* read, "Breaking the Silence: The Church and Sexual Abuse."[1] It was November 1992, and the story was about five hundred priests who had met in a seminary in Brighton to "discuss the draft of a sexual abuse policy for the Catholic Archdiocese of Boston." The unusual gathering was as a result of public pressure. By then, cases of sexual abuse by American priests had been reported for some time, in places as far flung as Minnesota, Louisiana, and California. Finally, there were "a spate of Massachusetts cases beginning last year and culminating in the most notorious," the scores of accusations against a former priest from Fall River, James Porter.

At the time of his ordination, Father Porter was described by his superiors as a "manly priest," who was a "leader." But years later it was disclosed that between 1960 and 1972 he had molested some two hundred minors, many of them now claiming "violent rape, cruel humiliation, and punishment that can only be described as sadistic."[2] In the end he pled guilty to the charges against him, and in 1993 he was sentenced to eighteen to twenty years in prison. It was this case more than any other that drew attention to the problem of clerical abuse in the general Boston area.

The Roman Catholic Church had always treated clergy sex with minors as an internal problem, one for bishops, religious superiors, or spiritual confessors to handle "out of public view." Scandal was to be avoided at all costs, which meant the image of the priest as celibate, observant, and sexually abstinent was "never to be questioned openly."[3] But by the early 1990s more church secrets were being revealed, particularly regarding sexual abuse by clergy, which was now being uncovered across the United States and Canada and elsewhere in the world as well. In 1992 Dutch television aired a program on the victims of child sexual abuse in the United States. In the days immediately following, some three thousand viewers called the station, "alleging that they too had been sexually abused by priests in the Netherlands."[4]

As a result of all the unwanted attention, the church was now being pressured as it never was before to address the problem of priests who abused children, especially in Massachusetts, where Father Porter's crimes had been allowed to go on for so long. But there was no clear consensus on how this unaccustomed challenge to clerical authority should be met. In fact, as the meeting in Brighton confirmed, among the participants there were considerable differences. Fall River's Bishop Sean O'Malley tried but failed to convince the others to "mandate bishops to act on sexual abuse in their dioceses." Boston's Cardinal Bernard Law, on the other hand, insisted the conference could not "take on the responsibility of an individual diocese." He wanted to preserve his freedom to deal with cases of abuse as he saw fit, which is why he declared that he, in any case, would go to the civil authorities "only when compelled by the law." Law made plain his preference, which was to develop "a policy that can effectively deal with the issue without gearing it into a legal mode."[5]

The Catholic Church may be imagined as an enormous ship, now being urged to change direction, at least slightly. For an ancient and venerable institution, with well over a billion members worldwide, this was no mean task, in particular for those who had been at the helm for so long. The church is hierarchically organized: ordained clergy are divided by rank into orders of bishops, priests, and deacons, with the pope, considered by Catholics to be the successor of Saint Peter, presiding over all. The actual management of this vast enterprise is at the level of the diocese, each of which has a bishop who is responsible for the religious welfare of the faithful in his particular area. The role of the laity, in turn, is equally clear: to be seen but not heard. In particular, throughout most of American history, with a very few exceptions, lay Catholics have been excluded from church governance.[6]

The church emphasizes hierarchy under all circumstances—the authority of priests and bishops and the supreme authority of the pope. This does not, however, preclude conflict within the church, especially in times of change. In fact, as the gathering in Brighton made clear, there were then, as there always had been, debates and disputes on matters of both theory and practice. Given the gradually growing pressure to address problems pertaining to sexual abuse, especially of minors, it is not surprising that while some clerics were rather more open to change, others, like Cardinal Law, dug in their heels.

Clerical celibacy, which is considered by some related to clerical abuse, has been core to the identity of the Roman Catholic Church since the fourth century, when various popes and church councils mandated that it be obligatory. The original reasons for the separation between the clergy and the secular society in which they are embedded were more grounded in the politics of the day, in the politics of the Roman Empire, than they were in spiritual aspirations. As one scholar of historical theology, Margaret Miles, put it, "The universalization and institutionalization of celibacy testifies to its importance at a particular moment in history when leaders of a recently marginalized and persecuted church felt the need for gathering social power."[7] In other words, by institutionalizing celibacy, by requiring it of all clergy, the church chose a path different from that associated with, for example, Saint Augustine, who viewed sexual abstinence as a gift to be acquired rather than a mandate to be imposed.

The German monk who became pope in 1073, Gregory VII, further contributed to the idea that clerical celibacy was all-important. He envisioned celibacy as a "force of moral regeneration from below—celibate clergy serving as an example of restraint to the semi-Christianized people of Europe—while a papal theocracy would rule over kings and princes."[8] Despite sporadic protests over the years—for example, when the archbishop of Rouen forbade clerical marriage, priests rioted—the demand that all Catholic clergy be celibate took root. Decrees issued in 1123 and 1139 (at the Second Lateran Council) made clerical marriage a crime, reduced wives of clerics to the status of "concubines or prostitutes," and rendered clerics' children illegitimate.[9] From then on, the mandate that all Catholic clergy should be celibate was reaffirmed over the years, never again to be seriously questioned.[10]

This comment on the importance of celibacy to the life of the Roman Catholic clergy is not to suggest a causal connection between it and sexual abuse. As Jason Berry put it, "Clerical celibacy, an unmarried life that assumes chastity, does not cause aberrant sexual behavior any more than the institution of marriage can be blamed for incest."[11] But celibacy is central to the governing of the church, and it constitutes an ecclesiastical culture that, particularly in the late twentieth century, seems to have become something of a magnet both to men with pathological problems and to homosexuals.[12] At a minimum, we now know that the number of priests who were sexually abusive during this period was not insignificant. An estimate provided in 1993 was that some twenty-five hundred members of the Catholic clergy, or 6 percent of all American priests, had abused approximately one hundred thousand children in the last generation.[13]

Again, this is not to equate either celibates or homosexuals with pedophiles. But the culture to which Berry and others have alluded, and the power structure that came about as a result, proved to be inseparable from the problems of priests who abused children and the cover-ups their behaviors engendered. An argument certainly has been made that both homosexuality and pederasty bred an obsession with secrecy and with avoiding scandal that, in turn, "bred a mentality of criminal deception."[14]

In the event, the meeting in Brighton, and the hard line that Cardinal Law took even then, foreshadowed the future. In retrospect the decade that followed, 1992–2002, seems a gathering storm. A growing number of cases of sexual abuse of minors by members of the priesthood were revealed, while the church failed to respond fully and satisfactorily. Finally, the rains came and the dam burst. Finally, there erupted what the Reverend Andrew Greeley referred to as "perhaps the most serious crisis Catholicism has faced since the Reformation."[15]

LAW AS LEADER

The crisis began with yet another headline, again in the *Boston Globe*, this one on January 6, 2002: "Church Allowed Abuse by Priest for Years."[16] The article described how since the mid-1990s more than 130 persons had come forward with "horrific childhood tales" about former priest

John J. Geoghan, who had allegedly "fondled or raped" them over a thirty-year period. Most of his victims had been grammar school boys, one as young as four. But the point of the piece was not to detail Geoghan's behavior. Rather, it was to raise questions about what the church did and did not do in response. In particular, the *Globe* wondered, "Why did it take a succession of three cardinals and many bishops 34 years to place children out of Geoghan's reach?"

The story made clear that Geoghan's record of abusing children was appalling; and that in spite of this record, he was transferred from parish to parish before being pulled from the pulpit. Father Geoghan was molesting minors even in his first post, after being ordained. His second assignment lasted only a few months, for reasons never explained. He continued to abuse young boys in his third parish, where he was from 1967 to 1974. In 1974 Father Geoghan was transferred yet again, this time to a parish in a section of Boston known as Jamaica Plain. There he remained until 1980, again molesting children, including seven boys from a single household. According to court documents and as reported by the *Globe*, Geoghan performed oral sex on them, fondled their genitals or forced them to fondle his, occasionally as he prayed. The pattern continued, with occasional interruptions for what was described as sick leave—the church often dealt with sexually abusive priests by sending them to a psychiatric facility with which it had close ties—until 1993. It was at this point that Cardinal Law finally removed Geoghan from parish duty. Still, it took another five years, after scores of lawsuits against Geoghan were quietly filed and some quietly settled, and after police from two counties started closing in, for Cardinal Law to defrock Geoghan and remove his right to act as priest.[17]

During all the years Geoghan was molesting minors entrusted to his care, church officials left him more or less alone, more or less free to continue to sodomize, save the occasional stays for treatment, which, however, were manifestly ineffective. This was not for lack of information. The archdiocese had known for decades that Father Geoghan had a problem, and a bad one at that. To reiterate, what made the *Globe* article so incendiary, therefore, was not Geoghan's behavior per se but the woefully inadequate response of his clerical superiors, including the man who during the preceding eighteen-year period had supreme clerical authority in the Boston Archdiocese, Cardinal Bernard Law.

It turned out that Law was told even during his first year in Boston, 1984, that Father Geoghan had been removed from at least his two previous parishes for molesting children.[18] Still, in spite of the fact that he already had "substantial evidence of Geoghan's predatory sexual habits," and in spite of the fact that one of his own bishops considered the continuing assignments to be so risky that he wrote the cardinal a letter in protest, Law continued past practice. Beginning in 1984 it was he who approved Geoghan's transfers, from one parish to the next.

Once the *Globe* broke the story, it could no longer be contained. Similar such items had been in the news for years, and nothing much had changed in response. Now, though, the transgressions were so obviously egregious, and the evidence of cover-ups was so overwhelming, the church found it impossible any longer to control the damage.

When the *Globe* piece first appeared, Cardinal Law responded almost immediately by ordering priests and other church officials to report promptly to the authorities any instances of future abuse. But Thomas F. Reilly, attorney general of the Commonwealth of Massachusetts, was not so easily satisfied. He declared that not only should instances of future abuse be reported, but instances of past abuse as well.[19] "Given what's happened here," said Reilly, "the church should err on the side of complete disclosure . . . There shouldn't be a free pass on anything when it comes to the sexual abuse of children." Now it was the cardinal's turn to hang tough. A spokesperson declared in his name that it would be "inappropriate" for the church to disclose information about past clerical abuse, because it would violate the promise of confidentiality to victims who had already come forward.[20] And so began what was called "the year of the pedophile," the year in which the "sexual misbehavior of priests" and the "astonishing attempts by bishops" to hide what happened all came to a head.[21]

At the center of the storm was the cardinal, Bernard Law, born in Mexico in 1931, the son of a colonel in the U.S. Army. He was ordained in 1961, appointed by Pope John Paul II to become archbishop of Boston in 1984, and elevated to cardinal one year later.

When he first arrived in Boston, Law seemed "the perfect choice" to lead the faithful in this most Catholic of all major American cities. "A Harvard man with considerable charisma, Law charmed church leaders and thrilled the laity during an inaugural week of hope and celebration."

He was fifty-two at the time, with a "shock of thick, silvery hair," and a politician's gift for "addressing a large crowd while making each person feel he was speaking directly to them."[22]

Law's beliefs seemed a mix of liberal views on the one hand, especially politically, and conservative ones on the other, especially theologically. He spoke out in favor of affordable housing and against anti-Semitism; and in the early 1960s, his first parish assignment being in Vicksburg, Mississippi, he became an open champion of civil rights. At the same time, his views on other issues, such as AIDS, same-sex marriage, and especially abortion, were more traditional or, if you will, more conservative.

Apart from being a presumably honest reflection of what the cardinal really believed, this amalgam of liberal and conservative attitudes served him well in the culture and structure that constituted the American Catholic Church in the last few decades of the twentieth century. Law was considered an "ambitious priest," which seems a fair assessment.[23] He served as bishop for ten years in Missouri, where he was leader of 47,000 Catholics, 90 priests, and 63 parishes. From there he was sent to Boston, where the numbers were quite different: some 2 million Catholics, 1,100 priests, and 408 parishes. This step up, from Missouri to Massachusetts, was huge. It "was like going from running a car dealership to running General Motors."[24]

There is no evidence that during his years as cardinal in Boston, Law was in any way memorable as a leader. He clearly had considerable gifts, intellectually as well as interpersonally, and he was deeply pious. Moreover, he had a specially affinity for certain groups who in the past felt shortchanged—Jews, for example, and immigrants, including many from Central and South America to whom he could speak in fluent Spanish. However, in retrospect at least, the consensus seems to have been that Cardinal Bernard Law never quite lived up to his early promise. Some said he was too isolated, "shut off from the flock, living in a palatial mansion, surrounded by advisers who gave him bad advice."[25] Others declared him a "compulsive micromanager," a workaholic who spent too much time at his desk, buried in bureaucratic detail.[26] And still others looked back at his tenure overall and concluded that Cardinal Law never really got it right, even at the start. "He believed it to be a bishop's duty to be a father to his priests, to be especially compassionate to them . . . and he did so, the record shows, most unwisely, and in the end destructively."[27]

As indicated, Cardinal Law's response to the 1992 scandal surrounding Father Porter was cautious, measured. He obviously did not want to turn the existing system—geared to protecting priests and the reputation of the Catholic Church—on its head. In particular, he continued to resist instituting a policy that would oblige the archdiocese to turn allegations against priests over to the civil authorities.

However, as his very presence at the conference in Brighton testified, he did not want to, nor could he afford to, appear completely unresponsive to what he termed "the sin of sexual abuse." So he agreed to establish a nine-member board to advise him on how to respond to priests accused of being molesters; and he met, once at least (in May 1993), with a group of experts on sexual abuse to listen to their recommendations regarding what by now was a glaringly obvious problem. However, as one of the experts put it years later, "Whatever we had just told him didn't seem to be registering." The cardinal and the two priests who were his point men on this issue seemed "determined to keep this problem and their response to it, within their culture."[28] In short, there is no evidence that either the nine-member board or any of the other modest measures ostensibly intended to make a difference did.

Flash forward ten years—to another meeting called in response to another crisis, this one also triggered by a priest who abused children. In their book titled *Betrayal: The Crisis in the Catholic Church*, reporters for the *Boston Globe* describe the meeting, which was called by Cardinal Law about a month after the shocking story about Father Geoghan hit the front page. The point of this gathering was to assemble a group of savvy and sympathetic counselors, in order to advise the cardinal on how to "steer his way through the burgeoning crisis." The meeting was sober, for it seemed the first time that Law really understood the seriousness of his situation. Those in attendance were nearly all Catholics, who were deeply devoted to the church generally and to the Boston Archdiocese in particular. But they did not mince words. Law spoke first, for about twenty minutes. When he finally acknowledged that his handling of Father Geoghan had been "flawed," he was interrupted by one of the commonwealth's best-known citizens. "Flawed," is not the word, he told the cardinal in no uncertain terms. "It's been disastrous."[29]

This blunt assessment constituted a turning point. It signaled that the cardinal's authority, even among members of his own flock, was now open to question. And it signaled that the crisis, for the cardinal and his archdiocese, was only now beginning to escalate. After further exchanges that spoke to the seriousness of the situation, the meeting broke up. The results were inconclusive. All that happened in the end was that Law promised, lamely, to "consider what he had just been told."[30]

Followers into Activists

The conservative Catholic thinker Michael Novak argues that Boston's Roman Catholics have long been difficult, as in difficult for church authorities to manage and control. According to Novak, Boston's laity has a history of "living in open dissent." In fact, he writes, "one can hardly be certain, listening to them parade their utterly self-confident convictions, why they don't become Congregationalists . . . or Baptists, or Unitarians, or, at least Episcopalians. They seem to abhor the most-distinctive features of the Catholic Church, most notably full communion with Peter, the bishop of Rome."[31]

Whatever the merit of Novak's comment, soon after the story about Geoghan hit the front pages, there were expressions of anger and disappointment among those whose support Cardinal Law would most need during the current crisis: lay Catholics. During the previous decade, laity in the Boston area had been quiescent more or less, prepared since the debacle of Father Porter to give church authorities, Law in particular, the benefit of the doubt. But this time around, it did not take long for their voices to be heard, in "open dissent."

A small group of lay Catholics made the decision nearly on the spot to get involved—deeply involved. They started by gathering on Monday nights in the basement of Saint John the Evangelist School in Wellesley. The room had a wall with letters spelling out their motto: on one side of a large cross were the words "Keep the Faith," and on the other side, "Change the Church."[32] Who were these people? According to the small group of *Globe* reporters who followed this story from start to finish, in the main they were churchgoing suburbanites, many of them graduates of Catholic schools and colleges, who were part of a "fast-growing group of heartbroken laypeople," determined to fix, or at least to try to, what they considered a problem of crisis proportions. Moreover, their commitment to the cause testified, implicitly if not yet explicitly, to their lack of faith in Cardinal Law's willingness to tackle the problem of sexual abuse by priests with the toughness and tenacity it now required.

One of the first significant signs of outrage among Boston's laity appeared on February 3, 2002. An op-ed piece written by Mary Jo Bane and published by the *Globe* described her dismay over the church's "culture of secrecy," and over the "excessive deference" paid clerical privilege. But Bane did more than describe, she prescribed, initially by declaring that she at least would put her money where her mouth was: "I will give no more money to the archdiocese until steps are taken to remedy structural and cultural flaws that created the current crisis."[33]

Bane was a member of the parish council at her church, in the Dorchester section of Boston, and professor of public policy at Harvard University's John F. Kennedy School of Government. So when she wrote of having concluded, after "prayer and reflection," that it was time "for lay Catholics who love the church" to challenge its culture, she did so both as a faithful Catholic and as an expert on leadership and management. Bane pointed out that other lay Catholics could similarly "withhold or postpone" for the time being their financial contributions to the archdiocese. And she urged them to abandon what she considered their "long ingrained deference to the hierarchy," and to help the cardinal "understand the responsibilities of a leader on whose watch tragedies have afflicted his organization."

Within just a few weeks some of the dissenters—lay Catholics in the Boston area who opposed the archdiocese in general and Cardinal Law in particular—began to protest on a regular basis. Thus they became Participants or Activists, who played important parts in the drama that quickly became a "national scandal."[34] While local media also carried stories about those who stood up for the church—a prominent example was Ray Flynn, former mayor of Boston and more recently ambassador to the Vatican—much more attention nationally and even internationally was paid to those who were strongly opposed.

The archdiocese, meanwhile, had good reason to be increasingly uneasy. Initially, Cardinal Law had stonewalled. But in early March he reversed himself—to an extent. Most important, he took responsibility and extended an apology: "And I stand before you recognizing that the trust which many of you had in me has been broken, and it has been broken because of decisions for which I was responsible, which I made . . . With all my heart, I am sorry for that. I apologize for all that and I will reflect on what all this means."[35] Still, there was a growing sense that what Law was offering was too little, too late. So the crisis continued to build, with some now calling on the cardinal to resign.

As winter became spring, the idea that the Boston Archdiocese was an archdiocese in trouble gained further momentum. Still more secrets were being revealed, and still more victims were surfacing, finally ready and in some cases even eager to tell their stories. Among them was Peter Pollard, who described his experiences and the consequences that were the result in a piece published by the *Globe* on April 7. "The crisis in the Roman Catholic Church is not about sexual desire," Pollard wrote. "It is about abuse of power: rampant, arrogant, and systematic. The perpetrators include the offending priests, the hierarchy that protected them, and perhaps hundreds of other priests who turned a blind eye . . . To those who ask that we forgive and forget, please understand . . . The betrayal may not be a chargeable offense in a court of law. But there is no statute of limitation on its impact. And there should be no forgetting."[36]

And there was none—there was no forgetting any longer. Among the many other reasons, the case of Father Geoghan had now been joined by the equally shocking case of Father Paul Shanley. The lawyer for the family of one of Shanley's victims released documents in April 2002 that confirmed the worst suspicions: here was another case of a priest who for some three decades had preyed on those who trusted him, on those who had come to him for help. And here was another situation to which the response of the Boston Archdiocese had been woefully inadequate.

Some sixteen hundred pages of previously secret church records revealed that in spite of Shanley's egregiously abusive behavior over a period of many years, Law and his deputies had "paid no heed" to the detailed 1967 allegations of misconduct against him. And they had reacted casually, if at all, to subsequent complaints, a few of which they agreed finally to settle. (In 1993, for instance, the church paid $40,000 to a man who had testified that when he was about twelve, Shanley repeatedly raped him.)[37] At one point, after a "medical leave," Law even shipped Shanley off to a diocese in California, without revealing his dismal and dangerous past. The *Boston Herald* responded to this latest bit of information by calling on the cardinal to quit: "Somewhere, somehow, Law will have to answer to his colleagues for the lies and half-truths told to make Shanley someone else's problem. But he can never explain to his own flock how he could cover up years of wrongdoing by a depraved priest. And if he cannot answer them, then it's time to leave."[38]

Around this same time the name of Dr. James E. Muller began to surface. Muller was an eminent cardiologist, fifty-nine years old, who up to then was best known for having cofounded the International Physicians for the Prevention of Nuclear War, an organization that in 1985 won the Nobel Peace Prize. It happened that Muller's previous experience as an Activist provided him with a template for how to respond to the current crisis. As he put it, "It's the same situation. Then, the people were disenfranchised from nuclear policy. Here, the people are denied a voice in the policies of their own church."[39]

Muller was a deeply devoted Catholic from an equally devoted Catholic family. But after reading about the crimes of Father Geoghan, and the church's longstanding practice of covering them up, he was badly shaken. Muller even considered leaving the church altogether but then decided to stay and fight from within. He became deeply involved with the group that met in Wellesley on Monday nights and soon became its president. Not incidentally, the group, which a few months earlier had consisted of only a few "heartbroken people who needed to talk," was expanding rapidly.[40] And it had a name: Voice of the Faithful. "We don't have to ask anybody if we can organize," declared Muller. "The faithful are designated by Vatican II to have a meaningful voice in the church; it just didn't create a mechanism. We will."[41]

In fact, they already had. Even by then, by May 2002, Voice of the Faithful was so well organized, it was beginning seriously to challenge the status quo. It had a twenty-five-word mission statement and that slogan, "Keep the Faith, Change the Church." Moreover, the "mechanism" of which Muller spoke was, remarkably, already in place. Within three months of its inception, VOTF had attracted over four thousand supporters in thirty-six states and nineteen countries. Hundreds of people visited the VOTF Web site (www.votf.org) every day, and dozens of debates and discussions took place on its electronic bulletin boards. VOTF was preparing to hire a full-time staff, working to establish chapters around the country, intending to incorporate as a nonprofit organization so money could be raised for Catholic causes it chose to support, and planning for a convention in July intended to draw some five thousand people. Muller, meanwhile, had a vision: "If I had a dream of what this would look like three years from now, our enrollment would be half of the Catholics in the world, every parish would have a chapter, and every diocese, every nation, and the world would too, and that organization would be a counterbalance to the power of the hierarchy—it would have a permanent role, a bit like Congress."[42]

Of course, members of VOTF constituted only some of those who became heavily involved, sometimes by sheer happenstance. Consider the role of Judge Constance M. Sweeney, who ruled, in what was described as "perhaps the most momentous decision of her judicial career," that ten thousand documents pertaining to eighty-four lawsuits against the now former priest, John Geoghan, be publicly released.[43] It was also she who obliged Cardinal Law to subject himself to a deposition by a lawyer representing Geoghan's alleged victims. Given her background, including sixteen years of Catholic education, Judge Sweeney seemed "an unlikely candidate to handle the Catholic Church with anything but the softest of kid gloves."[44] But she proved as independent as she was tough, which is how the part she came to play ultimately proved pivotal.

As time went on, the legal profession more generally assumed rather a prominent role in the proceedings. In other words, for all the cardinal's previous aversion to having the civil authorities intervene in cases of clerical abuse, this cause was now lost. In fact, Cardinal Law was himself deposed more than once, obliged to respond to questioning not only in the case against John Geoghan but in the case against Paul Shanley as well. Representing a client who was suing Shanley for molestation (by then he was also awaiting trial for raping an altar boy), attorney Roderick MacLeish Jr. was among those charged with questioning Law about his oversight of alleged clerical molesters. As well, it was MacLeish who pressed the church to release thousands of pages of damning files relating to other similar cases.

Nor was Reilly, the attorney general, disposed to walk away from what was turning out to be one of the biggest scandals in Boston ever. So he became and then remained an Activist as well. In June he convened a grand jury to consider whether there was sufficient evidence to bring criminal charges against the cardinal and several others in the Boston Archdiocese. While the general expectation was that in the end no such charges would be filed, Reilly was clearly determined to be part of the action. In April he agreed to an interview during which he refused to rule out bringing criminal charges against Law and other church supervisors, and during which he made plain that he considered that his office had an obligation to continue reviewing materials pertaining to the "sin of sexual abuse."[45]

All the while, during the spring and now summer of 2002, new information about sexual abuse in the church was being revealed, leading to still more charges and countercharges. During this entire period, the Boston media in general and the *Boston Globe* in particular contributed generously to creating a climate of crisis, but for good reason. The media, again the *Globe* in particular, assumed, correctly, that they were on to a story of major significance, and that interest in the story was sky high, especially but not exclusively in the Boston area. There were, in any event, countless news stories on aberrant priests throughout 2002, including many that amounted to not much more than tales of who said what about whom and when. Still, in the main, in spite of some criticism that the press was paying too much attention to this story of "sex, secrecy, and hypocrisy," the public was reasonably satisfied that, cumulatively at least, the coverage was balanced and in the public interest.[46]

Law, meantime, was starting to lose ground, including the support of several prominent lay Catholics who previously had been among the most loyal of his supporters. Once the Shanley shoe dropped, they let it be known that they no longer trusted the cardinal, and that, further, they were concerned the continuing scandal would erode their capacity to raise money for charitable causes.[47] At the same time, citizens, most of whom were likely Catholics, were taking to the streets. A group of protesters, small but vocal, gathered every Sunday in front of Boston's Cathedral of the Holy Cross, to demand that the cardinal resign. And in late June some three hundred people snaked their way through the streets of Boston, single file, holding signs with pictures of boys and girls, and men and women, all allegedly victims of sexual abuse. To be sure, the cardinal had his supporters—for example, another small group showed up on Sundays in front of the Cathedral of the Holy Cross, holding their own signs, in Spanish and

English, that read, "Stop the Attack on the Church" and "True Catholics Seek Unity, Love and Forgiveness."[48] But Activists as well as Participants had managed even by then to turn the tide against him. Some six months after the crisis began, the cardinal was going under.

ACTIVISTS TAKE THE LEAD

Throughout the spring of 2002 Law repented on the one hand but refused on the other to accept personal blame. In a letter distributed throughout the archdiocese, he admitted to his own sorry state: "I have become for some an object of contempt." And he apologized yet again: "I am profoundly sorry that the inadequacy of past policies and flaws in past decisions have contributed to this situation." But at the same time, he distanced himself from the case against Paul Shanley, claiming that his "first knowledge of an allegation of sexual abuse against this priest was in 1993."[49]

This delicate balance was evident in Law's relationship to Voice of the Faithful. In a general sense he professed support for the role of the laity in helping the church through the current crisis. But he was less open when obliged to actually deal with the organization that in short order had come to constitute the loyal opposition. In May VOTF was told by a top aide to the cardinal that while it had the right to meet, it should do so only "with and under the bishop of the diocese." The instruction was issued at a meeting at the chancery, which was the first between VOTF leaders and representatives of Law's administration. While the meeting was cordial enough, it was obvious there was a schism. VOTF president Muller said he and his colleagues were "pleased" to have had a chance to meet with Bishop Walter Edyvean, the Boston Archdiocese's top manager. But after the encounter took place, Donna Morrissey, who spoke for Cardinal Law, issued the following statement: "Bishop Edyvean pointed to the right of all the faithful to form associations . . . Likewise it is the diocesan bishop's role to exercise vigilance with regard to the way in which Catholic associations perform the tasks they set for themselves."[50]

From that point on, there was a clear line in the sand. During the second half of 2002, there was no longer any doubt that Voice of the Faithful, which had a rapidly growing membership worldwide, constituted the most serious challenge to Cardinal Law, and that although VOTF leaders did not so say outright, they meant to take him down.

In July 2002 VOTF mounted a full-court press. The group's first international convention, held in the Hynes Convention Center in Boston, had more than four thousand people in attendance. A reporter for the *Globe* noted there were "few firebrands among them." Instead, they were "soft-spoken" people, "with gray hair and conservative clothing."[51] But they were at the forefront of a movement, and they knew it. However careful their approach and conservative their demeanor, however excluded they had been up to then from the church's inner sanctums and inner circles, those present for the occasion came to be part of what they considered an event of historic significance. "We're planting a seed here," said one parishioner. "We're going to be the fertile soil the seed is planted in. There's not any way to stop this."[52]

For their part, VOTF leaders came loaded for bear. They set the stage by announcing important new initiatives even before the convention got under way. The most provocative among them was a report card of sorts, intended to evaluate bishops based on their compliance with the Charter for the Protection of Children and Young People, just recently approved by the U.S. Conference of Catholic Bishops. One VOTF leader, Paul Baier, said he anticipated that local chapters would soon be evaluating their bishops, and that shortly thereafter the results would be posted on the Internet. Baier also touched on the highly sensitive issue of fundraising. He announced that VOTF was set to launch its own Voice of Compassion fund, in order to accept money from those who wanted to contribute to Catholic charities, but only if they could circumvent the local archdiocese. VOTF leaders did their political homework as well, connecting before the convention with VIPs of all sorts, including, for example, the heads of the two major victim-advocacy groups, Survivors Network of those Abused by Priests (SNAP) and Linkup. Barbara Blaine, founder and president of SNAP, who said she was sexually abused by a priest beginning at the age of twelve, declared that this was the first time "a large group of Catholics has come together to say we support you and we believe you and we want you to be healed."[53]

At the time the convention was held, the president of VOTF was James Post, a professor of management at Boston University. He was described as a "life-long Catholic," educated in Franciscan and Augustinian traditions. In a speech delivered to the assembled, Post made four main points: first, that in just six months VOTF had become an organization to be reckoned with; second, that Cardinal Law's "breach of trust" had done the church "irreparable harm"; third, that VOTF nevertheless stood for "building up the church, not tearing it down"; and finally, that as baptized Catholics, members of VOTF had a "right" and a "responsibility" to "participate in the decision-making processes of each parish, each diocese, and the whole Catholic Church."[54]

Whatever the doubts up to then, after the convention was over there was no longer any question that VOTF would be satisfied with nothing less than a change at the top. Although Post still stopped short of calling on the cardinal to resign, his departure appeared the only remaining option. In fact, as many as two thousand VOTF supporters took matters into their own hands. They drafted a petition intended for Pope John Paul II, urging him to "hold accountable any bishop who reassigned an abusive priest or concealed his crimes."[55] Moreover, some sixty Catholic theologians, professors and advanced students, signed a second petition, this one declaring their support for the "rights and responsibilities of lay Catholics . . . to gather in the spirit of Christ, who dwells within the whole Church."[56]

James Muller, meanwhile, was now in the role of VOTF senior statesman. While he was passionate as ever about VOTF as an agent of change, Muller was considered the architect of what most viewed as the organization's "determinedly centrist posture."[57] It was he who urged VOTF to steer a middle course, which involved refusing to take a position on some of the church's most controversial issues, such as priestly celibacy, women priests, and sexual morality. However, there was one area in which Muller was militant, and it was an important one: money. VOTF had started its own fundraising operation. "No more donation without representation," declared Muller. "We have to gain financial power in this church. They say the laity are weak, but we are 99.9 percent of the church and 100 percent of the money, and we now have a structure where we can exert that power."[58]

Of course, neither the church nor the cardinal was without supporters. Conservative Catholics questioned Voice of the Faithful, arguing that instead of resisting the church, all Catholics should "willingly accept guidance from the bishops who are appointed to oversee local flocks."[59] C. J. Doyle of the Catholic Action League considered VOTF far too liberal, guilty of "unfaithfulness to Catholic principles."[60] Other conservative Catholics, some of them well known, flocked to the media, print and electronic, to vent their feelings and express their opinions. Patrick Buchanan wrote that the church needed to "restore its moral authority . . . to stand up to the moral confusion of modernity, not embrace it."[61] William F. Buckley and William Bennett had a different view. While both made it a point to support the church generally, they ultimately called on the cardinal to resign.

Two days after the VOTF convention, Law's spine visibly stiffened. He announced that he would not accept any funds raised by VOTF, whether for church agencies, schools, ministries, or hospitals. Moreover, Catholic Charities, the principal social service agency for the Boston Archdiocese, and Caritas Christi, a Catholic health-care network Law had founded, said they would similarly reject all monies given to them through VOTF. The importance of the cardinal's position on this issue was not to be underestimated, for donations to the Boston Archdiocese had dropped significantly, down to $4.8 million, compared with $7.5 million one year earlier. Still, VOTF would not be cowed. Post responded to the cardinal by declaring that VOTF would not be dissuaded from accepting funds for charitable causes and that, in any case, "the Cardinal's Appeal failed on its own, and it failed because of the reason we all know—the scandal in the church."[62]

The dispute over money continued—and it was messy. In late July officials representing Catholic Charities broke with Law, saying they would in fact accept VOTF donations. But just two days later they backtracked. A spokeswoman for Catholic Charities now declared that the organization would not be accepting money from VOTF, or at least not until its board voted to do so. Once again, it was left to the *Globe* to summarize the state of play: "The confusion of the week's events has left many potential donors unsure who will and won't take their money."[63] (The issue was not resolved until December, when the board of Catholic Charities did finally decide to accept VOTF funds.)[64]

During the late summer and fall, battle lines between the cardinal and those who opposed him hardened still further. Law's critics now felt free to ridicule his videotaped deposition regarding Father Shanley, saying he had "trouble giving straight answers to simple questions and [was] at pains to blame anyone but himself for permitting alleged molester priests [to] serve in parishes."[65] For its part, the *Globe* finally took a stand: it declared that the cardinal should go. An editorial dated August 17, 2002, read in part, "When WorldCom and other corporations find themselves in deep financial trouble because of unethical practices, the chief executive is expected to resign or be fired . . . For the sake of the institution to which he has devoted his life, Cardinal Law should make the decision to resign."[66]

In the main, the slings and arrows notwithstanding, the cardinal stayed silent. During this period he made no public statements about Voice of the Faithful, or about the similarly independent 250-member Boston Priests Forum, or about Father Walter Cuenin, perhaps the most visible of his clerical opponents. Instead, he pressed his case via various surrogates. For instance, the *Pilot*, the official archdiocesan newspaper, challenged VOTF members directly, questioning their credentials as centrists, including on such hot-button issues as birth control, divorce, and gay and lesbian rights. Read one *Pilot* editorial, "While the leadership of VOTF may assert that they take no position on matters of change in the Catholic Church, it is clear their backers do."[67]

Meantime, the crisis dragged on while at the same time reaching its inexorable conclusion. Why "inexorable"? Because the followers who became Activists refused to let up. The media—especially, of course, in Boston—remained fixated on and generally opposed to the cardinal. Attorney General Reilly also stayed in the game; in fact, by deciding to take on the Vatican, he raised the stakes. Reacting to Rome's decision to reject the abuse policies adopted by American bishops in June, Reilly said, "I think that canon law is irrelevant when it comes to crimes against children. I don't care about canon law. They can talk about canon law until the cows come home."[68] And Judge Sweeney continued to play her part as well. In October she threatened the archdiocese with heavy fines if it failed to comply with her order to turn over evidence against still another priest accused of molesting a boy. In her handwritten order she wrote, "If [the documents] are not turned over, I will enter a significant financial sanction, the amount to be determined after hearing."[69] Finally, there was VOTF, which was immovable and unstoppable. Throughout what was earlier called the year of the pedophile, VOTF remained a thorn in the cardinal's side. When Law said he would accept no money from VOTF, VOTF leaders tested him by offering a $50,000 donation to Catholic Charities. And when the archdiocese forbade certain VOTF chapters to hold meetings on church grounds, in order to "avoid further scandal and polarity among our parishioners," the president of VOTF countered immediately.[70] "Is it not absurd," James Post asked, "that this is the greatest Church crisis in 500 years. That [Law] is among the handful of men who are entrusted to resolve it. But the best they can do is ban Catholics from the buildings they and their money built?"[71]

Again, there were other kinds of Activists as well: Activists who strongly supported Law. A group calling itself Faithful Voice, in obvious contrast to Voice of the Faithful, was among the cardinal's staunchest defenders. But Faithful Voice was late to the game and relatively small in its numbers. And so its voice was weak and hard to hear, at least in comparison with that of its larger and louder predecessor, VOTF, which spoke against Cardinal Law, not for.

FOLLOWERS INTO LEADERS

By November it was clear that the end was near, in spite of the cardinal's trying one last time to repair his reputation. He came out of his self-imposed isolation, "slowly emerging in a series of choreographed steps, trying to see if the atmosphere has changed any and making what seem to be some tentative outreaches."[72] He stopped being defensive, finally engaging with unhappy priests, angry victims, restive lay people, and even with the press. As Donna Morrissey put it, speaking again for the cardinal, "We're in a lot different place today than we were earlier this year. Openness and speaking publicly about what we're doing, hopefully will add to the healing process."[73]

Law also performed what was described as a "stunning act of abasement on the altar of Boston's cathedral," asking victims of clergy abuse to forgive him for assigning sexual molesters to their parishes.[74] As he stood alone in front of the Cathedral of the Holy Cross, he extended the most direct, detailed, and heartfelt of his several apologies to date. In a voice intermittently choked with emotion, he pleaded with those who sat before him: "Particularly do I ask forgiveness of those who have been abused, and of their parents and other family members. I acknowledge my own responsibility for decisions which led to intense suffering. While that suffering was never intended, it could have been avoided had I acted differently."[75]

Withal, the drumbeat sounded by Activists who had marshaled against him did not abate. They would not, could not, now be mollified. Judge Sweeney, her patience wearing thin, said in late November that church records contradicted Cardinal Law's own sworn testimony—which was that neither he nor his aides had returned abusive priests to parish work without being sure they were no longer dangerous. According to Sweeney, there were "significant questions of whether the archdiocese was really exercising the care they claimed to use in assigning priests." The judge was especially incensed by a motion made by church attorneys to get the court to seal eleven thousand pages of documents submitted on behalf of plaintiffs who claimed they were victims of clerical abuse. Sweeney decried the archdiocese's "increasingly dreary effort" to slow or limit the release of information, and warned that the court "simply will not be toyed with."[76]

VOTF leaders were similarly determined to press on, to the end. Four of them had a face-to-face meeting with the cardinal, the first between him and any VOTF representatives. While both sides agreed the dialogue was quite cordial, there was no meeting of the minds either on the Voice of Compassion–Boston Fund or on the ban forbidding some VOTF chapters from meeting on church property. In other words, as 2002 drew to a close, for all the cardinal's belated efforts to calm the by now thoroughly roiling waters, the standoff between him and his opponents continued.

The straw that broke the cardinal's back was the release of over two thousand pages of previously secret documents that provided further evidence that the church's feckless, reckless handling of notoriously abusive priests was "standard procedure."[77] At least eight priests that had been protected by the Boston Archdiocese were guilty of criminal conduct. The Reverend Robert Meffan was an example: he admitted to fondling teenage girls preparing to become nuns by encouraging them to believe they were making love to Jesus Christ. The information was so damning that even Donna Morrissey had to admit the new revelations were "truly horrendous." (She added, though, that policies now in place evidenced the archdiocese's commitment "to the protection of children.")[78]

By now the cardinal's cause was lost. By now even the Vatican understood that nothing would suffice but his head.

- On December 9 it was reported that Law had secretly traveled to Rome.

- On December 10 it was reported that, in an unprecedented move, fifty-eight priests from the Boston area had signed a letter to Law, urging him to quit his post.

- On December 11 it was reported that Law would confer with the pope, who under canon law was the only one who could accept a cardinal's resignation.

- On December 12 it was reported that Law and at least five other bishops had received subpoenas to appear before a grand jury, already looking into their possible violations of criminal law.

- On December 13 it was reported that Pope John Paul II, "in a dramatic recognition of the damage done to the church by Law's repeated failure to remove abusive priests from the ministry," had accepted the cardinal's resignation.[79]

The reaction to the cardinal's unceremonious departure was mixed. Some church officials and prominent Catholics, especially in the United States, were visibly relieved, eager to declare the occasion a watershed moment that would allow for "healing and reconciliation."[80] Others—for example, the Massachusetts attorney general—were unwilling simply to let bygones be bygones. Reilly made it plain that so far as he was concerned, the depth and breadth of corruption in the archdiocese went "far beyond one person," and that, in any case, he intended to prosecute the cardinal and some of his subordinates insofar as the law would allow.[81] And still others, such as James Post, speaking on behalf of VOTF, were satisfied to move on, but not at the price of returning to the old ways. "What got us into this mess was a system of secrecy and authoritarianism," said Post. "And the only way we can get out of this mess is to turn that 180 degrees and bring sunlight and collaboration."[82]

As to Cardinal Law himself, he returned to Boston within a few days after having tendered his resignation to the pontiff, looking "beleaguered and a bit weary." He spoke to reporters, but only briefly, acknowledging "the course of events in recent months has certainly been different than anything I or others would have predicted on the occasion of my installation more than 18 years ago." He added that his personal plans for the future were not yet "fully developed," that he hoped his departure would help the Archdiocese of Boston to "experience reconciliation and to experience unity," and that he wanted one last time to apologize and beg forgiveness from all those who had "suffered" from his shortcomings and mistakes.[83]

As things turned out, some four years after that humiliating moment, Cardinal Law could be found living in Rome, presiding over a stunning basilica, mingling with admirers, and "enjoying as much power as ever."[84] Law was long known as one of Pope John Paul II's favorite American prelates, and it was obviously decided at the Vatican that Law should be "a highly respected member of the Catholic Church's hierarchy." And so after about a year and a half spent in obscurity—as chaplain of a convent in Maryland—the cardinal was once again placed in a high post, where he could readily express his "well-known flair for liturgical ceremony."

Still, the legacy of Activists who refused to stay silent in the face of clerical malfeasance lingers—and will for some time to come. Most on this list were, of course, Catholics themselves, including key players such as Judge Sweeney, Attorney General Reilly, a large percentage of Massachusetts legislators who ultimately changed the commonwealth's mandated reporter laws specifically to include clergy, the district attorneys who handled criminal complaints against specific priests, and many among the media.

Their immediate goals were, in any case, realized: first, to change the Boston Archdiocese's handling of cases of priestly abuse; and second, to force out the man many considered responsible for one of the greatest scandals in the history of the American Catholic Church. But they—Activists who became agents of change—had a longer-term impact as well. In particular, there is Voice of the Faithful, which now has two hundred parish affiliates across the United States and more than thirty-five thousand members worldwide. VOTF continues to play a part in church affairs, as a watchdog of sorts, or gadfly, if you will, particularly but by no means exclusively on issues of clerical abuse. For example, in 2006 some one hundred members of a New York chapter of VOTF marched, with seven thousand signatures in hand, to demand their archdiocese, located in Rockville Center, create an outside "finance council" to monitor its finances.[85] Similarly, at the first statewide VOTF conference to be held in

Connecticut (2006), President Mary Pat Fox made clear that one of VOTF's newest and most important goals was to obtain accurate information about how the church was spending its money. "We should be concerned about what we are funding," said Fox. "It is more than imperative that our church deal with this honestly and with truth."[86] In any case the church has now paid dearly for what is in this regard its sorry past. For example, in 2007, the Roman Catholic Archdiocese of Los Angeles agreed to pay hundreds of people by far the largest payout (to date) in the church's sexual abuse scandal: some $660 million.[87]

The Roman Catholic Church is now as it has always been. It is a hierarchical organization with those at the top wielding more power, authority, and influence—*much* more power, authority, and influence—than those lower down.

This time, though, things were different. This time Boston's lay Catholics, nearly all of whom previously were passive, had had it. They remained faithful, obviously, but they were fed up. The result was an upheaval of sorts, one in which even the most strictly structured of organizations proved vulnerable to pressure from below, from followers turned into Activists. During the year of the pedophile, people lined up against the Boston Archdiocese by the thousands. They joined groups, attended meetings, signed petitions, marched in the streets, and spoke out as the occasion allowed. Others were even more heavily invested and fully engaged, against the Boston Archdiocese generally and against Cardinal Law in particular. They were, so to speak, hell-bent on changing the church.

It is in the nature of things that a few followers played key—frankly, leading—roles. They included early Activists such as the editors of the *Boston Globe*, who broke the story about abuse and concealment and stayed with it straight to the end; Mary Jo Bane, fast out of the gate with a prominently placed opinion piece that made plain she, at least, would withhold her support for the church until it changed; Peter Pollard, one among a number of victims of clerical abuse willing to step forward; Thomas Reilly, the attorney general, who pressured the Boston Archdiocese with criminal subpoenas; Judge Constance Sweeney, who, her traditional Catholic education notwithstanding, was prepared to take on church officials she determined were corrupt; James Post, the public face of Voice of the Faithful during the time of crisis; and James Muller, an Activist of long and Nobel lineage, whose indignation now focused on the cardinal in his own community.

We can reasonably conclude that the pope never would have pushed one of his favorite cardinals to resign had not all of the aforementioned Activists been marshaled against him. It took the press and the priests and the people, not to speak of the law, to get the job done. But to read this story from start to finish is to be persuaded that it was lay Catholics at the grassroots level who finally made the difference. By tapping into the anger and outrage, Voice of the Faithful was able to grow with stunning speed, organize to great effect, press its case at every turn, stay the course until change was created, and remain viable long after Law left town. VOTF Activists to whom this change can be credited were followers—but only at first. At some point during the year of the pedophile, they became something else altogether. They became leaders.

Here in part, and in addition to the forced resignation of Cardinal Law, is their legacy. In 2002 John Geoghan was found guilty of indecent assault and battery. He was sentenced to nine to ten years in prison. (A year later he was strangled to death by a fellow inmate.) In 2005 Paul Shanley was found guilty of raping a minor. He was sentenced to twelve to fifteen years in prison. And in a report prepared by the Boston Archdiocese in 2006, it disclosed that as of 2005 it had expended $127.4 million to settle 895 sexual abuse claims. Another $8.8 million went to cover expenses related to abuse prevention efforts—and to promote "healing and reconciliation with survivors and others harmed by sexual abuse."[88]

Afterthought

While they lack the usual sources of power, authority, and influence, Activists can, under certain circumstances, constitute what amounts to an army. In fact, as we have just seen, if their timing is right, enough Activists enough engaged can go so far as to overturn the existing order. To be sure, this is never an easy task. Nor should it ever be undertaken lightly. But if the cause is deeply felt, and if the levels of energy and engagement are high, and if the numbers are sufficient, Activists can create great change.

So far as leaders are concerned, Activists are either a major resource or a major bane. In any case, Activists are stronger now than in the past, for two good and simple reasons: first, the cultural constraints against taking on people in positions of power, authority, and influence have been weakened—as what happened to Cardinal Law clearly confirms. And second, the new technologies make it simple to get information and disseminate it widely, and to communicate and connect in ways never earlier imagined.

To most followers, the very idea of going so far as to be an Activist is, simultaneously, enthralling and exhausting. On the one hand, we are inclined to admire those so strongly committed to an individual or an idea that they willingly, even eagerly, invest heavily in someone or something other than themselves. But on the other hand, we know by now that most of us prefer to be left in peace most of the time, to go our own way unless there is a compelling reason to do otherwise. Of course, there are those occasions when being an Activist and being self-interested are clearly one and the same. As the experience of Voice of the Faithful testifies, when this happens, the experience can be exhilarating and the outcome can be the payoff.

Still, there is this cautionary note—about Activists who channel their considerable energies into opposing their leaders, when to oppose them is to assume risk. To take on people more powerful than we is to consider that we might lose. Such a loss might cost little or nothing. But there are situations in life when to challenge or even question the powers that be can cost dearly. So those who would do so are advised to have eyes wide open.

8

Diehards

Operation Anaconda

Diehards are as their name implies—prepared to die if necessary for their cause, whether an individual, or an idea, or both. Diehards are deeply devoted to their leaders; or, in contrast, they are ready to remove them from positions of power, authority, and influence by any means necessary. In either case, Diehards are defined by their dedication, including their willingness to risk life and limb. Being a Diehard is all-consuming. It is who you are. It determines what you do.

FORETHOUGHT

Fortunately, I suppose, Diehards are rare. To ensure the survival of the species, we need normalcy, which implies self-preservation, especially among the young and healthy. But in the age of the suicide bomber— each and every one of whom by definition is a Diehard—this presumption is thrown into question. We wonder why ostensibly ordinary men and women are willing to blow themselves up because someone somewhere asked or ordered them to do so.

Of course, there are other kinds of Diehards as well: men and women with no obvious sources of power, authority, or influence, prepared to risk their lives for the sake of an individual or an idea, but in ways less dramatic. Consider Martin Luther King, whom we think of as a leader, but who in the beginning was a follower, determined nevertheless to change the existing order. King was willing to fly in the face of those more highly placed than he. He was ready to take his life in his hands. And he did in the end pay the ultimate price. So he was, was he not, a Diehard before he was anything else?

There are, in any case, only so many Diehards a society can take. And there are, in any case, only so many followers willing to play the part. However, to these general rules there is a single major exception: the military. Throughout the history of the modern nation-state, and even long before, armed forces generally have been organized along strictly hierarchical lines, and they generally have been predicated on two key assumptions. The first is that subordinates will follow orders issued by their superiors. And the second is that everyone, from top to bottom, is prepared if necessary to be wounded or even killed in battle.

To be sure, in times of peace, this second assumption is thrown into question. There is no reason to assume that Americans who enlisted in the military in the years immediately preceding 9/11 envisioned themselves just a short time later fighting for their lives in the streets of Baghdad. Nevertheless, to be a member of an armed force, whether conscripted or enlisted, is by definition to be prepared to defend something or someone to the death. In this all-important sense, the Diehards here described, the soldiers involved in Operation Anaconda, were no different from the countless millions who came before them or the countless millions near-certain to come after.

BACKGROUND

Afghanistan is an immense, landlocked country about the size of Texas. It was always poor but self-sufficient, until 1979, when everything changed, when for a range of reasons the Soviet Union decided to invade. Soviet troops eventually numbered some fifteen thousand, who came and then stayed.

During the ten-year period of the Soviet occupation, which coincided with the last decade of the Cold War, America's interest in Afghanistan was high. President Ronald Reagan backed Muslim anti-Soviet forces, and the CIA provided anti-Soviet Afghans with intelligence, military expertise, and advanced weapons. In fact, before it was all over, the United States had provided over $2 billion in money and weapons to seven different groups of Islamic resistance fighters.[1] But once the Cold War ended, and once the Soviets quit the country, the American spigot was turned off. U.S. economic and military assistance to Afghanistan declined dramatically.

The Soviet Union's occupation of Afghanistan was a disaster in every aspect. Previously existing political and economic structures were destroyed. Some 1.5 million Afghans went dead or missing. Another 5.5 million became refugees. And the capital of the country, Kabul, was half-flattened.

By the early 1990s the misery and chaos had led to factional fighting and then to near anarchy. These were the years during which the Taliban gained its first footing. It began as a grassroots movement, a modest militia composed largely of young men who were fiercely dedicated Islamic fundamentalists. The group had two main goals: to restore law and order and to enforce fundamentalist Islamic law. As a result primarily of the first, the Taliban grew surely and swiftly. By late 1994 it had the support of Pakistan. By 1996 it was in control of Kabul. And by 2000 the Taliban dominated more than 90 percent of battle-fatigued Afghanistan.

The West, meantime, grew increasingly uneasy. The Taliban was obviously extreme in its beliefs and behaviors, particularly as they pertained to women. It was also intent on destroying Afghanistan's historical heritage, in part by smashing to smithereens its artistic and spiritual treasures. Two ancient, irreplaceable, very large Buddhas situated just outside Kabul were, for example, demolished on the grounds that they were idolatrous and un-Islamic. Finally, the Taliban was harboring as a "guest" on Afghan soil a Saudi-born militant by the name of Osama bin Laden.

It was only a matter of time, then, before another U.S. president, Bill Clinton, came to conclude that however remote, Afghanistan was a country that had to be reckoned with. Under his leadership, American missiles destroyed what the Pentagon later described as an extensive terrorist training complex near Kabul. The complex was run by bin Laden, who even by then was seen as having masterminded the bombings of two American embassies, one in Kenya and the other in Tanzania.

In the immediate aftermath of the events of September 11, 2001, Osama bin Laden was declared by the United States to be public enemy number one. Bin Laden had claimed responsibility for the attacks on American soil; President George W. Bush in turn demanded that the Taliban turn him over to the United States. The Taliban refused—and so one month later the Americans and several of their allies began bombing Afghanistan. The idea was to get rid of the Taliban and its radical Muslim allies once and for all. The air strikes enabled the Taliban's Afghan opponents to quickly gain the upper hand. Kabul was retaken in November. By early December the Taliban had surrendered its stronghold in Kandahar. And by the end of the year, the Taliban and Al Qaida, bin Laden's organization, had been ousted from all of Afghanistan's major urban areas, giving way to a ruling coalition known as the Northern Alliance.[2] At the time, the Americans assumed that only three tasks remained: (1) to bring in bin Laden, dead or alive; (2) to bring in Taliban leader Mullah Muhammad Omar, dead or alive; and (3) to eliminate what was still left of the Taliban resistance.

However, a failed military mission, undertaken in November 2001 at Tora Bora in the White Mountains, which straddle the border between Afghanistan and Pakistan, proved the earlier assumptions wrong. American and Afghan troops had Al Qaida cornered, holed up in caves and crevasses. But since a few of the escape routes remained inadvertently open, about one thousand of Al Qaida's most hardened fighters, likely including bin Laden, managed to flee into the mountains to regroup.[3] Some considered the American loss at Tora Bora to be devastating evidence of how "scant intelligence, poorly chosen allies, and dubious military tactics fumbled a golden opportunity to capture bin Laden as well as many senior Al Qaeda commanders."[4] While others were less critical, there is no doubt the failed mission made a deep impression on America's political and military establishment. It persuaded the Americans that their mission in Afghanistan was not yet complete—and it set stage for Operation Anaconda.

ANACONDA

Plans for Anaconda were being developed at a time when many thought the war on terrorism was already over. But American policy makers, both civilian and military, saw things differently. They believed the last vestiges of both the Taliban 'and Al Qaida still had to be destroyed. First, they concluded the enemy was in a position to attack Afghanistan's newly installed and still fragile interim government. And second, they considered the enemy terrorists hell-bent on training more terrorists. Thus the decision to launch Operation Anaconda—intended to "squeeze the life" out of an enemy stronghold dug deep in the Shahikot region of eastern Afghanistan.[5] The number of enemy fighters was, I should add, not known. Estimates made by American intelligence fluctuated widely, from one hundred to a couple of thousand.

The details of Operation Anaconda, code-named for a Union Army plan to encircle and strangle the Confederate Army, were worked out at Bagram, formerly a Soviet base situated thirty miles north of Kabul. The base had billets for more than two thousand troops—American solders lived in twenty-man tents heated with diesel stoves—and long runways that could accommodate a fleet of aircraft including Apache, Cobra, Chinook, Black Hawk helicopters, and C-130 transport planes.[6] The original plan was to use some two thousand soldiers, half of whom were supposed to be Afghans, to isolate and encircle enemy territory, followed by attacks intended to destroy whatever was left of enemy forces. As the U.S. Army explained it, "The goal was to hit the enemy hard enough to kill or capture as many of the al Qaeda as possible and to squeeze the survivors out of the valley into the blocking positions where they would then be eliminated."[7]

Operation Anaconda was in keeping with the overarching military strategy earlier developed by Secretary of Defense Donald Rumsfeld. Rumsfeld was of the opinion that the American military should generally replace Cold War weapons such as tanks, armored troop carriers, and heavy artillery with light infantry, which he presumed more suitable to modern warfare. Light infantry was faster and more flexible. It could more easily reach the battlefield, usually by air. And it was judged more likely to be effective on terrain as treacherous as Afghanistan's.[8] In short, Rumsfeld's transformed military was intended to be light and lean and quick, with very few "boots on the ground." It would depend primarily on overwhelming firepower, directed by high technology.[9]

But while Operation Anaconda was being planned in keeping with both Rumsfeld's new strategic approach and Afghanistan's dangerous terrain, there were skeptics from the start. *Los Angeles Times* reporter Richard Cooper was one. He provided this early assessment, which was nothing if not grim:

> *For more than 2,000 years, the steep ridgelines, caves and ravines of the Shahi Kot valley in eastern Afghanistan had been the final redoubt, the ultimate sanctuary for Afghan resistance fighters. Driven from their cities, villages and fields, conquered in other mountain strongholds, generations of fighters had retreated to the shelter of this valley, whose name means "The Palace of the King." Tradition said no foreign army had ever successfully assailed it. Not Alexander the Great in 327 BC. Not Britain in the 1840s. Not the Soviet Union, which lost 250 soldiers on a single day in 1987—about 200 of them reportedly stoned to death after capture.*[10]

The enemy, especially Al Qaida, was as forbidding and formidable as was the terrain. In fact, there was a distinction to be made between the Taliban on the one hand and Al Qaida on the other. After they were pushed from power, most Taliban fighters not killed or captured had homes to which they could rather easily return—farms and villages in Afghanistan and Pakistan. But Al Qaida fighters were different. Most of them were on the run from the authorities, and so they could not simply rest or quietly retreat. Nor could they easily switch sides, to the Northern Alliance, as had many Taliban-affiliated militias. For Al Qaida consisted mostly of outsiders, foreigners from far-flung places such as Chechnya and Saudi Arabia, who could expect no more sympathy from their Afghan opponents than they could from the Americans. Moreover, Al Qaida's religious fervor provided strong motivation. Their fighters really hated the Americans, and now they were poised to directly confront them. "Many had traveled thousands of miles to learn the skills of jihad in Al Qaida's Afghan training camps. Now the infidels had come to Afghanistan. The prospects for jihad could not be better. With no way home and the chance for victory or martyrdom before them, they could be expected to fight."[11]

But as the planning for Operation Anaconda began in earnest, it became apparent that the intelligence required for an operation of this size and complexity was unreliable at best. Above all, because the estimated numbers of enemy fighters fluctuated so widely, three questions remained to be answered: What exactly should Operation Anaconda consist of?

How exactly should Anaconda be executed? And who exactly should do the heavy lifting?

CHAIN OF COMMAND

During the three-year period from July 2000 to July 2003, General Tommy Franks was ultimately responsible for Afghanistan and Pakistan. As commander in chief of United States Central Command, Franks oversaw American military operations in a twenty-five-country region that included all of Central Asia and the Middle East, save Israel. In 2001 he was the four-star general in charge of leading the successful attack on the Taliban in Afghanistan—as well as the unsuccessful attack at Tora Bora. In 2002 he was the four-star general who had full authority over Operation Anaconda. In 2003 he was the four-star general who led the invasion of Iraq. And until his retirement, he was the four-star general who presided over the American forces that occupied Iraq.

So far as Franks was concerned, it was his job to carry out, without any obvious signs of dissent, military policy set by the Pentagon, in particular by Rumsfeld. From the beginning, then, all operations in Afghanistan, including Operation Anaconda, were conducted under Franks's clear mandate, which was to keep to an absolute minimum the number of conventional forces sent into battle. To the dismay of junior commanders on site, this dictum amounted to an "arbitrary cap" on the number of U.S. personnel that Franks would permit on Afghan soil at any one time.[12] To be fair, the plan for Anaconda, which was to limit the number of conventional forces and to rely instead on unconventional warfare in combination with airpower, had worked well against the Taliban, at least initially. However, it had not worked at Tora Bora, and as Sean Naylor points out (Naylor wrote what is up to now the definitive account of Anaconda), the enemy this time around was the same. The enemy forces in Shahikot were not the Taliban's "farmers-cum-fighters." Instead, they were the hardened fighters of Al Qaida and other similar Islamic guerillas groups, all of whom were prepared, if necessary, to fight to the death.[13]

Reporting directly to General Franks was Lieutenant General Paul Mikolashek. During the war in Afghanistan, Mikolashek had commanded not only the army forces for which he was normally responsible but all of America's conventional ground forces as well, across the same twenty-five-nation area over which Franks presided. Unlike Franks, who conducted the Afghan war from his headquarters in Tampa, Florida, some seven thousand miles and ten time zones away, Mikolashek spent most of his time on the ground in the general area—that is, in Kuwait, where he served as a sort of middleman, between those responsible for planning and executing Operation Anaconda day to day and those higher up, Franks and Rumsfeld in particular. Mikolashek was deeply loyal to Franks, but since he was involved in decision making at the highest levels, he was also tasked with somehow negotiating between those making the decisions and those making the demands.

Mikolashek's point man for Operation Anaconda was, in turn, Major General Franklin "Buster" Hagenbeck, a West Point graduate who was now commander of the 10th Mountain Division, out of Fort Drum, New York. Appointed commander of the 10th only in August 2001, Hagenbeck had no more idea than did anyone else that one month later, on September 11, his life would change for good. It was Hagenbeck who would soon be assuming direct responsibility for nearly all U.S. forces involved in Operation Anaconda.

The 10th Mountain Division was a light infantry division of the U.S. Army, with something of a legendary history. It was first activated during World War II and fought valiantly, particularly in Italy, where among its troops was one of the most famous of all World War II veterans, former majority leader of the U.S. Senate Bob Dole. After the war, the 10th Mountain Division was deactivated, only to be reactivated years later as part of the military buildup mandated by President Ronald Reagan. In its modern incarnation, the 10th is a specially tailored infantry division, rapidly deployable by strategic airlift and prepared to conduct operations ranging from humanitarian relief to full-fledged combat. In fact, the 10th Mountain Division is judged to be so versatile that during the last decade it has been deployed more often than any other division in the U.S. Army.[14]

Given this illustrious history, when Hagenbeck arrived in Central Asia, he assumed that he and his troops would be where the action was, in Afghanistan. Instead, they were ordered to stay in Uzbekistan, which is where they remained while plans for Operation Anaconda were being finalized.

Described as an "even-tempered officer of patrician countenance," Hagenbeck was nevertheless, by his own admission, "chomping at the bit to do something." Although he did not have access to the most recent intelligence reports, he obviously knew that enemy forces remained in Afghanistan, and so told his staff to collect the available intelligence on who was where and doing what. Hagenbeck wanted to know how he and members of his team could get into the action—could command and control the conventional and special operations forces soon to be deployed in Anaconda. In short, his aim was to demonstrate his value to Mikolashek "in the hope of persuading the three-star general to give Mountain a combat operation to head up."[15]

After Operation Anaconda was over, Hagenbeck was asked by a reporter for a military magazine, "What's the most challenging part of combat operations in Afghanistan?" He replied, the "harsh environmental conditions," and then went on to describe the dirt and dust flying all around, helicopters taking off in brownout conditions, with rocks and rugged terrain beneath them and nearly no place to land.[16] But at the time, in December 2001, Hagenbeck did not yet know what he was in for. All he knew was that he was eager, very eager, "to do something."

Enter Colonel Frank Wiercinski. His brigade was composed primarily but not exclusively of troops from the 187th Infantry Regiment, which also had an illustrious if complicated history, as suggested by its nickname, the *Rakkasans*. The word is Japanese and it literally means "falling down umbrella," which is to say, parachute. It was given to the 187th years earlier, as a result of its performance in the Pacific theater during both the Second World War and the war in Korea. The Rakkasans are distinguished in several ways. They constitute the only airborne regiment that bears a name derived from a past enemy. They have a long and famous history of fighting especially hard, especially well, and with remarkable valor. And they are the only airborne warfare regiment in the history of the U.S. Army to fight in every war since the development of airborne tactics.

Wiercinski is a seasoned officer, tall and solidly built, who had been in command of his brigade for about one year. He had an extraordinary assignment. First, since there are only a relatively small number of army brigades (approximately thirty-three before 9/11 and forty-three by fiscal year 2007), only a fraction of the army's 320 infantry colonels can be brigade commanders at any given moment. Second, Wiercinski's brigade had a legendary history: they were the Rakkasans. As he himself remarked, the reputation of the Rakkasans was a great multiplier. "We knew where we came from, we knew who we were, and we knew what we stood for."[17] Finally, and most importantly, Wiercinski was in command during a critical period in American history. Soon after the attacks on 9/11, it became clear that the Americans were likely to undertake some sort of military operations in Central Asia, and that if they did, at some point the Rakkasans would likely be leading the charge, with Colonel Frank Wiercinski out in front.

PLAN OF ATTACK

As soon as the planning of Operation Anaconda got under way in earnest, there was conflict. As of early December it was clear the Rakkasans would in fact be tasked with going into Afghanistan and then with rooting out Al Qaida and other Islamic militants. But while men like Hagenbeck and Wiercinski were ready, willing, and able to take on the assignment, how exactly it would be accomplished remained unclear. On the one hand, there was the usual pressure from Washington to keep the operation mean but lean. But on the other hand, there were lower-level officers such as Wiercinski, whose soldiers' lives were on the line and who were anxious about going into combat with less than what they thought they needed. Less in this case meant too few munitions—and too few troops. Naylor's view of the disagreements on this particular issue, between Wiercinski and his higher-ups, is unambiguous: "It is hard to avoid the conclusion that Franks's and Mikolashek's orders to Wiercinski paid lip service to the need to be prepared for 'full-spectrum operations,' but did not equip him for such, and that the reason was that senior U.S. commanders thought the war was all but won, and that combined arms battles were not in the cards."[18]

To further exacerbate the situation, conditions in Afghanistan during the early months of 2002 were, to understate it, difficult. For the soldiers of Task Force Rakkasan, overriding everything else was the knowledge that, unlike other recent operations—in Somalia or in Haiti, for example—

this time they were being flown into a war zone. This was not about peacekeeping or about nation building. This was about direct confrontations with enemy fighters. This was about defending the United States of America hard on the heels of 9/11. Moreover, in addition to the natural fear and loathing, there were immediate difficulties to contend with, such as the cold, the bitter cold, and the long weeks of doing nearly nothing. As it turned out, while those at the top of the chain of command were busy making the big decisions, those farther down were in effect idle, which made a bad situation worse. In fact, the restlessness of the men and women who had trained hard to fight hard, and who had flown halfway around the world with a mission in mind, only to find they were (literally) cooling their heels, was palpable. Hagenbeck, among others, still felt frustrated. Weeks after having landed in the region, he was eager to see some action. "We thought we'd gotten there at the tail end of the war in Afghanistan, and we weren't gonna see much action. So when we heard that there was some Al Qaida there, we wanted to be part of the fight. When [the offer] was extended, we jumped at the chance."[19] In other words, for all the extreme stress and discomfort, seeing some action remained for many, if not most, of these Diehards their paramount goal. They had come to do a job, and they were impatient to go ahead and do it.

Finally, on February 14, 2002, Hagenbeck and his staff were given full responsibility for Operation Anaconda, which signaled their forward deployment from Uzbekistan to Afghanistan, in particular to the base at Bagram, which would serve as headquarters. Anaconda had by then grown unusually complicated, if only because of the heterogeneous group that had been hastily assembled and was now was under Hagenbeck's command. The fighting team finally in place was called the Combined Joint Task Force Mountain. By definition, a combined joint task force includes elements of more than one service and more than one nation—and this one certainly qualified. Hagenbeck's task force included troops from the 10th Mountain Division, the 101st Airborne Division, the 75th Ranger Regiment, U.S. Special Forces, Navy SEALs, British Royal Marines, Canada's 3rd Battalion and Princess Patricia's Light Infantry, and the Afghan National Army. Hagenbeck's task force also had additional support from the U.S. Army, Air Force, and Navy, and from other countries, including Germany, France, Denmark, Norway, Australia, New Zealand, and Saudi Arabia.

Hagenbeck's job, therefore, was not only to fight the enemy but also to mediate among the different demands made by the different players under his own command. Still, the growing size and complexity of Anaconda notwithstanding, the basic thrust of the operation remained the same: to kill or capture enemy forces, particularly Al Qaida; to intercept their movements; and to identify and disrupt their support mechanisms and escape routes.[20]

Wiercinski, meantime, was again embroiled in conflict. The original plan called for the Rakkasans to fly into the Upper Shahikot under the cover of darkness and then, silently, to walk west, to block the passes. Wiercinski, though, along with some of the other senior Rakkasans, was, in Naylor's words, "fiercely resistant" to the idea. He "wanted the entire air assault to go into the Lower Shahikot in the daylight," mainly because the mountains in the area are snow-covered, which makes it difficult to see where to land an aircraft.[21] The issue was especially contentious. After all, American lives were at stake, and the plan was to launch Anaconda within just a few weeks or even days. Hagenbeck made the decision, siding finally with Wiercinski. But there was a cost to all the infighting. And there was the sense even then that had Tommy Franks not insisted on assembling the Anaconda force "in piecemeal fashion from a grab bag of units," strategic planning and tactical decision making would have gone more smoothly and been more effective.[22]

Perhaps the major concern was firepower—too light and too little to do the work that had to be done. Officers from the 10th Mountain Division and the Rakkasans had wanted more artillery all along. But, again, Tommy Franks repeatedly refused their request. While his response was in keeping with the Pentagon's overarching strategy, it was also a reflection of recent history, in particular of the Soviet experience. Under no circumstances did the United States want to convey to the Afghans that they, like the Soviets before them, would use heavy artillery as they deemed necessary, the consequences be damned. Still, this did not mollify men like Wiercinski, who continued to feel that his superiors were withholding sufficient support. After all, to be a Diehard means you are *ready* to die—it does not mean you *want* to die. History, in any case, was on Wiercinski's side: Operation Anaconda was the first time in sixty years that the U.S. Army had sent a brigade-sized infantry into battle against prepared enemy positions with no supporting artillery.[23]

ATTACK

As commander of the Rakkasans and in charge for the purposes of this operation of troops from the 10th Mountain Division, Frank Wiercinski knew he had to keep his soldiers motivated, especially given the weeks of waiting, which were now being succeeded by the tensions inevitable immediately before a major battle. On the morning of February 25 he met with his commanders to give them a pep talk: "You're making history here. You need to be proud of yourselves; you need to be proud of your soldiers. Do not slacken up."[24] But it was on the eve of battle that Wiercinski's tongue turned silver. It was, as Naylor wrote, "quite an occasion." The brigade commander spoke to his entire seventeen-hundred-soldier task force, "each battalion lined up in formation on an empty patch of ground in tent city, colors fluttering in the breeze." Wiercinski told those standing before him that this was a defining moment, a moment to avenge the firefighters, police, and other emergency workers who had gone into the burning towers of the World Trade Center to save the lives of others. He continued: "A lot of you are thinking, 'I've never been in combat, I don't know how I'll do.' . . . [But] you will be good in combat for a lot of reasons. The first one is because of who you are. You volunteered. You've got it in here," he intoned, pounding his chest. "And you'll be good in combat because of comrades . . . You will do it for each other." He went on to admonish his troops not to be afraid to kill the enemy, not to be afraid to pull the trigger. And then he concluded: "I wouldn't want to be anywhere else, anywhere else in the world today, than right here with you . . . Today is your 'Climb to Glory,' today's another chapter in Rakkasan history. Today's your 'Rendezvous with Destiny.' You should all be proud of yourselves. God bless each and every one of us. I'll see you when we come back. Remember our motto: 'Let Valor Not Fail.' Rakkasans!"[25]

The start of Operation Anaconda was delayed by forty-eight hours due to bad weather: snow, sleet, rain, sandstorms, high winds. So the battle was finally joined on March 2, 2002, when Afghan fighters joined U.S. troops and allied warplanes to attack hundreds of suspected Al Qaida and Taliban holdouts in eastern Afghanistan. The plan was for some three hundred Afghan militiamen, who had all of three weeks' training, to rout out the hundreds of terrorists hiding in the mountains. Then the U.S. troops were supposed to come in, to ambush and vanquish.

But the Afghan effort collapsed within hours, which meant the entire plan unraveled almost immediately. The U.S. infantry deployed into their blocking positions nevertheless, only to take fire as soon as they landed, from an enemy that was as well equipped as it was well positioned.

- On day one of the battle, one American solider was killed and sixteen soldiers were wounded, as allied forces met "unexpectedly fierce resistance."[26] In fact, things went so badly that first day that Hagenbeck was on the verge of pulling everyone out. Persuaded to stay in place by the special operations commander, he decided instead to bring in a second group of air assault forces from the north.[27]

- On day two, U.S. aircraft dropped 270 bombs on Al Qaida and Taliban hideouts in the Shahikot valley. An additional fifteen hundred allied solders were sent in, with firefights erupting as the troops pushed toward the mountains. Rough terrain further slowed their progress.

- On day three, there was another crisis, notwithstanding that by then allied fighting forces had grown to number two thousand. A series of mistakes and the cascade of events that followed led to the downing of two helicopters and a pitched battle on top of the highest mountain in the area. The fighting lasted all day. When it was over, seven Americans were dead, and an additional forty-eight were wounded.[28] By then Al Qaida and Taliban forces included, among others, Arabs, Uzbeks, and Chechens, which further explains why American and Afghan troops were up against an enemy far fiercer than anticipated.

- On day four of Anaconda—the whole operation was originally supposed to have lasted no more than seventy-two hours—the situation had become so difficult and so uncertain that allied commanders were obliged to revise their predictions of a quick victory.

- On day five another three hundred U.S. troops were called in.

- On day six the Afghan government decided it too had better add more men to its fighting forces, in this case another one thousand.

- And on day seven, the fighting still had not let up. Further, there was no end in sight. Defense Secretary Rumsfeld explained the enemy's tenacity. They were "extremely well dug in," he said, and very "well supplied." Military officials, meanwhile, said they hoped the fighting would end in the next week. But they went on to repeat they would not make predictions of any kind.

By March 12 most of the enemy had made their way through the rugged terrain to flee the fighting. This enabled U.S., Afghan, and allied forces to finally sweep through the valley with little remaining resistance. It was later reported that there were 517 enemy casualties, with another 250 estimated killed but unconfirmed.[29] (Most of the fatalities were caused by attacks from the air.) For their part, the Americans lost 8 men; another 82 were wounded.

On March 18 General Tommy Franks declared that Operation Anaconda was officially over. He described it as "an unqualified and complete success."[30] But others judged it differently even then. On March 10 *Time* magazine declared that the battle had gone "awry."[31] And on March 24 an article in the *Los Angeles Times* concluded that part of the plan for Operation Anaconda had been "blown to pieces—with cascading consequences."[32]

Put another way, long before the war in Iraq, the Bush administration was tainted by what during the Vietnam War had been called a *credibility gap*: a gap between what the American people were told by their government and what they ultimately came to believe. In this case, whatever Franks's optimistic assessment, it was clear from stories being told by those on the ground that Operation Anaconda did not go according to plan. As it later turned out, there were several reasons for the military's disappointing performance. But even at the time, it was widely understood that the number of enemy fighters, which turned out to be about one thousand, was greater than the number anticipated right before launch. And even at the time, it was widely understood that their resistance, tenacity, and willingness to die made them especially fearsome and ferocious. The bottom line was that after several days of combat, Al Qaida and Taliban fighters were still in place, neither eliminated nor dislodged. Sergeant Major Frank Grippe, from the 10th Mountain Division, who took shrapnel wounds in his legs on the first day, put it this way: "The picture Intel painted was just a little bit different from what was happening on the ground."[33] Grippe, who to his surprise found hundreds of enemy fighters lying in wait, reported that "they came at us with mortars, RPGs, and light and heavy machine guns. From a blocking mission, it turned into a reconnaissance force on an al-Qaeda stronghold. My men were whacking people from 400 to 500 meters, but there were also gunfights. We're talking nose to nose."[34]

In Europe as well it was known almost immediately that Anaconda had run into trouble. On March 10 a British paper reported the operation, which was supposed to have encircled Al Qaida and Taliban fighters in an area of some sixty to seventy square miles, was not the surprise attack it was intended to be. On the contrary: the enemy was waiting, lying in ambush. The *Observer* quoted several soldiers, some of whom were hit, and all of whom said they were surprised by the large number of enemy fighters. One of the first to be wounded, by shrapnel in his thigh and elbows, Army Specialist Robert McCleave, said he was hit from no more than about ten feet away. "One of the soldiers with us took the bulk of that blast," he went on. "The rest of us got pretty well wounded. A fellow soldier of mine stared right at me in the eyes and started screaming." Concluded the *Observer*, "The picture that has emerged—in particular from the 18 hours that 10th Mountain Division's troops were pinned down—has privately shocked American commanders confronted with the image of wounded soldiers being forced to run from one hiding place to the next under withering fire while enemy fighters, tucked away in the caves, were able to escape massive bombardment from American warplanes."[35]

Even one of the military's own house organs did not gild the lily. To be sure, *Army Magazine* did not find fault. But neither did it shy from reporting in April 2002 that Operation Anaconda was "bloody and personal," a "a close-in, small-arms, mortar and rocket battle in an area south of Gardez, Afghanistan, called Shahi Kot." The story described mountain peaks rising to an elevation of twelve thousand feet, caves by the hundreds hidden in the slopes, fighting fierce and prolonged, and an enemy that was prepared to "fight to the death." It also quoted General Hagenbeck, who sounded properly gung ho in spite of the challenge he now recognized was daunting: "As long as they want to send them here, we'll kill them here. Should they go somewhere else, we'll go with our Afghan allies and coalition forces and kill them wherever they go."[36]

Subsequent assessments of Operation Anaconda have been even more critical than those made at the time. An analysis published in 2004 in *Inside the Pentagon* concluded that the "sloppy" chain of command for which Tommy Franks was directly responsible made combat failures in Operation Anaconda "almost inevitable from the start." There was particular criticism of the "serpentine" command structure, with reporting mechanisms too complex to be clear, even to those most directly involved. Based on research conducted by a thirty-eight-year-old army special operations officer, who was writing a thesis for his master's degree, the piece pointed out that while Hagenbeck was the joint task force commander, even he did not have "operational control over all the forces necessary to effectively prosecute the mission assigned" by his direct superior, Mikolashek. The result: a situation where three days into the operation Hagenbeck found himself unable to "cope with the unforeseen events that normally occur in combat."[37]

A careful study of Operation Anaconda, conducted under the auspices of the Rand Corporation, was just as damning. The analysis was similarly critical of the "poorly defined command relationships," which explained in large part why even the preparations for Anaconda "were off to a bad start."[38] But the operation fell short for other reasons as well. For example, the air force's performance was less than optimum, for the simple reason that most of its officers had made the mistake of assuming that the dirty work of fighting terrorism was already over. This contributed to their "operating in a more relaxed mode during the weeks that preceded Anaconda."[39] And it explained why by the time Anaconda got under way, many of its most experienced staff members had already been rotated back to the United States, only to be replaced by relative newcomers, who in March 2002 were still learning on the job. There was also the failure of intelligence, with particular regard to the numbers of enemy fighters. As noted, these estimates changed throughout the planning process—which is why just before Anaconda was launched, a careful count was conducted one last time. The results of this final review persuaded Hagenbeck and his commanders that the number of enemy fighters was at the low end, perhaps one hundred fifty to two hundred men. But, as it turned out, the final count was wrong, way wrong.

Years later, by 2006, even the U.S. Army conceded that Operation Anaconda went badly from the get-go, which was "fatal" to the momentum of the attack. "It was soon apparent that the original main effort under [the Afghan commander] was not going to make any headway against the tenacious foe." Moreover, the planned U.S. air strikes intended to assist the Afghans were "poorly coordinated and generally ineffective." The enemy, meanwhile, had "particularly effective" mortar fire; well-camouflaged, dug-in fighting positions with overhead cover; large stocks of food and ammunition; and excellent forward observation posts; all of which provided, among other things, important information on where exactly to attack the coalition forces now streaming into the valley. In short, according to a report prepared by and for the U.S. Army, "The initial U.S.-led Afghan ground attack failed in part due to poor air support, a lack of artillery, and, most damning, a more numerous and aggressive enemy than anticipated."[40]

Several years after the fact, both Tommy Franks and Buster Hagenbeck conceded at least some of the errors of their ways. In his memoirs Franks claimed that the plan for Anaconda was "very credible," but then went on to admit that it was "not completely coordinated."[41] Hagenbeck was more forthcoming. Some two years after Operation Anaconda he acknowledged that organizational and command-and-control problems accounted for most of the confusion that bedeviled the battle, particularly early on. He further conceded that the lack of coordination, with the air force in particular, was costly. Air cover would have been invaluable as soon as it became clear that Anaconda was in trouble. In short, General Hagenbeck himself confirmed that with the benefit of hindsight, he would have done things differently. "We weren't idiots," he said, "but we weren't asking the questions we needed to."[42]

AMERICAN SOLDIERS

As usual in these matters, it is the soldiers on the ground rather than those stationed thousands of miles away who bear the brunt of the burden. Operation Anaconda was no exception to this general rule.

Two Officers

On February 27, 2006, Secretary of Defense Donald Rumsfeld announced that President George W. Bush had nominated Lieutenant General Franklin L. Hagenbeck to become the fifty-seventh superintendent of the U.S. Military Academy at West Point. As his extraordinarily successful military career would seem to confirm, Hagenbeck has played his professional part to near perfection—as it pertains both to leadership and to followership. The military hierarchy is like other hierarchies, especially when it is rigidly enforced. This is to say that those ranked somewhere in the middle—as in not at the top or at the bottom—are leaders and followers *simultaneously*.

During Operation Anaconda Buster Hagenbeck was the commander in charge of nearly all U.S. forces. (The exception was classified special operations forces.) But notwithstanding his imposing title and his important position, he was, as we have seen, not fully in charge of his own fate. Naylor's book has several depictions of Hagenbeck as frustrated by his marching orders, ranging from where he was stationed for weeks on end, in Uzbekistan, to how and when his troops would be given permission to see some action. In other words, given his rank and position, it is easy enough to see Hagenbeck as a man in charge, as a leader, as *the* leader of Operation Anaconda. But the other way to look at this selfsame man is to see him as a follower. Viewing Hagenbeck from this perspective, we can learn other things about him, such as his adaptability (he moves easily from being a leader to being a follower and then back again) and his interpersonal skills (he is able to manage those lower positioned than he and to ingratiate himself with those higher positioned than he).

Even in his new position as superintendent at West Point, which, as these things go, bestows on him a high degree of autonomy, Hagenbeck has to be comfortable with deference as well as dominance. Obviously he will continue to dominate his subordinates, at least as *dominate* is broadly defined. But at the same time, he will have to continue to defer to his superiors. In fact, the military is all about signs and symbols—bars and stars on uniforms, all those salutes, and all that standing at attention—that communicate rank order.

Obviously, someone like Frank Wiercinski is also, simultaneously, a leader and a follower. During Anaconda he was, on the one hand, commander of Task Force Rakkasan; but on the other hand, he had no choice but to bow to his superiors, even when he was in strong disagreement. When they feel they must, good commanders can, and sometimes do, take issue with those positioned above them. But of course, colonels nearly never challenge, or even come into contact with, those in charge of developing overall strategy, with four-star generals, for example, or with secretaries of defense.[43] So even though we are talking here about matters of life and death, in the end a colonel would have nearly no choice but to demonstrate what was earlier called "obedience to authority."

A few months after Anaconda was over, Wiercinski gave an interview about the operation that reflected his dual role as superior and subordinate. Wiercinski said then that he and his men had met with "a lot of mass firepower and surprise," but that they had "got right on top of" the enemy. Moreover, he spoke confidently about the excellence of his equipment— for example, the Chinook helicopters that were "very powerful, incredibly powerful"; and he spoke positively about the overall plan, which balanced "safety risk assessment with combat capability."

But the interviewer did not let Wiercinski off the hook so easily. He asked him point blank about the "tv talking heads," who had "second guessed" the mission, in particular "since you didn't take in field artillery." We know, of course, from Naylor's account that this was a major sticking point, that Wiercinski had all along been unhappy with Franks's mandate forbidding the use of what he, the colonel, considered the requisite hardware. But on the occasion of the interview, Wiercinski played the good soldier. This was his reply: "We had to watch what we were carrying . . . A lot of people do ask [why] not an artillery battery. I've thought about that over time. I don't know where I would have put it, how I would have lifted it, and I don't know how I would have secured it."[44] Wiercinski did admit that in some respects the American military fell short, saying it had to improve training to "add flexibility, ingenuity." But otherwise, he staunchly defended every aspect of Operation Anaconda and, by implication, the decisions made by his superiors, right straight to the top. When he was reminded again that some considered Anaconda a failure, he replied, "I've read some of those articles myself. I quite honestly don't understand their definition of [failure]." And then he went on to tell about how when he asked Hagenbeck for more Apache helicopters, his request was immediately approved: "63 hours. 16 more birds in the battle. Look at what had to happen. The helicopter had to be broken down, loaded on the Air Force C-17s, flown to Afghanistan, reassembled. That's the way it's supposed to work."

Four Noncommissioned Officers

Noncommissioned officers (NCOs) in the U.S. Army have a creed that invokes (1) their commitment to their country, (2) their commitment to being good leaders, and (3) their commitment to being good followers. The creed reads in part:

> *No one is more professional than I. I am a Noncommissioned Officer, a leader of soldiers. As a Noncommissioned Officer, I realize that I am a member of a time honored corps, which is known as "The Backbone of the Army." I am proud of the Corps of Noncommissioned Officers and will at all times conduct myself so as to bring credit upon the Corps, the Military Service and my country regardless of the situation in which I find myself . . .*
>
> *All solders are entitled to outstanding leadership; I will provide that leadership. I know my soldiers and I will always place their needs above my own . . .*
>
> *Officers of my unit will have maximum time to accomplish their duties; they will not have to accomplish mine. I will earn their respect and confidence as well as that of my solders. I will be loyal to those with whom I serve; seniors, peers, and subordinates alike.*

The descriptions that follow are of four NCOs who were part of the 10th Mountain Division's Charlie Company. They depict the first twenty-four hours of Operation Anaconda, which constituted the fiercest fragment of the fiercest battle fought by American troops in a generation.[45]

We have already seen that Command Sergeant Major Frank Grippe made no bones about the fact that "the picture Intel painted was just a little bit different from what was happening on the ground." A strapping man of thirty-nine who had joined the U.S. Army some twenty years earlier, Grippe recalled that just before Anaconda was launched his men had "a feeling of elation that we're actually finally going to go in and do the overt offensive operations that we're so well trained in."[46] But after the fact was different: after he and his men saw battle, that "feeling of elation" vanished in a heartbeat.

Five days after going in, on March 7, 2002, Grippe described the scene to a group of American reporters. "The actual valley that we're engaging the enemy in, the base of the valley is approximately 8,500 feet. It's totally surrounded by mountain peaks that rise up to 11,000 feet. The terrain itself is very rugged, a lot of spurs and ridges running off the peaks." Grippe told of how the moment his chopper landed, he and his 125 men sustained a barrage of fire for which they were simply not prepared. "After about the first ten minutes of combat, I guess the al Qaeda came out of their caves and their well-fortified positions and we experienced a heavy volume of fire from the actual mountains above us. As the day progressed . . . we started receiving mortar fire, rocket propelled grenades . . . heavy machine gun fire, light machine gun fire, small arms fire, from the hills above us. So if you can picture that, we're out in the open. Even when we're behind this ridge line there's still mountain peaks to the north and to the south of us and the peak lay to our front where we were receiving heavy volumes of fire." Although he was injured early on, Grippe stayed with his troops. "I didn't leave with the wounded. And I didn't extract myself out of Afghanistan either, like most of the doctors wanted me to. I'm down here. My injury's okay, I can walk and so forth. I just have to get it healed up enough, scabbed over enough so I can get up in the mountains with my men."[47]

Grippe gave another interview about Operation Anaconda, this time to the *NCO Journal* about a year after it was all over. Now he spoke from his home base, Fort Drum, New York, and was more reflective. He spoke of collegiality: "The commanders that I've worked with and I have thought a lot alike. We all worked together." And he spoke of the importance of good training: battle-drill training, shooting skills, combat lifesaver training, and physical fitness. And he spoke of the mission during which his soldiers suffered—twenty-two out of the eighty-six at Grippe's position were wounded—but which he considered critically important nonetheless. "No matter how elite our officer corps is, no matter how elite our senior NCO corps is, if the junior NCOs and junior enlisted fail in their missions, the country fails. Can you imagine if we were not successful in all of our operations in Afghanistan?"[48]

One of the soldiers in Grippe's battalion was Sergeant First Class Thomas Abbott, a thirty-two-year-old father of four. He had been in combat before, in the bloody firefight in Mogadishu in 1993. Still, he was, as were most American soldiers in the wake of 9/11, "pumped" for Anaconda.[49]

But Abbott was like Grippe: the thrill was gone the moment he landed. Later he recalled that seconds after getting out of the back of his Chinook, there was a yell, "Incoming!" Enemy fire rained down on him and his comrades from a fortified ridgeline partway up the mountain. Simultaneously, they were being shot at by two dozen black-uniformed Al Qaida, who appeared to them "like ants, climbing the ridge to the west."[50] Abbott and his fellow fighters took cover in the shallow ditches and began returning fire in both directions, many of them ditching along the way their eighty-five–pound rucksacks, packed with food, cold-weather gear, and extra ammunition.

Abbott was not spared. He was hit. His right arm was deeply lacerated—which did not stop him screaming at his men to get up and move before another mortar round struck. "If you don't get up, you are going to die," he yelled. Ann Scott Tyson, writing for the *Christian Science Monitor*, describes the scene: "One soldier stared back blankly, slipping into shock. 'Snap out of it!' Abbott shouted. He radioed for cover, and led the band of wounded as they hobbled and dashed 40 yards to the [protective] bowl. As he lay in the dirt, unable to shoulder a weapon, Abbott felt defenseless. Worse, more than half of his platoon was wounded and he blamed himself. His mind drifted to thoughts of his children, and his wife's parting plea: 'Don't be a hero. Come back to us.'"[51]

In the end, Abbott got out safely, recalling with pride some months later that the Americans had "fought them off"—that his savvy soldiers had refused to be lured by the enemy into a deadly ambush.[52] But as Tyson observed on the basis of her interviews with Abbott and others, the lessons of Operation Anaconda were sobering: deficient planning, shortfalls of intelligence, and the costs of U.S. military efforts to spare civilians.

Time magazine wrote about thirty-year-old Staff Sergeant Randal Perez that he "didn't join the army to be a hero," but that in Operation Anaconda "he became one."[53] Perez and his wife had just had a baby, ten-week-old Ramiro, whom Perez had never seen and who was uppermost on his mind, even as he was going into battle. But two years earlier Perez had wanted so badly to lead troops in combat that he pushed to get out of the army supply corps and into the frontline infantry. Abbott had been something of a mentor, recognizing that Perez's enthusiasm and determination more than made up for his lack of infantry experience.[54] So now, here he was, Perez up to his neck in what he thought he wanted.

Perez clambered down the ramp of his chopper into what was described by Mark Thompson, reporting for *Time*, as the natural equivalent of a giant stadium. There, then, stood Perez, vulnerable and exposed like his fellow soldiers, while from up the half-mile-high mountains that surrounded them on three sides, Al Qaida fighters began firing away: "Operation Anaconda had just begun—and Perez and his comrades were already playing defense."

That's when, as Grippe later recalled, "all hell broke loose." And that's when Abbott and the other leader of the First Platoon got hit—leaving Perez suddenly, instantly, in charge. By this time, nine of what were now Perez's twenty-six men had already been wounded, which meant his immediate task was twofold: getting them to safety and not endangering the lives of those who were left. "I'm the quarterback now," Perez thought. "Whatever I decide, I'm going to have to live with it, right or wrong."[55] What he decided was to do two things at the same time. He did what he could to take care of his wounded men while staying simultaneously on the offensive, blazing away at Al Qaida with his M-4 rifle. All day long he walked the line of his men, making sure each had sufficient ammunition, handing out more to those who needed it, and checking on the casualties, including those of Abbott, his mentor and superior.

After the fact, everyone agreed Perez was a hero. One of his soldiers wondered that Perez showed "almost no concern for his body. He's up there, and rounds are flying all around him, in between his legs, and he doesn't flinch. He keeps firing."[56] Grippe, who earlier was skeptical about the former supply officer turned infantryman, now freely acknowledged that Perez had "kicked ass as if he was a combat vet from numerous firefights. He just did a spectacular job that day." And Captain Nelson Kraft concurred as well—Sergeant Perez had acted like a seasoned platoon leader. "If I were to write down the perfect platoon leader in a combat situation, that was Sergeant Perez."[57]

Perez was in charge for fifteen more hours before he and the last of his men were flown back to safety. His behavior in battle was recognized by the U.S. Army: on March 18, General Tommy Franks personally awarded him the Bronze Star for valor. Interviewed on the occasion by a reporter for CNN, Perez spoke briefly of Operation Anaconda as a "hairy situation." But, he continued, "The remembrance of September 11 kind of gears us up and gets us motivated for the next operation."[58]

Some months later, Perez summarized the experience, reflecting on his time in combat, which he claimed made him a better man. "It changed me. It made me more attentive to everything. It made me more serious about life and family, more patient. Combat makes you value your family more; you think about them a lot when you're there. They may not be in the trenches ducking bullets with you, but they're always there."[59]

Specialist Eddie Antonio Rivera went nearly unnoticed until August 2002, when *Esquire* magazine published a story on Anaconda, in which Rivera was the main character. He was described physically: "his hair curly black, his brows black too, his mustache a thin black streak that at one end broke up into shapeless bristles." He was described professionally: "he was usually a no-show at Ellenville High," who nevertheless managed to graduate and join the army. And he was described personally: he had a girlfriend, Krystal, an army reservist he met while training in Texas to become a medic. Krystal was "black, round-faced [and] long-haired." She was a "girl whose smile melted artillery pieces," and so it was that Rivera fell in love. But then came September 11, and Rivera, who by then was the one and only medic in one of the platoons in the 10th Mountain Division, told Krystal, "I may have to go somewhere."[60]

And he did—first to Uzbekistan and then to Afghanistan, as part of Operation Anaconda. But like all the others in this particular platoon, Rivera was victimized by the part of Anaconda that went "awry," which is how he was caught right in the middle of a firefight. Within minutes, he heard someone cry out, "Doc! Doc! Doc!" And within a few minutes more, there was a critical need for anyone with any medical training at all. Mortars now chasing them, Rivera and another medic ran and stumbled, along with two wounded sergeants, to a safe haven behind a small knoll. Rivera started ministering to the first, Abbott, and then to the other, McCleave. John Sack, who wrote the piece for *Esquire*, describes the scene:

> *Abbott's got a piece of a mortar round in his triceps, and Rivera treats it by the book, wrapping it in Kerlix, while saying, "You're all right," but it's impenetrable what's wrong with McCleave. On his clothes is no blood, but in back of the knoll he sits as though wearing a sign saying HOME-LESS . . .*
>
> *"Sergeant McCleave," says Rivera, "What's wrong with you?" . . . "Where am I?" "Sergeant McCleave!" Rivera screams, shaking him vigorously. Some slobber comes to McCleave's lips, and he says audibly, "I . . . don't . . . know."*
>
> *"Sergeant McCleave!" says Abbott, the shrapnel-suffering sergeant. "Tell the doc what's wrong with you! Or you'll die!"*

Now Rivera rips off McCleave's gloves and says, "Good." He looks at McCleave's Interceptor and says, "Good." He cuts McCleave's pants, and on both of McCleave's legs, both upper and lower, he sees dozens of holes from the same indiscriminate mortar round that hit Miranda and Abbott. Now, shrapnel is painful wherever it is. Unlike a bullet, it enters red-hot, and starts burning the flesh, fat, muscle, nerves of the boy who haplessly caught it. McCleave's state of shock isn't in any way overwrought. He can't raise either leg, so Rivera props each leg on his knee like a two-by-four that he's sawing as, with his hands, he wraps on the Kerlix, lest his good buddy bleed to death and, at their camp, his cot right next to Rivera's become unoccupied."[61]

Later in the day Rivera is spent. His day began at two in the morning, and he hasn't eaten since then or had hardly any water. His face is gray-black from being close to all the mortar rounds, and on his hands is other people's blood. "What am I doing here," he thinks to himself. And then he remembers the World Trade Center—so much worse than Operation Anaconda, so much more dreadful in its consequences, and he is becalmed. And he begins to pray, clutching the small white cross in his pocket. "Lord, if I can't make it out of here, please take care of my mom and dad and please take care of Krystal."

Rivera's division, the 10th Mountain Division, comes home to the Adirondacks in April. "Undead," as Sack puts it, "thanks to Rivera," are, among others, Abbott and McCleave. Rivera receives the Army Commendation Medal with a *V* for valor and goes home to Krystal's new apartment, close by, in Liverpool, New York. "I love you," he tells Krystal. But, he adds, "I love those guys. So much that I might have died for 'em. Even those guys in cowboy hats and big-buckled belts, I love 'em. I don't listen to country music with 'em. I don't do the two-step with 'em. But when they cry, 'Doc!' I run like they're my own brothers. Because they are."[62]

DIEHARDS DUTY BOUND

The U.S. military is subject to civilian control. Every member of the armed services is therefore subordinate to someone more highly positioned than they. Even those at the highest levels of the chain of command are obliged ultimately to obey their civilian superiors. Legally, morally, there are exceptions to this general rule, in particular because members of the military swear allegiance not to any single individual—to the president or the secretary of defense, for example—but rather to the Constitution. (The oath they take is to "support and defend the Constitution of the United States.") But these exceptions are so rarely realized, they play only a small role in military life.

Even during the Vietnam War, when several of the nation's highest-ranking military officers, the Joint Chiefs of Staff (JCS), had major reservations about American involvement, they chose to stay silent rather than to speak up. While some would argue that this was a dereliction of their duty, others, including the generals themselves, clearly thought, at least at the time, that their primarily loyalty was to President Lyndon Baines Johnson. Given this presumption, they believed they had no choice other than to follow his lead.

Their dilemma was memorably depicted by Active-Duty Army Colonel H. R. McMaster, to whom it was clear the president had lied about the level of American engagement in Vietnam. Yet in spite of this, and in spite of the fact that it was up to the people through the Congress to determine whether the "freedom and independence" of South Vietnam was worth the risk to American lives, the JCS supported their commander in chief by "misrepresenting their own estimates of the situation."[63] In other words, faced with a decision between being loyal to the president and being loyal to the people, the JCS chose the former over the latter. McMaster was censorious, concluding that the JCS did not effectively exercise their intellectual independence and insist "to the point of resignation if necessary, that their professional military judgment be heard and accorded due weight by political leadership."[64]

This raises the question of why: why did the chiefs not challenge the commander in chief? The reasons are several, including the standard prohibition against political activity by a military officer, their personal and professional loyalty to the president of the United States (the earlier-described struggle between Harry Truman and Douglas MacArthur had warned of the hazards of violating civilian control), and their loyalty to their own services.[65] For example, Army Chief of Staff Harold K. Johnson decided not to resign because he judged it in the army's best interest that he remain in his leadership role. As his biographer put it, "During the course of his stewardship as Chief of Staff, he had on a number of occasions contemplated resignation in protest, but each time he drew back, concluding that he could do more good by continuing to serve."[66] The point, in any case, is clear: the chain of command is so strong that even the nation's highest-ranking military officers find it difficult, if not impossible, to stand up to someone higher ranked than they, the commander in chief.

Operation Anaconda was of course no exception to this general rule. Part of a larger initiative called Operation Enduring Freedom, intended to "drain the swamps" of terrorists, it was thought at the time to be as just as it was necessary.[67] Recall that this was in the months immediately succeeding 9/11—so it was widely considered right to risk the lives of a few to protect the lives of the many.[68] In fact, whatever the reservations about Anaconda, they did not center on whether the operation itself was justified. This is evidenced by a number of the soldiers here described, who invoked the attacks on the World Trade Center to sustain their conviction that what they were doing was right and in the national interest.

But if the mission per se was just, at least so far as the majority of Americans were concerned, what can be said about its planning and implementation? Put another way, is it possible to launch a military operation that is just in theory but unjust in practice?

In these matters the division of labor is supposedly this. The decision to commit forces to conflict is made by political leaders. But once the decision to commit has been made, it is military leaders who are responsible for implementing it. Military leaders, officers and noncommissioned officers alike, train and discipline those beneath them. Military leaders determine which strategies and tactics to use. And military leaders decide when and where to press forward, or for that matter to pull back.[69] This bestows on them a great responsibility—and places on them a great burden. Why? Because the consequences of bad leadership in combat can be grave, even fatal. And because given the chain of command, given Diehards who submit to their superiors, including in the heat of battle, there is virtually no open dissent. Almost always orders are obeyed, even the bad ones, no matter the consequences.

We know now that Operation Anaconda suffered from poor planning and implementation. There was the unreliable intelligence, the "serpentine chain of command," and the too few troops and too meager munitions.[70] As a result, American and allied soldiers were trapped in situations for which they were ill prepared. And as a result, Combined Joint Task Force Mountain failed to successfully carry out its original mission: to rid the immediate and surrounding areas of enemy fighters.

We also know now that Operation Anaconda was used to score political points. I refer particularly to the rosy assessment provided by Tommy Franks in the immediate aftermath. Even at the time, close observers knew full well that Anaconda was by no stretch of the imagination the "unqualified and complete success" that Franks claimed. At a minimum it was self-deception, a misplaced optimism that, among other things, foreshadowed what happened in Iraq. Mark Danner has referred to the conflict in Iraq as "the War of the Imagination," conducted on the basis of false hopes rather than on hard-nosed assessments of what "staying the course" would come to mean.[71] By General Hagenbeck's own testimony later, Anaconda was similarly deprived of the requisite reality checks, before, during, and immediately after.

Whatever the judgment of history, the soldiers here named were Diehards. Some were deeply dedicated to their superiors. All were deeply dedicated to supporting and defending the Constitution of the United States— and to safeguarding each other. To this end, they put their lives on the line willingly, and in many cases even eagerly. Diehards like Hagenbeck, Wiercinski, Grippe, Abbott, Perez, and Rivera were all fired up for Anaconda. They wanted to defend and protect the United States of America. They wanted to uphold the reputations of soldiers who came before them. They wanted to do what was expected, to obey their military superiors, even when they found them wanting. They wanted to protect their buddies, even at risk to themselves. And more than anything else, above all, they wanted to catch, to kill, the enemy responsible for the attacks on American soil.

The U.S. military is not oblivious to the importance of having superiors take account of their subordinates. The Marine Corps, for example, makes it clear that while effective followers accept "the necessity for compliance," effective leaders treat their followers "as individuals," whose independence remains intact.[72] Moreover, officially at least, the military recognizes the tension between the rigidity of command on the one hand and the need for honest feedback on the other.[73] Still, as we have seen, in practice even high-ranking officers nearly always defer to those more highly positioned than they.

This brings us to the more than half dozen generals who, although deeply unhappy over the course of the war in Iraq, waited for months, if not years, to call for Rumsfeld's head.[74] More specifically, in part because the Uniform Code of Military Justice prescribes punishment by court-martial for using "contemptuous words against the president, the vice-president, Congress, the secretary of defense," they made their real views known only after they had retired from active military service.[75] This is not to say they were too late to have an impact. In fact, the so-called revolt of the retired generals contributed to creating a climate in which Rumsfeld's continuing service as secretary of defense finally became impossible. However, at the time it mattered most, before the U.S.-led invasion of Iraq even took place, of the top military brass it was only Army Chief of Staff General Eric Shinseki who told Congress that for the operation to succeed, a much larger force was required. (For telling truth to power, Shinseki was marginalized.[76] He retired soon after.)

As to the hundreds of thousands of soldiers closer to the bottom of the military hierarchy, once they volunteer to serve, they have no voice, none whatsoever, in making the strategic decisions that could cost them their lives. Here they are, during Anaconda's hardest hours: "Pinned down and surrounded by an enemy that outnumbered and outgunned them, and who were fighting with a ferocity that no one had predicted, the young infantrymen responded to the chaos and confusion with a courage that surprised even their NCOs."[77] It is Diehards like these who give followers a good name. It is Diehards like these, subordinates without sources of power, authority, and influence, who place on their superiors the moral obligation to lead wisely and well.

AFTERTHOUGHT

I told the story of Operation Anaconda to dissect this particular operation—and to get at questions Anaconda raises about relations between followers and leaders. Clearly, leaders have a special responsibility in those situations in which lives are at risk. I quote James Webb, decorated marine combat veteran of the Vietnam War, former secretary of the navy, and most recently senator from Virginia. Senator Webb recalled that when he was on active duty, he, like most soldiers, trusted the judgment of our national leaders. "We owed them our loyalty, as Americans," Webb said, "and we gave it." In turn, Webb continued, our leaders "owed us sound judgment, clear thinking, concern for our welfare, a guarantee that the threat to our country was equal to the price we might be called upon to pay in defending it."[78]

In these few spare lines, Webb described a reciprocal relationship, in which both followers and leaders have the right to expect something from the other. Followers, soldiers, are expected to be loyal, which presupposes being prepared to die. Leaders, in turn, are expected to be as sensitive as they are smart, as ethical as they are effective. Above all, leaders, both civilian and military, are presumed to weigh carefully the threat to our national security against the price of blood and treasure.

What, though, happens when things go wrong, when one or the other, followers or leaders, fails to meet this commitment? Members of the armed services are inclined always to obey orders even if they are questionable—but what can we say in this regard about civilians? Clearly, they have more leeway. So the question I would finally ask is, When it comes to matters of war and peace, and civilian superiors are seriously lacking, how, if at all, should civilian subordinates respond?

Let me respond to my own question by turning to Colin Powell, secretary of state under George W. Bush, and George Tenet, director of the Central Intelligence Agency under George W. Bush. Both men knew before the American invasion of Iraq was launched that the administration's case for going in was, in part at least, bogus. Yet neither one of them took strong issue with the commander in chief or, for that matter, with his closest advisers. Nor did either man decide to quit the administration, to challenge the president, by taking their case directly to the people. As Maureen Dowd put it, "If Colin Powell and George Tenet had walked out of the administration in February 2003 . . . they might have saved the lives and limbs of all those brave U.S. kids and innocent Iraqis."[79] But they did not walk out, and they did not speak up. They stayed silent, putting their loyalty to the president ahead of their loyalty to the people. Consider it a lesson in how *not* to follow.

PART III

Future Followers

The fault, dear Brutus, is not in our stars,
but in ourselves, that we are underlings.

—SHAKESPEARE

CHAPTER 9

Values

JUST AS THERE ARE GOOD LEADERS and bad leaders, many of whom are familiar, there are good followers and bad followers, less familiar perhaps but no less important. The question before us is, What do good and bad followers look like?

First, though, a reminder of how followers are defined in this book: *followers* are subordinates who have less power, authority, and influence than do their superiors, and who therefore usually, but not invariably, fall into line. The thing to recall at this point is that some of the time superiors, leaders, are nearly irrelevant. That is, some of the time followers react not to what leaders do but to what they do *not* do. On such occasions they simply take matters into their own hands and follow each other rather than those more highly positioned than they.

BYSTANDERS

As I indicated in the chapter about Bystanders in Nazi Germany, there is nearly no circumstance in which to be described as a Bystander is to be described in a way that is flattering. And when circumstances are dire, the need to do something, as opposed to doing nothing, is obviously more urgent. As Martin Luther King put it, "Man's inhumanity to man is not

213

only perpetrated by the vitriolic actions of those who are bad, it is also perpetrated by the vitiating inaction of those who are good."[1]

I am reminded of the famous/infamous story of Kitty Genovese, who was murdered in 1964 on a tree-lined street in Kew Gardens, an ordinarily pretty and placid section of New York City. Arriving home from work late one night, she walked from her car to her apartment, soon to be stalked and stabbed by an assailant cloaked in the dark. The attack on her lasted longer than thirty minutes and was either seen or heard by no fewer than thirty-eight "respectable, law-abiding citizens"—none of whom took it on themselves to call the police. Why? No one did anything because no one else did anything. There was no leader—and there was no one else who did anything more than stand by.

After the fact, one man willing to talk about what happened admitted he and his wife had heard Genovese scream. They went to the window "to see what was happening, but the light from our bedroom made it difficult to see the street." So, his wife interjected, "I put out the light and we were able to see better." When they were asked why, given what they had seen and heard, they did not call the police, the woman replied, "I don't know."[2]

One of the reasons we continue to find the story of Kitty Genovese so compelling is that the crime was up close and personal. Americans can relate to the lone young woman who was brutally murdered and to the otherwise safe and friendly neighborhood in which the murder took place. It is more difficult for people to connect to calamities far from home, as *New York Times* columnist Nicholas Kristof has been the first to remind us. Kristof has been writing for years about the genocide taking place in Darfur. In column after column he expressed shock and dismay that so little was being done to stop the killing; and in column after column he urged, cajoled, pleaded with his readers to somehow intervene. Here is Kristof on bad followers: "Perhaps the most extraordinary aspect of Darfur isn't that gunmen on the Sudanese payroll heave babies into bonfires as they shout epithets against blacks. It's that the rest of us are responding only with averted eyes and polite tut-tutting."[3] Clearly, he is especially outraged by Bystanders, by those among us who know about the murder and mayhem but who do nothing in response.

At the same time, Kristof is inspired by and admiring of good followers, particularly by Activists who do whatever they reasonably can about the murder and mayhem in Darfur, even though they themselves lack power, authority, and influence. Kristof writes about grassroots efforts such as the one led by students at California's Santa Clara University, who replicated and then resided in a mini refugee camp, to raise money and awareness. And he names young Activists such as thirteen-year-old Rachel Koretsky, from Philadelphia, who distributed circulars and organized a rally, in the process raising some $14,000 for victims in Darfur; and Tacey Smith, a twelve-year-old from a small town in Oregon who, after seeing the movie *Hotel Rwanda*, formed a Sudan Club and raised money by selling eggs, washing cars, and asking for donations instead of birthday presents; and Jason Miller, an MD/PhD student who in his spare time became the foremost expert on how investments by foreign companies "underwrite the Sudanese Genocide."[4] Finally, Kristof provides the kind of information that makes it easy for his readers to act, such as the Web addresses www.savedarfur.org and www.genocideintervention.net.

Progress with regard to Darfur is glacially slow. Still, different people in different places have made a difference. Grassroots efforts have been especially important—case in point: those targeting China. China has a long record of protecting the Sudanese government against efforts by the United Nations to send in peacekeepers. But soon after grassroots Activists the world over, finally also including celebrities such as Mia Farrow and Steven Spielberg, threatened to tag the 2008 Beijing Olympics the "Genocide Olympics," the Chinese government pulled back, at least slightly. It sent a high-ranking official to push the Sudanese government to agree to accept a United Nations Peacekeeping Force, which several weeks later it actually did. As an editorial in the *Boston Globe* put it, "There are signs that officials in Beijing are beginning to get the message . . . not from other governments but from a grassroots movement to shame China by characterizing the 2008 summer games in Beijing as the 'genocide' Olympics."[5] By the summer of 2007 there was in fact "a first step to save Darfur."[6] A potentially groundbreaking agreement was struck to send a twenty-six thousand member United Nations–African Union joint peacekeeping force to the area.

The general consensus on matters like these is this: good followers are ready and willing to put their money where their mouths are. Bad followers, in contrast, are not. Of course, the divide between good and bad followers is more complicated than this simple formulation would seem to imply. Some followers do stand up for what they believe—but what they believe is morally wrong. Other followers are reluctant to stand up and be counted— but only because the risks of so doing are high. To more fully understand what now constitutes the conventional wisdom, at least in the United States, consider these further examples of Participants, Activists, and Diehards, all of whom are engaged in public life. This is not to say that I agree with every one of the positions taken in the following pages. Rather, it is to say that these particular followers were in some way dissatisfied with the status quo—and so they invested time and energy in creating change. Together, they support the idea that *for followers to do something is nearly always better than for followers to do nothing.*

PARTICIPANTS

We have seen that ordinary people are more willing now than they were in the past to stand up and be counted. We have also seen that they are more willing now than they were in the past to take matters into their own hands. Again, this is not to suggest that generations past were altogether silent. Quite the contrary—countless times they fought for what they believed in ways that put succeeding generations to shame. For example, many observers have compared the Vietnam generation to the Iraq generation, finding the former bold and impassioned and the latter distant and detached.[7] Still, the twenty-first century is even at this early stage singular—there are many people in many places willing to speak out.

Sometimes the voices belong to the downtrodden—to women in Africa speaking out finally in greater numbers against what their leaders have tolerated for so long, genital mutilation; or to gays and lesbians in the Middle East, unwilling any longer to conform to the prevailing norm, which is to treat them as if they were invisible. In the United States, evidence of this kind of energy can be found among illegal aliens, whose fight to be integrated into the system evolved into a powerful political protest, notwithstanding the contentiousness of their claim to what some call "amnesty."[8] In 2006 hundreds of thousands of people in Los Angeles and in some sixty other cities around the country marched against congressional efforts to crack down on those who had entered the United States illegally. By the time it was all over, the numbers were huge, a half million or so, and Californians had witnessed the single biggest demonstration in the state's history. John Cassidy, writing for the *New Yorker*, was a sympathetic observer: "Even more stunning was the sound of a once marginalized community finding its voice . . . Here, finally, were the janitors, maids, dishwashers, babysitters, garment workers, office cleaners, shelf-stackers, busboys, cooks, gardeners, pool boys, and fruit pickers who do the work that American citizens generally won't do—at least, not at the wages being offered."[9]

In the United States and in many other places around the world as well, we are witnessing members of another previously marginalized or even persecuted group intent on planting their flag: homosexuals. Consider these numbers, all from 2007: a gay pride parade in São Paolo attracted some 3 million people; a gay pride parade in Warsaw drew twenty thousand, in spite of the need for heavy security; and a gay pride parade in Paris had some seven hundred thousand marchers, including the city's openly gay mayor, Bertrand Delanoe. This is not to speak of the gay pride parade in Rome, in which one hundred thousand participants were led by transgender member of parliament Vladimir Luxuria; or of the fifteen thousand people who took to the streets in Tel Aviv, in spite of nearby signs that read "God hates debauchery."[10]

More often than not, though, Participants are ordinary people who came to feel so strongly about an issue on which their leaders were absent that they decided to do something about it. Animal rights advocates, for instance, now constitute a mass movement. In addition to animal rights Activists and Diehards, such as Ingrid Newkirk, founder of People for the Ethical Treatment of Animals (PETA), Participants in the animal rights movement are now countless in number, especially in the United States and Europe. Their mission: to protect animals from unnecessary cruelty and provide them with good care. Testimony to their enormous and still-growing clout are dramatic changes in the food industry, with chains like McDonald's and Burger King recently imposing guidelines on their meat and egg suppliers, including extra water, more wing room, and fresh air for egg-laying hens. In 2007 Burger King went even further, announcing that it would begin to buy eggs and pork only from suppliers that did not confine their animals in crates or cages.[11] Legal arguments, which claim that animals should no longer be regarded as property, are being advanced as well. Until rather recently animal law courses were virtually unheard of. Now they are taught in more than half of all American law schools.

Along similar lines, people are taking into their own hands problems related to the environment. Alarmed by the rate at which planet earth is being degraded, aware that their political leaders are doing too little too late, nongovernmental institutions and individuals the world over have led the way, engaging often in Herculean efforts to reverse or at least slow the damage. An example is the World Wildlife Fund, which recently struck a landmark agreement with Asia Pacific Resources International, a company that for years was destroying some of "the most biodiverse lowland forest on the planet." The idea was to get Asia Pacific to expand exponentially a recently designated Indonesian national park and to encourage it to preserve forests in future logging.[12] The fact is that public pressure to strike such deals is now so great that environmentalists and corporations now work together in "a new spirit of compromise."[13] Put another way, followers have obliged leaders, in both business and government, to pay attention. Many of the largest and best-known companies, including FedEx, Tyson Foods, BP, and General Electric, have announced they're signing on. And CEOs in growing numbers are boasting that they too are eager to get green. Wal-Mart's chief executive, Lee Scott, has declared that he is determined to turn the world's largest retailer into the world's greenest. Said Scott of company founder Sam Walton, who, I should add, has been dead for over a decade, "I think Sam Walton would, in fact, embrace Wal-Mart's efforts to improve the quality of life for our customers and our associates by doing what we need to do in sustainability."[14]

In part our recently heightened awareness of the environment is the consequence of work done for decades by organized groups such as Greenpeace, which was one of the first to draw our attention to issues such as global warming, endangered forests, and dirty waters. But the response by individual followers to the inefficacy of individual leaders has had a far greater impact, especially in recent years. Membership in the Sierra Club went up by about one-third (to eight hundred thousand) during the four-year period beginning in 2002. The number of Americans who say they worry about the environment "a great deal" or "a fair amount" has, according to the polls, also increased, up from 62 percent in 2004 to 77 percent in 2006. The numbers of students dedicated to cleaning up the environment has climbed even faster, their ranks representing a wide swath of disciplines and beliefs, "from the 3,000 member Engineers for a Sustainable World to the Evangelical Youth Climate Initiative to Net Impact, a green business school network with 130 chapters."[15] In fact, all across America the virtues of "sustainability" are now being trumpeted loudly and clearly, which explains the newfound interest in everything ranging from alternative sources of fuel to cleaner dry cleaning.[16]

Of course, one of my main points is that the number of Participants is growing not only in the United States but in countries all over the world. In the remote hamlet of Tamga, residents frustrated by corruption and the sorry legacy of a chemical spill "did something that would have been unthinkable in Kyrgyzstan not long ago: they rose up."[17] In the United Arab Emirates, eight hundred foreign workers, most of them Indians and Pakistanis, marched down a main highway to protest how they were being treated. Their demonstration was "unprecedented in its scale and high profile, laying bare a Dickensian underworld of poverty and exploitation in the shadow of a gleaming city of high-rise buildings and luxury hotels."[18] In Cambodia, eight hundred of the country's poorest people did the unthinkable: they left behind their crops and animals to pour out publicly and passionately their complaints and demands, which included the "demand for free speech and democratic rights."[19] And in Minsk, the expected landslide victory of President Aleksandr Lukashenko, widely considered Europe's last dictator, motivated thousands of Belarusians to protest in the streets. These particular Participants were prepared to go for broke, to ignore the "swirling snow and official threats of arrest to denounce the election as a clumsily orchestrated sham."[20]

Even France, "which has a strong tradition of often violent demonstrations and paralyzing strikes that is largely tolerated by the broader population," was unnerved in recent years by what could fairly be described as a double whammy.[21] On the one side were the riots, arson, and vandalism instigated primarily by Muslim youths, furious at what they considered their deliberate exclusion from mainstream French society. And on the other side, after the French government had responded to Muslim demands with a law aimed at easing high unemployment, were the counterprotests.

Strikes and demonstrations broke out in more than two hundred fifty towns and cities, led by students and unions opposed to the new law, which, they were sure, threatened their interests. More than a million people marched in the streets, and many of France's universities, schools, post offices, banks, government offices, and shops were forced to close.[22] In the end, President Jacques Chirac bowed to public pressure. He was forced by his followers to rescind the very law he had championed only weeks before.[23]

ACTIVISTS

We have seen how Activists in the corporate sector recently impinged on business as usual. To be sure, some things are resistant to change—for example, executive pay, which continues to be sky high in spite of all the griping. But shareholder Activists have already had an impact; and there is evidence their determination to "bore from within" is increasing rather than decreasing. For example, managers of socially responsible investment (SRI) funds are taking this sort of activism to a new level—some now making it a point to invest in companies with bad track records, precisely to effect change from within. Green Century Funds, for example, a group of SRI funds owned by nonprofit environmental groups, used its shareholder status to persuade Whole Foods to fully and accurately label all in-house products that contain genetically engineered ingredients. "Green Century had filed repeated shareholder resolutions calling on the company to disclose such information, and apparently the pressure finally paid off."[24] Their efforts were similarly effective with other companies—for example, with Apple Computer. When a Green Century representative suggested at the company's annual meeting that it launch a free recycling program for obsolete iPods, Apple went ahead and did it.

Activists are all over the place now, including, as mentioned earlier in passing, at Harvard University. The faculty's deep involvement in a crucial matter of university governance, in the presidency of Lawrence H. Summers, was so unusual, and so indicative of the times in which we live, the case merits a closer look.

Summers, who became president in 2001, did not take long to alienate key members of the campus community. Their ranks included at least one well-known faculty member of the African-American Studies Department, Cornel West, who soon quit Cambridge for what he came to consider the greener grass of Princeton. After another series of what might politely be described as diplomatic gaffes, Summers made his last major mistake. In January 2005, in speaking to the question of why women were underrepresented in science and engineering, he suggested that part of the problem might be innate differences—that is, between men and women. In response to the instant furor over his being, at the least, politically incorrect, Summers apologized, repeatedly, for what he said and how he said it. But it helped not in the least: within days Activists in the opposition had lined up against him.

Members of a university faculty are not, in the usual sense of this word, *followers*. Certainly, members of Harvard's tenured faculty are not in any way beholden to Harvard's president. But in matters of institutional governance, they generally do go along with what the president decides; and they generally do not, in any case, instigate the equivalent of a palace coup. This case, though, was different. Within weeks thirteen professors publicly attacked Summers at a faculty meeting. And within months Harvard's Faculty of Arts and Sciences passed a vote of no confidence in the president, dealing him what most considered a "stunning" and certainly unprecedented rebuke.[25] Everett Mendelsohn, a professor of the history of science, declared that the vote of no confidence was a signal from the faculty to the Harvard Corporation (which has the power to hire and fire the president), which had to be "taken seriously." And J. Lorand Matory, professor of anthropology and of African and African-American Studies, was even more pointed: "There is no noble alternative to [Summers's] resignation," said Matory. "This is about his management style. He is dictatorial and autocratic."[26]

Little more than a year after he made his comments on women in science and engineering, Larry Summers was effectively obliged to resign, making his the briefest Harvard presidency since Cornelius Conway Felton died in office—in 1862. The year preceding his resignation had turned into the political equivalent of a gathering storm. Harvard faculty were increasingly emboldened to speak out, now joined by others including, for example, a member of the Harvard Corporation and a former dean, who told the *Boston Globe* that Summers had said things "that appear less than truthful."[27] The situation came to a head at a faculty meeting held in February 2006. According to an account in *Harvard Magazine*, fifteen people spoke out against Summers, questioning not only his competence but his character. A specter appeared—"the specter of a second vote of no confidence in the administration"—but not a person in the room spoke in Summers's defense.[28]

The news of Summers's resignation was announced on the university's Web site on February 21, 2006. The message was accompanied by a letter from Summers, who wrote that the "rifts" between him and "segments of the Arts and Sciences faculty" had made it "infeasible" for him to continue to serve in his current role.[29] Meanwhile, the Activists who had toppled the president were gracious in their victory. Professor Matory: "I admire him for the humility and dignity that it took to step down. In stepping down he deserves our collegiality and support."[30]

If Activists at Harvard seem somehow esoteric, Activists in other places are nothing if not approachable. In fact, like the Activists who invested so much of themselves in Voice of the Faithful, they encourage us, each and every one, to sign on.

Uganda's women's rights movement is one of the oldest in Africa and one of the most impressive in the world. After years of suppression, the movement began to flourish again in the late 1980s, when women were actually encouraged by the government to keep their daughters in school, to start small businesses, and to challenge laws and practices that restricted their property rights, failed to protect them from rape, and maintained divorce statutes that favored men. Once AIDS started to spread, women's rights Activists redoubled their efforts. They organized marches against rape in the city streets and urged women across the country to band together to confront abusive men. In time, "Uganda's widespread social mobilization against AIDS and gender violence touched every corner of society, from the president's office to the remotest villages. But it started with frank, open discussions among friends, relatives, and neighbors, some of whom became the policymakers and activists who shaped the nation's response to AIDS." Progress against the disease was so striking in Uganda that AIDS experts could not help but be impressed, in particular by the power of ordinary people to spread new ideas and information, to transform gender relations, and to change sexual behavior.[31] Is there better evidence of follower power—of the power of the people to make a difference?

Americans with Alzheimer's disease are creating another kind of grass-roots movement, this one intended to improve services and change public perceptions of the 5 million similarly afflicted. They too are tired of waiting for their leaders to do what they want them to do, and so have taken matters into their own hands—and they are making a difference.[32] Early-stage Alzheimer patients are themselves leading the charge. Determined to create change, they travel tirelessly around the country, telling their stories, speaking to groups and organizations, pushing for more patient-support groups, creating new social networks, and of course lobbying their leaders, state and federal lawmakers in particular, to get their attention and enlist their support.

These are the kinds of political action groups, advocacy groups, and even support groups now springing up all over the place. When seen through the lens of followership, they are no more, and no less, than people without conventional sources of power, authority, and influence making a single, simple, significant decision: *not to depend on those in charge to take charge.*

Diehards

Diehards dedicate their lives to their cause, whether an individual or an idea. They draw on their convictions, their passions, to drive them, to urge them forward, against all odds. Some of the time Diehards are members of groups, such as the soldiers who were part of Operation Anaconda. But there are other times, when Diehards are individuals acting alone, half-crazed, if you will, by the fierceness of their determination and dedication to getting one thing or another accomplished or to sending one or another kind of message.

Here is a wonderful example, a man who ranks among the most eminent of twentieth-century Diehards: Russian scientist Andrei Sakharov. Although he began his career as a nuclear physicist, "Sakharov not only thought his way out of the totalitarian system he'd grown up in, he learned to exploit its weaknesses. To put it differently, Sakharov was not merely a beneficiary of the international human rights movement, but one of its founding fathers."[33] For his troubles, Sakharov was arrested by the Soviet authorities, sent into internal exile, and forced for six years to live under close, constant police surveillance.

Not infrequently, and for reasons about which we can only speculate, many Diehards are women. And not infrequently, they are driven to become Diehards because of a tragedy that befell their children. Candy Lightner started Mothers Against Drunk Driving (MADD) after her twelve-year-old daughter, Cari, was killed by a drunk driver. Amilya Antonetti founded Soapworks after discovering that conventional household cleaners made her infant son seriously sick. Elizabeth Margulies (along with her husband) started a public relations campaign against Aetna, for refusing to pay expenses incurred by her baby boy, who had Tay-Sachs disease. Sorrel King started a grassroots movement on behalf of hospital safety after her eighteen-month-old daughter, Josie, died as the result of medical mistakes made at Johns Hopkins Children's Center in Baltimore. When Johns Hopkins offered a financial settlement, King asked the hospital to take some of the money and start a children's safety program. Then she created the Josie King Foundation to fund safety initiatives at other hospitals. Most recently, in order to reach consumers as well as medical professionals, King launched a Web site, at www.josieking.org, "with her own blog on patient safety; an online community where families can post their medical-error experiences and provide emotional support; advice from medical and legal experts on how to avoid error and deal with it when it occurs; and resources for hospitals seeking to improve safety."[34]

Then there are the war stories. In Israel, Rachel Ben Dor, whose son was a soldier in Lebanon, founded Four Mothers—Leave Lebanon in Peace. For years her group was dismissed—derided, even. But ultimately it was honored for having started what the *Jerusalem Post* called "one of the most successful grass-roots movements in Israeli history."[35] The recent experience of the United States is even more telling, for among the few followers who regularly protested the war in Iraq, most were women, notably a few mothers of a few soldiers who were called on to serve. Some of these women were Activists, such as Celeste Zappala, from Philadelphia, who cofounded Gold Star Families for Peace after her son was killed in Baghdad; and Jean Prewitt, from Birmingham, Alabama, whose son similarly died and who remembered that "the first year I was rather numb, and then I got angry."[36] But the Diehard among them was Cindy Sheehan, who started a grassroots movement that remained meager in size, but who nevertheless did more than any other ordinary American to take on President George W. Bush and his conduct of the war in Iraq.

Cindy Sheehan is the mother of Army Specialist Casey A. Sheehan, a twenty-four-year-old Humvee mechanic who was killed in Sadr City on April 24, 2004. Whatever her grief in the wake of Casey's death, her anger was fueled during a private meeting she and her family had with President George W. Bush two months later. As she later described it, Bush did not know the name of her son; acted inappropriately, as if the meeting were a party; and called her "Mom," which she considered disrespectful.[37] A short time later Sheehan started giving interviews and making public appearances, all in an effort to marshal the American people against the war. Before long she became the nexus, such as it was, for antiwar protesters. In August 2005 she took herself to Crawford, Texas, to establish "Camp Casey," a muddy outpost set up just a few miles down the road from the ranch Bush calls home. White crosses were hammered into the dirt, pink banners were strewn across the trees, and flowers were delivered to what was, in effect, a round-the-clock campsite built to accommodate antiwar protesters who came from around the country. The numbers Sheehan pulled in were not large, and she aroused the ire of local residents who found her and the accompanying media circus intrusive. But Sheehan's effort had its compensations. A woman from Dayton, Ohio, drove two days to Crawford to be with her, just because she "wanted Cindy to know I support her."[38] (Sheehan did not let up. In 2007 she took on House Speaker Nancy Pelosi for not trying to impeach President Bush.)

In the United States, among the most familiar of Diehards is the whistle-blower. Whistle-blowers are subordinates desperate to fix what's broke. The typical trajectory involves an initial attempt to do so in-house; then, if the problem continues, whistle-blowers go outside the organization that employs them to complain in public. To use the word *whistle-blower* is to imply there is or there might well be retaliation of some kind, punishment for undercutting one or more superiors by disclosing a serious mistake, a significant misjudgment, or an activity that legally or morally is unethical.

Whistle-blowers are Diehards simply because the risks they take are so high. Some studies suggest that between a half and two-thirds of all whistle-blowers lose their jobs, and that for many the costs are even higher. One expert on whistle-blowers reports that of the several dozen whistle-blowers he studied closely, most lost their houses and many lost their families.

Moreover, cases against whistle-blowers can drag on for years, which is why so many suffer from depression and alcoholism and why roughly half go bankrupt.[39]

Some stories about whistle-blowers are well known. The case of the *Challenger*, the NASA space shuttle that exploded in the skies over Cape Canaveral seventy-three seconds after liftoff, was dreadful for many reasons, above all because seven astronauts died in the accident. But there was a twist to the tragedy, for as it turned out, two senior spacecraft engineers had spent six hours the previous day with NASA officials, pleading with them to delay the launch because they feared the rockets might malfunction in the unusual, below-freezing cold. For years thereafter, at least one of the two men, Roger Boisjoly, a senior engineer at Morton Thiokol, was a wreck. He walked away from Thiokol and, since corporate America dislikes a whistle-blower, struggled for years to find meaningful work. "I beat myself up for a long time over what happened that night," said Boisjoly. "Maybe I hadn't done enough. Maybe I should have gone home and called the *New York Times* or something."[40]

Sherron Watkins, who warned Enron CEO Kenneth Lay that the company might well implode, is another well-known whistle-blower, although she walked away from the mess smelling like a rose. In fact, in 2002, *Time* named Watkins, along with two other women—Coleen Rowley, who became known as the FBI's public conscience, and Cynthia Cooper, who had signaled loudly and clearly that things at WorldCom were terribly wrong—"Persons of the Year." All three had similar stories to tell, including their motivations for exposing the flaws of their institutions, their shock when the actions they took were publicly exposed, and their dismay at being condemned for what they did, at least by some.[41] Whether or not Watkins was in the usual sense of this word a *whistle-blower* has been a matter of modest debate. Among other things, her protest was registered in an anonymous letter to Lay, which was not the "classic whistleblower screed about right and wrong." Rather, it reflected a mix of motives, including the fear of being found out.[42] Be that as it may, Watkins's letter to Enron's chief executive officer was a long and carefully worded warning, "a dead-on prophecy about what lay ahead."[43]

Whistle-blower stories are almost always compelling—follower against leader, the powerless against the powerful, David against Goliath. But almost always they are also sad—an object lesson to followers, to subordinates, of how risky it is to go out on a limb, especially alone. Christoph Meili was the former night watchman at Zurich's Union Bank of Switzerland who in 1997 rescued from the shredder documents describing property seized from Holocaust victims—documents that Swiss banks had denied they had. For his troubles, Meili was fired, investigated by the police for violating the bank secrecy act, and hounded out of his homeland. But his action made it possible for Holocaust victims and their heirs finally to receive from the banks their due, a $1.2 billion settlement.[44]

Dr. Peter Post, a vice president for marketing at Pfizer, was increasingly isolated by the company for publicly criticizing the pharmaceutical industry over the pricing of drugs. First, his subordinates simply stopped reporting to him. Then his superiors stopped returning his calls. Then his secretary went elsewhere. Then his office was moved, far from the action. Then he was denied access both to his Pfizer e-mail account and to his corporate cell phone.[45] Finally, he was fired. The case is complicated, for Post had earlier filed a lawsuit against Pfizer on a matter other than pricing, which ultimately was dismissed. Nevertheless, the trajectory is typical: marginalization, humiliation, and, in a good number of cases, exile.

Bunnatine Greenhouse, an army contracting official who criticized a large, noncompetitive contract with the Halliburton Company for work in Iraq, suffered similar ignominy. In the beginning Greenhouse registered her complaints internally. When that didn't work, she went public, describing the contract as "the most blatant and improper contract abuse I have witnessed."[46] Incensed, and citing poor performance, the army demoted her, removing Greenhouse from the elite Senior Executive Service and reassigning her to a lesser job. Greenhouse, who had worked in military procurement for twenty years, hired a lawyer who charged that she was demoted not because of her work, but because the army prefers to "sidestep" strict procurement requirements when "it suits their needs."[47]

Private-sector whistle-blowers have benefited in recent years from a provision in the Sarbanes-Oxley Act, which provides legal protection against retaliation to employees of publicly owned companies, if what they suspect is corporate fraud.[48] But for those in the public sector, the situation has, if anything, deteriorated. A 2006 congressional report found that in spite of the 1989 Whistleblower Protection Act, federal employees did not have adequate safeguards.[49] Nevertheless, in May 2006 the Supreme Court scaled back protections for government workers who blow the whistle on official misconduct. In a 5–4 decision (which was a victory for the Bush administration), the justices said that 20 million public employees did not have free-speech protection for anything they say regarding their jobs. Supporters of the ruling claimed that it would protect governments at every level against frivolous lawsuits filed by disgruntled employees. But critics predicted that the impact would be negative as well as sweeping, "from silencing police officers who fear retribution for reporting department corruption" to subduing federal employees who otherwise would be inclined to report a threat to the public welfare.[50]

Issues relating to whistle-blowers might appear on the surface to be trivial, in part because some whistle-blowers are in fact "quirky," somehow at the margins of the institutions they inhabit.[51] But a good deal of the time, Diehards like these are simply truth tellers, who dare to defy the authorities in spite of an organizational response likely to be punitive, likely to twist their words into "an act of private disobedience and psychological disturbance."[52] Whistle-blowers like Jon Oberg—who warned years before it became widely known that student loan companies were collecting millions of dollars in federal payments to which they were not entitled, only to be told by his supervisor to work on something else—are the equivalent of the canary in the coal mine. When their professional lives are brought to an end, it confirms our worst suspicions: modern organizations not only fail to foster civic virtues, they go on to destroy those who display them.[53] Of course, when they succeed, as Oberg finally did, whistle-blowers are transformed, changed from followers into leaders.[54]

Which brings me to this final point: of all the different types of followers, the most likely to become leaders are Diehards. Diehards are, after all, driven to create change—they are consumed by their commitment. No wonder that some who succeed become legends in their own time.

Bad Followership

By and large, the Participants, Activists, and Diehards so far discussed in this chapter are "good." Environmentalists, for example, and shareholder activists, and whistle-blowers such as Bunnatine Greenhouse, are generally considered admirable for taking the time and the trouble and in some cases the risk to speak truth to power and right a wrong. People like these may be said, then, to exemplify good followership. They refuse to permit their relative lack of power, authority, and influence to preclude them from doing something they think should be done.

But as earlier suggested, the willingness to engage is not in and of itself "good." The question is, Willingness to engage to what end, for what purpose? In some cases, the answer is clear. Nearly none of us would consider Diehards ready to die for dictators like Pol Pot or Saddam Hussein, or for cult leaders like Jim Jones or David Koresh, in any conventional sense of this word *good*. But most cases of Participants, Activists, and Diehards are obviously more ambiguous than these. To return to some of the recent examples, for every advocate of animal rights, there are many more who consider the cause to be trivial or even misguided. For every advocate of the right of illegal immigrants to remain in the United States, there are countless others who would just as soon see them sent back.[55] And for every member of Harvard's faculty who wanted President Summers out, there were others who cared not at all, one way or the other, and others still who strongly believed he should stay. Even whistle-blowers are ambiguous figures, because for every one we ultimately honor, we permit many more to be marginalized or even punished for daring to cross their superiors and for deviating from group norms.

Engaging in the group or organization of which you are a member thus testifies to no more and no less than that you are, well, engaging. Where does this leave us? If Participants, Activists, and Diehards are in and of themselves neutral, value free, how do we distinguish good followers from bad ones? To this question there is, obviously, no single answer. Where you stand depends on where you sit—on what are your basic beliefs, on what are your fundamental values, and on what you think of this leader and these followers in this situation in particular.

Still, just as we have some sense of what distinguishes good leaders from bad ones, so, similarly, should we have some sense of what separates good followers from bad followers. Two criteria particularly pertain: one about means and the other about ends. The first criterion relates to level of engagement—some engagement being better than no engagement.

The second criterion relates to motivation—being motivated by the public interest is better than being motivated by self-interest. Five axioms follow from these two criteria:

- To do nothing—to be in no way involved—is to be a bad follower.

- To support a leader who is good—effective and ethical—is to be a good follower.

- To support a leader who is bad—ineffective and/or unethical—is to be a bad follower.

- To oppose a leader who is good—effective and ethical—is to be a bad follower.

- To oppose a leader who is bad—ineffective and/or unethical—is to be a good follower.

By and large, followers who are uninterested and inactive are bad. They include Isolates and Bystanders, who do nothing to support good leadership, or to slow bad leadership, or to contribute in any way to the group or organization of which they are members. The damage done by doing nothing is, of course, greatest when the leader is bad in the extreme—but by then it is usually too late: "By the time Kim Jong Il, the Dear Leader, took over from his father as the absolute rule of North Korea, the country was a slave society, where only the most trusted caste of people were allowed to live in sullen obedience in Pyongyang, while vast numbers of potential class enemies were worked to death in mines and hard-labor camps."[56]

The stakes are less high in corporate life. At least life and limb are not at risk. Still, even in the workplace, our tendency to go along with bad leaders rather than to openly oppose them remains strong. Jean Lipman-Blumen argues that we put up with bad leaders because we are afraid that "we are incapable of overthrowing such strong figures all by ourselves."[57] She points out that subordinates often say they had no idea that others felt the way they did: "I wish I had known at the time," said one of those she interviewed. "I probably would have pulled up my socks and gone to my boss's boss. Or, at least, gone with a few others to complain. But I thought I was all alone . . . so I just decided it was better to leave."[58]

The problem, incidentally, is by no means confined only to subordinates in the middle or at the bottom of the corporate ladder. Lipman-Blumen also writes about corporate boards "completely under the spell" of corporate leaders, no matter the quality of their performance. Such boards not only do not intrude on bad leaders, they rubber-stamp their proposals and pay their astronomical salaries, even when people are being fired and the stock price is plummeting.[59] So the problem of the passive follower pertains not only to subordinates but also to those who do, in fact, have at their disposal some power, authority, and influence.

I myself have written about William Aramony, once the much-admired CEO of United Way, who deviated wildly from the straight and narrow while board members averted their eyes. Much like the boards of many other organizations, Aramony's "was populated by well-intentioned but overextended executives, lawyers, and financiers who had neither the time nor the inclination to exercise meaningful oversight."[60] The same thing happened at the Smithsonian Institution, which eventually had to issue a high-profile apology admitting that its board of regents "failed to provide the oversight that might have prevented extravagant spending by its former chief executive." This particular board was not so much under the spell of the chief executive officer, Lawrence M. Small, as it was disengaged from him: "The Regents did not routinely receive, nor did they demand, the information necessary to support vigorous deliberation and well-reasoned decision making."[61]

The point is this: members of boards are not typically conceived of as followers. Quite the contrary: they are ultimately responsible for what happens to the organization over which they have, in theory, at least, final say. But if they fail to do what they are supposed to do, if they fail to monitor management, they are, for all practical purposes, Bystanders.

So far as followers are concerned, then, silence is not golden. It can signify only one of two things, neither of which is a particular virtue. Silence signifies that followers are withdrawn to the point of ignorance and apathy; or it signifies that they are aware and informed but choose for some reason not to speak up. I earlier noted that the army chief of staff under President Lyndon Johnson, Harold K. Johnson, chose to stay silent rather than go public. But given his real opinion of the war in Vietnam, and given the outcome, second-guessing his decision is fair game. We know that General Johnson agonized over what to do, particularly because President

Johnson continued to refuse, against all advice, to call up the reserve. Later, one of the general's subordinates remembered him saying, "Every night I go home, and I wonder if I should resign. They're asking me to do things that frighten me. But if I resign, they'll just put somebody in who will vote the way they want him to."[62] Repeatedly, then, the army chief of staff thought about taking a public stand, thought about telling the American people the government was pursuing a policy he thought dangerously flawed—only repeatedly to decide against it.

In any case, the mantra now is different, especially in business. Today's corporate experts are urging today's corporate leaders to get their followers to speak up. Superiors are being advised to provide a friendly environment, in which subordinates feel free to provide honest feedback. In fact, bosses are being told actually to concern themselves with "silent employees," who have concluded "the risk of speaking up—the chance that they would be ignored, shot down or labeled a troublemaker—outweighed the potential benefits." In short, in the current climate, failing to "actively solicit input from people at every level" of the organization is considered bad leadership and bad management. As Jim Grenier, a vice president for human resources at Intuit, put it, "It's not about a consensus culture. You're looking for more input so you can make a better decision. Employees know that we are serious about asking for their feedback, and we listen and we do something about it."[63]

But of course, the other way of looking at this selfsame phenomenon is as I am doing here: not from the perspective of superiors tasked with getting their subordinates to speak up, but from the perspective of subordinates who should not need their superiors to give them license.

Then there are followers who are bad not because they hang back—quite the contrary. These followers are engaged—engaged with bad leaders. As always, there is the extreme, as in this picture painted by Ian Buruma: "The terrifying thing about dictatorship is people's willingness to believe in the divine aspirations of dictators. The hundreds of thousands of screaming, crying, praying, book-waving, flag-waving men and women in Beijing, Berlin, Moscow, or Pyongyang, worshipping their leaders, are not only doing so because they are forced to; many, perhaps even most, really are caught up in the hysteria."[64] It is, in turn, this craziness, this contagious craziness, that leads to political violence and to the bureaucracies that support it. The trouble with Nazi functionary Adolph Eichmann, Hannah Arendt wrote in her seminal work on the banality of evil, was precisely that "so many were like him, and that the many were neither perverted nor sadistic, that they were, and still are, terribly and terrifyingly normal."[65] We witnessed this again, more recently, in Rwanda, where Hutu villagers who had been instructed by their leaders to kill Tutsis "approached the task much as they would a 9-to-5 job."[66] One of the villagers later admitted that while the killing continued, life seemed nearly ordinary. "We sang on the paths . . . We chatted about our good fortune. We soaped off our bloodstains in the basins, our noses enjoyed the aromas of full cooking pots . . . We made fun of every 'Mercy!' cried by someone we'd hunted down. We counted up and stashed away our goods."[67]

Most bad followers are, of course, less extreme in their behaviors. Nevertheless, for one or another reason of self-interest—for a reward of some kind, perhaps, or to preclude punishment for failing to comply—followers follow leaders who are, for example, incompetent, or intemperate, or corrupt, or even all of the foregoing. Some of these followers are situated up close, while others engage from a distance. They are, in any case, enablers: *for bad leaders depend absolutely on bad followers to sustain them.*

Consider the case of Marion Barry Jr., the erstwhile mayor of Washington, D.C. In a previous book, I described how, in spite of his being addicted to sex, drugs, and rock and roll, and how, in spite of his being notoriously ineffectual, Barry nevertheless was reelected to office no fewer than four times.[68] How to explain it? Barry survived politically because he was protected on the one side by family, friends, and close personal associates who were the most important of his enablers. And obviously he was supported on the other by Washington's electorate, many of whom, like him, were African American, and who chose to stand by Barry to the end of his sad, failed political career.

Or consider, for that matter, the case of Enron. During the years of crisis, the names and faces of Enron's bad leaders, particularly former CEOs Kenneth Lay and Jeffrey Skilling, became familiar. But how many of us paid much, if any, attention to their dozens of bad followers? I am thinking, for example, of Ben Glisan Jr., once Enron's treasurer, who helped craft many of the company's fraudulent financial transactions. Glisan was a protégé of Andrew Fastow, Enron's chief financial officer, who ended up pleading guilty to two counts of wire and securities fraud and is serving a sentence of six years in prison. Fastow's crooked directives notwithstanding, where he led, Glisan followed. As he testified in court, Glisan did have misgivings: "I started to believe the company was headed for some very serious financial straits."[69] Nevertheless, in part because Fastow was a superior telling him what to do, and in part because he stood to gain financially, Glisan never blew the whistle. In fact, he later acknowledged that among the many other benefits he received from going along with Fastow was a $1 million return on a $5,000 investment.[70] Incidentally—ironically, if you will—Fastow was himself a bad follower. In his various court appearances, he made plain that what he wanted, maybe more than anything else, was to please his boss, Skilling. As Fastow put it, "I thought I was being a hero for Enron."[71]

Here is another example: Wesley H. Colwell, former chief accountant of Enron's wholesale energy-trading unit. At the direction of his various superiors, who in turn were acting on orders from Skilling, Colwell admitted to manipulating earnings on two separate occasions. Why? Because Enron's corporate officers had made clear to those beneath them they wanted to beat the analysts' estimates for each quarter, which required Colwell to fudge the numbers. And then there is Paula H. Rieker, secretary to Enron's board, who came to board meetings to keep the minutes. Testifying in court years later, Rieker was able to recall key details, including Skilling's order to make "last-minute changes in earnings results to put them in line with analysts' expectations."[72] In testifying against Skilling and Lay, Rieker revealed her own craven role: a bad follower who, of her own free will and with her eyes wide open, followed bad leaders.

GOOD FOLLOWERSHIP

Good followers are the antithesis of bad followers. Good followers are in some way involved in the groups and organizations of which they are members: they do something, as opposed to doing nothing. Good followers also support good leaders, those who are effective and ethical. And they oppose, insofar as they reasonably can, bad leaders, those who are ineffective, or unethical, or both. By this measure, neither Isolates nor Bystanders are good followers. Similarly, by this measure, Participants, Activists, and Diehards are good followers only if they support good leaders and/or oppose bad ones.

Two more points, both of which return to ones I made earlier. The first is that what followers do and do not do does not depend only on their leaders. All of us react to a range of different stimuli, of which leaders are only one. For example, given what we know about social contagion, followers might decide to engage (or disengage) simply because other followers, especially those who resemble them, are similarly engaged. Many of the students who took part in the antiwar protests of the 1960s and 1970s did so more as a response to what other students were doing than to anything else. Similarly, many of those who played a part in the modern civil rights movement did so not only because they were against racial inequity, and not only because they were inspired by leaders such as Martin Luther King and Malcolm X. They also participated because they wanted to be part of an exciting community committed to a common cause.

The second point goes back to the difference between *followers* and *followership*. I defined *followers* as subordinates who have less power, authority, and influence than do their superiors. Similarly, I defined *followership* as the relationship between a subordinate and a superior, *as well as* the response of the former to the latter. Thus values are about followership rather than followers, for what followers do and do not do, in response to what leaders do and do not do, has normative implications.

In 1988 Robert E. Kelley published an article in the *Harvard Business Review* titled "In Praise of Followers," in which he made a path-breaking pitch for the importance of good followership.[73] While he does not emphasize, as I do here, the importance of the end as opposed only to the means, he nevertheless argues persuasively for the "effective" follower, who is "enthusiastic" and "intelligent" in "pursuit of an organizational goal." Effective followers, Kelley writes, manage themselves well, commit to the group or organization of which they are members, and they are "courageous, honest, and credible." Kelley's subsequent book on the subject (1992), which was discussed in chapter 4 and is titled *The Power of Followership*, made the same case, now more expansively.[74] Kelley's primary argument was that followers matter, not only leaders. Kelley's secondary argument was that followers can matter more if they are "exemplary," if they are actively engaged, while at the same time maintaining their independence, both from the leader and the rest of the group.[75]

In *The Courageous Follower*, also discussed in chapter 4, Ira Chaleff makes more or less the same points.[76] He too writes mainly about the workplace, and he too emphasizes the subordinate over the superior. Chaleff argues that followers should be more aware of their power, more willing to engage, and more ready to challenge those more highly positioned than they. To be sure, Chaleff no more than Kelley has any intention of upsetting the status quo, of having subordinates go off half-cocked, taking on superiors at every turn. To the contrary: both men generally advocate followers who work for their leaders rather than against them. Nevertheless, they want to stiffen the spines of those whose resources are meager, so that if the occasion arises, they have the nerve to challenge and even to quit the organization altogether "if the offending situation is not corrected."[77]

I could conclude this chapter about values by making a list of the traits and capacities of good followers, like all those other lists we have of the traits and capacities of good leaders. But I will refrain from so doing for two simple reasons. First, ideally such lists should be situation specific. For what it takes to be a good follower (and leader) is different in different circumstances. Second, such a list would, in any case, strongly resemble those with which we are already familiar, those that name the traits and capacities of good leaders. In other words, curiously, counterintuitively, what it takes to be a good follower looks a lot like what it takes to be a good leader. Like good leaders, good followers should be informed, energetic, independent, and so on. And, like good leaders, good followers should have the capacity to cope with complexity, to manage change, to exercise good judgment, and so on.

So I will avoid doing the obvious and conclude instead with a story about two men, both of whom were good followers. On the one hand, they were, simultaneously, leaders, men of high rank who under normal circumstances were in charge and in control. But on the other hand, they were subordinates pushed by their superiors into what finally became an untenable position. The first was Jeffrey M. Johnson, the publisher of the *Los Angeles Times*. And the second was Dean Baquet, the editor of the *Los Angeles Times*. Their time of troubles began in the late summer of 2006, when Johnson openly defied his bosses at the Tribune Company by refusing to make the additional layoffs—eighty-five people had already been cut—they insisted were necessary.

For a while Johnson's defiance was tolerated, in large part because he had strong support from fully 400 members of the 940-member editorial staff, who among other things had signed a letter on his behalf.[78] But the uneasy truce between him and those who were above him was short-lived. Within just a few weeks he was forced out of his job, punished for refusing to obey orders. Still, Johnson refused to slink away in silence. In fact, he seized the day and reiterated his strongly held view: "I still believe that you have to balance economic realities, which have all of us cutting as many dollars as we can, with how you're going to grow in the future."[79]

Just a few weeks later, Baquet, who had sided with Johnson but who in his absence was thought indispensable, was similarly shown the door.[80] He was said to have been fired not because of the dispute per se but because his defiance was open—which was true. One month earlier, during a speech in New Orleans, Baquet had gone so far as to encourage editors everywhere to "push back"—to push back against owners who had ordered them to cut newsroom staffs.[81]

Neither Johnson nor Baquet is a typical follower. Both were highly positioned. Both were extensively experienced. And both were impervious to the sad fate that can befall others who stand up to those with more power, authority, and influence than they. At the same time, they resisted their superiors at considerable risk and, ultimately, at considerable cost. Moreover, although the pressure to cut costs in the newspaper business is real, they demonstrated the courage of their convictions. So, while on the one hand they are exemplars of how good followers can have bad outcomes, on the other hand they are exemplars of how good followers can do good work.

10

Transformations

ALL MY PROFESSIONAL LIFE, I have worked in the field of leadership. So far be it from me to bite the hand that feeds me, to diminish the importance of leaders. But it's time to grow the business. It's time to adopt a more expansive approach to leadership, to include followership. I am not arguing that the two be joined only occasionally. I am arguing that leadership and followership be thought of in tandem—as inseparable, indivisible, inconceivable the one without the other.

On the one hand, I am suggesting something new and different in that our analyses of how power, authority, and influence are exercised have been leadercentric, fixated on those who rank high. But on the other hand, synthesizing leadership and followership, leaders and followers, involves no more than a natural progression. For it is also true that we have known all along there is no leadership without followership, no leader without at least one follower.

Folding followership into leadership is intended not only to be an intellectual exercise—there are practical implications as well. But for this synthesis to take place, two things have to happen. The first is consciousness-raising: the growing understanding that followers are not second to leaders, not merely their appendages, but a force, a phenomenon, to be reckoned with in their own right. The second is followership education in addition to, as part of, leadership education. As it stands now, for all the care and feeding we provide our leaders and managers, followers get nearly none. For all the countless books, videos, courses, classes, coaches, seminars, and workshops aimed at those *with* power, authority, and influence, hardly any are intended for those *without*. As a result, those of us who are followers—which most of us are most of the time—generally have not much impetus and even less of an idea of how to harness our own considerable resources.

We know by now that followers are like leaders: they are unalike. Not only do they demonstrate different levels of engagement, there are regional and cultural differences, differences between being a follower in a small group or in a large organization, differences between being a follower who is high up the hierarchy and one who is far down, and so on. Moreover, things change. No one would argue that relations between superiors and subordinates are the same now as they were a hundred, not to speak of a thousand, years ago.

Withal, it would be a mistake to exaggerate these differences to the point of paralysis. We take it for granted that most leadership courses can and do accommodate different kinds of leaders from different kinds of places. In fact, at Harvard University's John F. Kennedy School of Government, which is where I teach, such courses are among the most popular and heterogeneous in the school. (Over 40 percent of Kennedy School students are non-Americans.) So I presume the same for followers. I presume that subordinates of all kinds are enough similar to consider them a group, arguably even an interest group. I further presume that followership education would be every bit as rigorous an intellectual exercise as is leadership education. Finally, I presume that developing good followers is important, as important as developing good leaders.

I want to be clear: this is not about transforming followers into something else altogether. It is not about encouraging or empowering followers to become leaders. Recall that I define followers by rank—so by definition they are subordinates who have less power, authority, and influence than do their superiors. What I am talking about, then, is follower*ship*—which does not mean changing the *rank* of followers but changing their *response* to their rank, their response to their superiors and to the situation at hand. As a consequence, this final chapter makes six all-important assumptions:

- *Followers constitute a group* that, although amorphous, nevertheless has members with interests in common.

- While followers by definition lack authority, at least in relation to their superiors, *they do not by definition lack power and influence.*

- Followers can be *agents of change.*

- Followers ought to *support good leadership and thwart bad leadership.*

- Followers who *do something are nearly always preferred* to followers who do nothing.

- Followers can create change by *circumventing their leaders and joining with other followers* instead.

As earlier indicated, times are changing. Among other things, the leadership literature is beginning to get real—to reflect the fact that followers matter. For example, an article in *Leadership Quarterly* proposed a model for "authentic" follower development, albeit one predicated on leader development.[1] So the leader was the cause and the follower merely the effect—but, still, at least followers were not excluded from the discussion altogether. Another, perhaps better, example is an article in *Leadership Quarterly* that looks at followers in their own right, independent of leaders. The author concludes that under certain circumstances followers are "increasingly skilled manipulators of self and information."[2] And he sounds a cautionary note, warning leaders that their followers can create changes they "may not anticipate, be aware of, or indeed even understand."[3]

Other materials disposed to followers, as opposed to leaders, include books such as Robert Cialdini's well-known *Influence: The Psychology of Persuasion.*[4] Cialdini is a social psychologist who wants to stop people from saying yes when what they really mean is no. The book is not about relations between leaders and followers per se. Rather, it is about the "psychology of compliance" more generally, and about stiffening the spines of those who too readily do what other people want them to do.

One of the chapters is about what I call "resistance to authority." Cialdini points out, as I do here, that there are reasons why we normally accept hierarchies, including those that rank us nearer the bottom than the top. Among other things, we learn from birth that obedience to authority is more likely to get us what we need and want than is resistance to authority. What worries him, though, is how often we comply with people in positions of authority without giving our compliance so much as a second thought. Why do we go along so mindlessly? Well, again, we follow because following is so much easier than not following, so much easier than taking the time, the trouble, and sometimes the risk of saying no. Small wonder that Cialdini seems only a little bit helpful—he is going against the grain of human nature. He recommends that we develop a "heightened awareness of authority power," which in turn will enable us to develop a "properly guarded approach" to "authority-influence attempts."[5] The bottom line, in any case, is by now familiar: we tend to take the easy way out, to go along, even when going along could turn out badly.

Let me return one last time to what has become, somewhat to my own surprise, a running theme. We consider that the relationship between leaders and followers is of signal importance. It is—to leaders. What I am suggesting is that from the evidence here presented, *followers are more important to leaders than leaders are to followers.* Of course, many leaders are immensely important to their followers; and many leaders care not a whit about their followers. But it turns out that follower-follower relationships are much more important than we generally assume. In fact, leaders are often quite incidental to the action.

The social psychological literature is full of information about how ordinary people influence other ordinary people, or, in the parlance of this book, how followers influence other followers. But those of us with an interest in leadership have by and large disregarded what in other areas of inquiry is considered significant: that what happens in life can have little or even nothing to do with people more powerful, more highly positioned, or more influential than we. In "Shooting an Elephant," the police officer, the authority figure, fast became a tool in the hands of others. At Merck, Raymond Gilmartin, the CEO, was almost incidental to the aggressive development and marketing of Vioxx. In Boston, it was Voice of the Faithful that drove the action, not Cardinal Bernard Law. And after Operation Anaconda was over, it was Specialist Eddie Antonio Rivera who made it blindingly clear that those who mattered most were not his military superiors but his buddies, his peers, his fellow followers: "I love those guys. So much that I might have died for 'em."

Along similar lines, we know there are "innumerable social and economic situations in which we are influenced in our decision making by what others around us are doing."[6] Consider Zagat Survey, which publishes that stunningly successful series launched in 1979 as something of a hobby and now contains the cumulated opinions of some 250,000 people worldwide on restaurants, resorts, and so on. Based only on these surveys, with no additional information of any kind, people just like us decide where to eat and where to stay. We think of this as rational behavior—even though it smacks of herd behavior. What matters, in any case, is that not only leaders "trigger group action" but followers do as well.[7] Moreover, the "contagion" effect goes a long way toward explaining not only what we do but also how we feel.

No book on followership should fail, therefore, to reference the importance of followers to other followers. I would go even further: I would argue that no book on leadership should fail to reference this relationship either. In other words, the evidence suggests the exercise of good leadership as well as of good followership depends not only on the nature of the relationship between superiors and subordinates but also on the nature of the relationship between subordinates and other subordinates.

To enable understanding of follower power—and the limitations thereof—the next two sections provide practical pointers. They take into account leader-follower relationships and follower-follower relationships as well. Again, the idea is not to transform followers into leaders but to encourage followers to engage in spite of, or, if you will, because of, their subordinate rank. Remember, they are us. None among us is always a leader and never a follower.

In the Workplace

We know by now that during the last fifty years or so, relations between superiors and subordinates in the workplace became more equal. The reasons include cultural changes, such as those demanding less deference to authority, including from children to their parents and from students to their teachers. And they also include the information revolution, which of itself made organizational hierarchies flatter. Some, in fact, are flat to the point where relations between leaders and followers are fluid (they trade places); and others are flat to the point of having no immediately obvious leaders (or followers) at all. Such groups and organizations are "leaderless" by design, the idea being that people are happier and more productive if they are autonomous.

Withal, leaders are in no danger of becoming extinct. Debian Project is an open source software community with over one thousand members in forty countries, with a history of having had nine different leaders in thirteen years (1993 to 2006). Community members always understood that a governance structure of some kind is necessary. But they were loath to having anything remotely resembling a traditional organizational hierarchy. So they went the extra mile. They drafted a constitution that defined and delineated what it means to be a leader at Debian Project. Debian's constitution limits positional authority by requiring leaders to "make decisions which are consistent" with the views of the majority. It further requires that leaders adhere to the same rules that apply to other members—no special privileges. Finally, it requires a system of checks and balances. The power to make major decisions is divided between the rough equivalent of an executive committee and a technical committee.[8]

Notwithstanding a constitution that virtually ensures that Debian is governed by democratic rule and that its leaders are carefully constrained, leaders still manage somehow to emerge and in some way to take charge. Moreover, they rise to the top not only on the basis of their technical skills but also on the basis of their leadership skills. In other words, even at Debian, where such pains are taken to level the playing field, some people lead and other people follow. "The informal work of coordinating individual efforts and linking them to community goals [is] a vital source of leadership."[9]

Along similar lines is a book written by Ori Brafman and Rod Beckstrom titled *The Starfish and the Spider: The Unstoppable Power of Leaderless Organizations*.[10] Brafman and Beckstrom consider the model of the traditional CEO outdated or, at a minimum, suboptimal, which of course it is. Conventional CEOs are described as leading by command and control, as being powerful and directive, and as considering their task to be the maximization of profits. The problem is that none of these skills and capacities are especially well suited to the changing face of business.

However, rejecting the old model of leadership is not tantamount to rejecting leadership altogether—to being "leaderless." In fact, Brafman and Beckstrom admire "the catalyst"—who turns out to be a leader by another name. Catalysts are not necessarily in positions of high rank— that is, they are not necessarily superiors as this word is usually used. But much of what they do—initiating, facilitating, and inspiring, for example—is so leaderlike that before the book is over they are in fact described as a "leader type."[11] (This is an example of the lines between leaders and followers being blurred.)

Here is my point: major changes, good intentions, and new nomenclatures notwithstanding, what inevitably happens, in the workplace as everyplace else, is that some people lead and other people follow. Even the most deliberately democratic of our workplaces are *informally, if not formally*, rank ordered. Moreover, in many organizations, traditional hierarchies still prevail. In most teaching hospitals, for example, there still remains a division of labor reminiscent of nothing as much as times past. On the highest rung of the hospital hierarchy are physicians who are, simultaneously, senior administrators. Right under them are senior physicians who make rounds once or twice daily. Somewhat lower down are residents and interns, who spend countless, sleepless hours mastering the medical trade. And at the bottom of this particular ladder are the medical students, still inhibited, if not prohibited, from challenging those higher up than they.[12]

The effects of rank ordering are sometimes benign—and sometimes not. Rank ordering can be pernicious. Here, then, is a question to which all of us should know the answer: does the mere fact of being a follower, of being subordinate, impact on our well-being? The answer is *yes*, being subordinate does, or at least it can, have an impact on our health and welfare, and in potentially significant ways.

Consider the concept of "relative deprivation," which involves comparing ourselves to others to whom we are similar. A survey of sixteen thousand workers conducted in Great Britain found their "reported levels of job satisfaction had less to do with . . . salaries than with how their salaries compared with those of co-workers."[13] Moreover, feeling somehow deprived, which derives from feeling somehow powerless, is bad not only for our mental well-being but also for our physical well-being. Another British study found that civil service workers who were promoted to the top ranks lived longer than did their colleagues in lower-ranking jobs. More precisely, midlevel civil servants were more likely than their bosses to develop a range of potentially deadly conditions, including heart disease, high blood pressure, lung cancer, and gastrointestinal ailments.[14] A recent study conducted in the United States came to more or less the same conclusion, particularly as it pertained to subordinates obliged to endure miserable superiors: "Employees stuck in an abusive relationship experienced more exhaustion, job tension, nervousness, depressed mood and mistrust."[15]

While no one fully understands the connection between feelings of relative deprivation and people's health, it appears related to stress. There is evidence to support this hypothesis in the animal kingdom, where fights over status are common. For example, Robert Sapolsky, a preeminent student of baboons, found that blood samples taken from low-ranking baboons have higher levels of a hormone associated with stress; similarly, dominant rhesus monkeys have lower rates of atherosclerosis than monkeys further down the social hierarchy. The bottom line is this: "The degree to which low rank is harmful to an individual is likely to depend on the number of people of higher rank, because each such person is in a position to deliver the threats, insults, enforced obeisance, or ultimate violence that generate stress. Individuals who are insulted by those immediately above them insult those immediately below them, generating a cascade of threats and violence through which low-ranked individuals feel the burden, not just of their immediate superiors, but of the whole hierarchy above them."[16]

What is to be done? How to empower people who feel powerless? How to engage people who are disengaged? How to get followers to do something, as opposed to doing nothing? How to get followers to support good leaders? How to get followers to stop or at least slow bad leaders?

I might add that the importance of this last question—how to stop or at least slow bad leaders—is wildly underrated. Our focus is nearly always on developing good leadership; our focus is nearly never on diminishing bad leadership, likely because it is so tough a nut to crack. In any event, we know full well, even based on our own experience, that bad leaders are ubiquitous.[17] In the 1980s and 1990s Robert Kelley conducted workplace surveys that confirmed the high level of follower dissatisfaction. He found that less than half of all leaders instill trust in their subordinates, two out of

five bosses lack leadership skills, and only one in seven superiors are considered by their subordinates to be role models.[18] A recent study out of
Florida State University confirmed the so-called bad boss was everywhere
to be found: nearly 40 percent of the seven hundred workers surveyed
said their superiors failed to keep promises; more than a third complained
their bosses did not give credit where credit was due; and just under one-
third of subordinates reported that in the last year they were subjected by
their superiors to the "silent treatment."[19] (The problem, by the way, is
overarching. In 2006 fully seven in ten Americans agreed or agreed strongly
that "there is a leadership crisis in the United States today.")[20]

The good news is this: subordinates do have some arrows in their quiver,
some workplace tactics and strategies that may make a difference. Let me
be clear: I do not for one moment mean to minimize the task, mean to imply
that exercising power and influence from the bottom up is easy. As already
discussed, we have good and sound reasons for wanting to stay safe, for
avoiding rather than engaging those who have more power, authority, and
influence than do we. Still, we do know something about what followers
can and should do both for their own good and for the common good.

Supporting good leaders is the easy part. It requires little more than
common sense and the determination to step lively and do well. Try, for
example, to develop different sorts of workplace skills, to be productive
and participatory, and to meet collective goals as well as individual ones.

Sometimes, in fact, we can support good leaders simply by taking matters into our own hands. Here is an example—two women at Best Buy
Company who changed a key component of the corporate culture, more
or less on their own. CEO Brad Anderson had encouraged "bottom-up
stealth innovation"—so Cali Ressler and Jody Thompson, who were based
in human resources, seized the day. Their goal was to create a workplace in
which fixed schedules went out the window, in which all Best Buy employees would be free to set their own hours, to come and go as they
pleased, so long as their work was done. Their experiment began "as a
covert guerilla action that spread virally and eventually became a revolution." In short order, average voluntary turnover fell dramatically, produc-
tivity went way up, and so did employee engagement.

How did Ressler and Thompson do it? To begin with, they did *not* go
to their superiors seeking approval. Instead, they met privately, quietly

strategizing about how to implement their ideas in small pilot trials. Once they saw some openings, they forged ahead and quickly "gained social networking heat." At first participants avoided talking about their new-found autonomy, especially to higher-ups, for fear the perk would be taken away. But in time the word got out, and to loftier and loftier levels of management. To be sure, the remarkable changes unleashed by Ressler and Thompson were not conflict-free. Some at Best Buy resented the shift, and others worried that before long it would prove disastrous. In fact, if Best Buy's business does go south at some point in the future, the company may yet beat a hasty retreat. But whatever happens in the long term, what Ressler and Thompson accomplished in the short term, without the usual trappings of corporate power and authority, was "a radical reshaping of the workplace."[21]

Of course, not all bosses encourage innovation from the bottom up or, for that matter, from the top down. Many fail to respond as we would have them respond, not even to the best of our intentions. What to do then? This can get tricky, requiring of followers that they become strategic by learning to *lead up*, or, if you prefer, to *manage up*. (Both terms have been used in recent years; both obviously take pains to avoid the "f" word, the word *follower*.) Leading/managing up is considered a soft skill that enables subordinates somehow to influence their superiors. To be sure, managing up can be seen as unattractive, as self-promotion or as manipulation. Nevertheless, for followers who want to get traction, managing up is key. Says Jeffrey Pfeffer, a professor at Stanford University's business school, "Many people believe that if you are doing a good job and accomplishing something, your bosses necessarily know this, but they don't." Since the only people who can help you are above you, this means you have to "tell your boss about your accomplishments and tend to the relationship, including face time, flattery and asking for advice." While such gross ingratiation may seem demeaning, "How else," asks Pfeffer, "are you going to fare in a competition against people who have fewer inhibitions?"[22]

The point is that those who have less power, authority, and influence *do* have ways of impacting on those who have more. What's more, the question of how to lead or manage up—of how to be a good, smart follower—is getting more attention than it ever did before. First, subordinates themselves are being targeted in new and different ways, as in the Harvard Business School publication *Working Knowledge*, which features articles with titles such as "Understand What Motivates Your Boss" and "Do I Dare Say Something?"[23] Second, it is more widely understood that leaders themselves are often followers, superiors in subordinate roles, as evidenced in an article published in *Harvard Business Review* titled "Surviving Your New CEO."[24] The piece is clearly targeted at those in upper-level management, at "executives" and at members of "senior teams," who, now that they have a new boss, need their own advice on how to succeed. Not incidentally, this advice—for example, "show your goodwill," and "study your [boss's] working style," and "be on your 'A' game"—applies as well to those further down the corporate ladder. Third, as another article in the *Harvard Business Review* testifies, we expect now some sort of reciprocity, from leaders to followers. Titled "What Your Leader Expects of You—and What You Should Expect in Return," the piece is not new and different in its description of what superiors have a right to expect. But it *is* new and different in its description of what subordinates have a right to expect, including bosses who "provide clarity of direction," who "set goals and objectives," and who "demonstrate honesty and candor."[25] Fourth, I would not underestimate the power of the 360-degree evaluation. The mere fact that some number of subordinates are now in a position to regularly evaluate their superiors is of consequence, in some cases actually, and in all cases symbolically.

Finally, CEOs themselves are being told in no uncertain terms to encourage their followers to, yes, well, lead. Why? Because, according to the *Wall Street Journal*, "CEOs can't change companies on their own." Instead, "change will have to come from those leading from below," specifically, managers who "make the shift from service and governance to a leadership role." Managers who themselves are eager to make such a change— are eager, that is, to become leaders—are given advice that, again, is the sort of advice that would apply as well to subordinates at nearly every level of the organization. It includes, "make the decision to be a leader," and "focus on influence not control," and "make your mental organization chart horizontal rather than vertical."[26]

One last time: I do not underestimate the difficulties of "leading up," or of "leading from below," or, to use the term being used here, of being a good follower. There are risks associated with behaving in ways that are contrary to convention. In fact, if such an effort is inept, it can "prove little more than reckless abandon, a career-shortening or even career-ending move."[27] But under the right circumstance, the benefits of being a bold subordinate are likely to outweigh the costs.

Another professor at Stanford University's business school, Debra Meyerson, also tells people in the middle how to change the organizations in which they work—in particular, how to make them hospitable to most, if not all, in their employ.[28] (An example might be working parents trying to get their employers to offer flextime.) Meyerson identifies five strategies useful to *tempered radicals*—to subordinates who strike a balance between conformity and rebellion. The strategies are resisting quietly, turning threats into opportunities, negotiating, leveraging small wins, and taking collective action.

Resisting quietly means sticking up for who you are, even if you are somehow different; making your points without antagonizing the powers that be; and working behind the scenes, beneath the radar, to do what you want and intend. The ability to turn a threat into an opportunity involves employing tactics such as diverting and delaying—but of course at the right time and in the right way. Questions to ask beforehand include, Is this a good time to take a risk and mount a challenge? Is this a fight worth starting? How likely is the intended result? Negotiating requires that you objectively assess the interests of others and, if necessary, bring in a third party to mediate. To leverage small wins means to use them wisely and well, in order to achieve greater goals later on. Finally, there is collective action—nearly always the most effective strategy of the powerless against the powerful. More about this later, but for now, here is Meyerson's position: while individuals can and do create change, it is collective action that broadens the impact and deepens the benefit.[29]

Of course, being a good follower is more difficult and dangerous when it involves stopping a bad leader: a leader who is ineffective, or unethical, or both. The title of an article on the subject warns of "The Perils of an Office Coup," and makes plain that while you may think the boss should be fired, "the job that's lost could be yours."[30] The advice that's provided is sound—for example, it's time to "speak up when your frustration with your manager affects your ability to do your job," and it's good to share your thoughts "as long as you have colleagues you can trust." But it only hints at the heavy lifting that thwarting bad leadership in the workplace usually entails.

For good reason those most directly affected, subordinates in the workplace, as opposed to consultants looking in from without, tend to doubt their capacity to create change. In an informal series of conversations I've had with working adults, they generally report that however reasonable the idea of challenging a bad leader or manager may sound, it seems to them far-fetched. As they experience it, self-interest motivates what happens in the workplace, which means we do what we are expected to do, what we are ordered to do. We toe the line because chances are that we will be rewarded for doing so or, alternatively, punished for not doing so. Ira Chaleff (author of the aforementioned *The Courageous Follower*) responds to such concerns by arguing that followers tend to "inflate the danger involved in taking a courageous stand." His point is that while subordinates who stand up to their superiors take a risk, they also take a risk by doing nothing, especially if they acquiesce to inappropriate leadership behavior. Think, for example, of subordinates at Enron, sent to prison for going along with their superiors; or for that matter of subordinates at Abu Ghraib, taking the heat for superiors who turned a blind eye. Moreover, Chaleff argues, there are benefits to speaking up: "If a stand is taken appropriately and effectively, this often changes the perception of the follower in the eyes of the leader. The follower is no longer a mere functionary but becomes a player who is invited into the circle of advisors the leader relies on when weighing competing courses of action."[31]

This said, there is no question that followers who would take on bad leaders had best be cautious and clever and keep their eye on the prize. What more precisely does this entail? Two points particularly pertain. First is the importance of good timing—the earlier the better. My own study of bad leadership suggests it's a slippery slope—the more deeply it is rooted, the more difficult it is to upend.[32] The second point pertains to being well prepared—well armed, well defended, and well protected. Subordinates who would challenge their superiors should gather their facts, find allies, and get good counsel. In the event of serious resistance, they should go to a higher authority (if there is one) and protect themselves by having both emotional and financial reserves and, if necessary, by having legal representation.

In taking on a bad leader, in the workplace or anyplace else, no decision matters more than whether to go it alone or in concert with others.

If at all possible, collective action is better: it is far better to join forces with fellow followers than to play the lone ranger. First, it is safer. And second, it is more likely to be effective. To repeat: the single strongest weapon of the powerless against the powerful is the power of numbers. As Jean Lipman-Blumen noted, when one follower confronts a bad leader, the follower is in danger of being ousted, seduced, or bought off. Coalitions, in contrast, "are the key to success."[33]

Sometimes, though, coalitions are not possible. Sometimes, for whatever individual or institutional reasons, going it alone is, or seems to be, the only way to go. This brings us back to the whistle-blower, to a single follower determined to take on a single leader (or more), no matter the cost. We know by now that blowing the whistle is really risky. To preclude it from also being foolhardy, Tom Devine, at the time legal director of the Government Accountability Project, wrote a small, fine book titled *The Whistleblower's Survival Guide: Courage Without Martyrdom*. To would-be whistle-blowers he provides this advice. First, before you do something you cannot undo, talk to your family and friends. Second, try to have your employer react to you rather than the other way around. Third, find out whether other people are similarly upset about the wrongdoing. Fourth, before formally breaking ranks, consider whether there is any reasonable way to stay, to work within the system. Fifth, keep careful records of what you do and when you do it. Sixth, find allies, both inside the organization and out. Finally, get a good lawyer.[34]

It is good to know that most followers have some options, even in workplace situations that appear on the surface to be daunting. Leaving, of course, is the ultimate option—quitting when the costs of staying outweigh the benefits, when leaders and managers mislead and mismanage, remaining all the while hostile or simply deaf to our concerns. But sometimes quitting is a last resort, which makes it more important that we be active and even proactive, as opposed to being merely reactive.[35]

One last point, one last reiteration of an observation I made earlier and on which virtually every observer of American business in the first decade of the twenty-first century has come to agree: big bosses are less big than they used to be. Leaders have less power, authority, and influence, which is to say that, in some cases at least, followers have more. How many more times will we hear that in contrast to the "authoritarian, contemptuous" Robert Nardelli, the former CEO of Home Depot, his successor, Frank

Blake, is a breath of fresh air, sounding a "new tone from the top." Not only is Blake "folksy, disarming, sincere, occasionally funny and often self-deprecating," he is also, at least in comparison with his greedy predecessor, modest. Blake's salary was $8.9 million, in contrast to Nardelli's, which was $39.7.[36] But this is, of course, about much more than what happened at one company. This is about "creating a new CEO" altogether, if only because of others, who give them no choice.[37]

Jim McNerney, CEO of Boeing, speaks freely of having to depend on his "power to persuade." Martin Sullivan, who succeeded the imperious Hank Greenberg as head of American International Group (AIG), claims not to mind that he, unlike Greenberg, has to share power. And Mark Hurd, who succeeded Carly Fiorina at Hewlett-Packard, denies even having a vision. "I'm not a big vision guy," he insists. Here, in the words of long-time *Wall Street Journal* reporter Alan Murray, is the bottom line: CEOs like McNerney, Sullivan, and Hurd "are less powerful than their predecessors. They are on shorter leashes, more beholden to their boards of directors and more susceptible to the influence of a broad range of outsiders—regulators, accountants, attorneys general, hedge fund managers, union bosses, proxy advisory services, trial lawyers, public pension funds and nonprofit activists." So there we have it—workplace leaders who need a deft touch so that "nobody revolts"; who are afraid to fire workers "because it has never been easier for U.S. workers to go to court and allege that they've been sacked unfairly"; and who, however handsomely paid, are not, it appears, perfectly happy. In 2006, "more than 28,000 top executives lost, left, or changed jobs, up 68% from 2005."[38]

IN THE PUBLIC ARENA

Being a follower in the public arena is obviously different from being a follower in the workplace. Among other things, in the workplace if we do nothing, we are likely somehow to be punished. In contrast, in most modern democracies there is no penalty whatsoever for being a Bystander or even for being an Isolate.

Consider what happened during George W. Bush's two terms in office. Toward the end of his second four years most Americans no longer approved of Bush's performance as president. But the fact is that with few exceptions, those who were opposed to the president—in October 2007 his approval rating was only 33 percent—and especially to his conduct of the war in Iraq said little and did less. Once they signed on to the president's initial decision to invade, which they did in large numbers, the American people, like the American president, "stayed the course." Put directly, in spite of our serious misgivings, we followed where he led from start to finish.

Did we have another choice? Is there anything the American people could have done differently? Yes, absolutely. They, we, did not have to go along, or, at least, we did not have to go along quietly. We could have openly opposed sending troops into the Middle East in the first place; and then at any point thereafter we could have loudly demanded they be sent back home. Not to speak of the fact that in 2004 we could have elected another president, a Democrat, entirely. Which brings us back to this: to be a good follower is to actively support leaders you favor and to actively oppose leaders you do not.

Looked at from this perspective, the problem with the American political system is not any single individual, not even the president. Rather, the problem is the high level of political detachment and the low level of political engagement. "Nearly half (48 percent) of the adult population can be characterized as disengaged from both the civic and political realm."[39] Not only do roughly half of eligible voters fail even to cast a ballot, many of those who do go to the polls are otherwise uninterested, or at least not interested enough to do anything much more than vote for president once every four years. In fact, one might reasonably speculate that the most powerful single reason for our perennial frustration in this general regard is the gap between the real and the imagined. On the one hand, the American political culture extols the virtues of participatory democracy, which presumably enables and even encourages people to take an active part in public life. But on the other hand, for a variety of reasons that range from being busy to feeling powerless, we live in a time in which political activism in the conventional sense of this word is meager. This in spite of the fact that in January 2007, when President Bush announced he was sending an additional twenty-one thousand troops to Iraq, no more than about one-quarter of the American people approved of the way he was handling the conflict.[40]

To be sure, the level of participation in the 2004 presidential election was, by recent American standards anyway, relatively high (about 60 percent of eligible citizens went to the polls). But our political involvement, such as it is, typically stops at the ballot box. While there was, as we have seen, some grassroots activity reflecting widespread dissatisfaction over the war in Iraq in particular, the truth of it is that during this most recent war, the opposition was muted. The question is why. Why in this day and age, when people the world over are speaking out more often and more insistently than they ever did before, has the war in Iraq been an exception to the general rule?

The reason for this discrepancy is, as mentioned earlier, generally ascribed to the draft. In particular, there was a draft during the war in Vietnam, when the American people obliged the U.S. government to finally withdraw, and there is none now. Still, this difference does not seem to fully explain the degree to which Americans this time around have shunned large-scale political protest. *New York Times* columnist Frank Rich has offered an alternative explanation, one that suggests that being on the computer is a substitute for being in the streets: "As our country sinks deeper into a quagmire . . . we the people, and that includes, yes, you, will seek out any escape hatch we can find. In the Iraq era, the dropout nostrums of choice are not the drugs and drug culture of Vietnam but the equally self-gratifying and narcissistic (if less psychedelic) pastimes of the Internet. Why not spend hour after hour passionately venting in the blogosphere . . . about our 'state of mind or the state of the nation or the steak-frites at the new bistro down the street'?"[41]

There is another reason why twenty-first-century Americans are politically detached rather than politically engaged: we are, quite simply, out of the habit. Many of us, especially young people, have had little or no experience participating in the political process. Nor is such experience especially encouraged. In recent years high schools and colleges have strongly supported their students getting involved in community life; but they have been less supportive of their students getting involved in political life. As a result, many of today's young people are turned on to public service but turned off by politics. So they are more likely to be civically engaged and less likely to be politically engaged. "This new mix has privileged civic engagement over more traditional forms of political engagement such as voting, and focused on civil and corporate organizations rather than government institutions as the central arenas for public action."[42] Young people now are less likely to vote, to get involved in campaigns and elections, to contact public officials, to identify with a major political party, or to be a member of any type of explicitly political organization. "They are also less likely to express interest in politics and public affairs, to follow such issues in the media, or to be knowledgeable about them."[43]

This lack of interest has been further sustained by a president who, in spite of leading a nation at war, has neither asked for nor been offered national sacrifice other than that of the military. As a result, young people today do not think of followership, of citizenship, as entailing obligations of any kind, including voting. None of this is inconsequential, neither the theoretical implications of what it means to live in a participatory democracy deprived of widespread political participation, nor the actual outcomes. In fact, the evidence strongly suggests that if younger Americans did participate in the political process in greater numbers, public policies pertaining to at least some issues—such as the environment, health care, immigration, and gay marriage—would be different.[44]

The research suggests that the most active citizens, the most effective ones, are those who take part in civic *and* political life. Assuming that we consider such engagement to be important, to be desired, the question is how to cultivate it. How to cultivate followers who engage in the civic domain and also in the political one, both to support who and what they are for, and to oppose who and what they are against? We know that adults are more likely to participate in public life if they did so when they were young, and if they have the "motivations, skills, resources, and opportunities to do so."[45] Our task, then, is to foster all of these through a variety of initiatives ranging from parental modeling, to formal and informal school programs at every level, to outreach by nonprofit and political organizations. Given the decades-long decline in trust in American government, given a culture in which denigration of government and of government officials is considered cool and even funny, small wonder that political engagement has suffered, especially, again, among young people. Still, past is not necessarily prologue, which means there is work that could be done, and should be done.

Those of us used to the privilege of participating in political life tend to take it for granted. But elsewhere in the world, in places where the very idea of being able to politically participate is new, things are different. Consider this item, in a 2006 issue of the *South China Morning Post*: "Hong Kong has already demonstrated 'people power,' with hundreds of thousands marching in the streets ... Chief Executive Donald Tsang Yam-kuen has realized the existing government structure must evolve to adapt to today's new reality of an engaged citizenry. Hong Kong is no longer only a model of laissez-fair economic development. It is now a test case for peaceful political transition. On the issue of Hong Kong's democracy, the whole world is watching."[46] Or this item, an article titled "In Chinese Boomtown, Middle Class Pushes Back," in a 2006 issue of the *New York Times*: "When residents here in southern China's richest city [Shenzhen] learned of plans to build an expressway that would cut through the heart of their congested, middle-class neighborhood, they immediately organized a campaign to fight City Hall. Over the next two years they managed to halt work on the most destructive segment of the highway and forced design changes to reduce pollution from the roadway. It became a landmark in citizen efforts to win concessions from a government that by tradition brooked no opposition."[47]

Of course, it's one thing to support a good leader or oppose a bad one in a democracy. It's quite another to oppose a bad leader in a system less benign. While in a perfect world followers can always find some ways to resist, in this imperfect world it is hard to do much of anything when the leader is bad to the point of being evil.[48]

The Scottish philosopher David Hume was astonished if not appalled by the "implicit submission with which men resign their own sentiments and passions to those of their rulers."[49] Here, then, are ways to stiffen the spine, to stiffen the spine of men and women who too readily "resign their own sentiments and passions to those of their rulers."

- Be aware of being a follower.
- Be informed.
- Be engaged.
- Be independent.
- Be a watchdog.
- Be prepared to analyze the situation, the leader, and the other followers.

- Be prepared to judge the situation, the leader, and the other followers.

- Be open to allies and to forming coalitions.

- Be prepared to be different.

- Be prepared to take a stand.

- Be prepared to defend yourself.

- Be loyal to the group, not to any single individual.

- Know the importance of timing.

- Know the slippery slope—bad leaders who over time become more deeply embedded and more difficult to uproot.

- Know tactics and strategies such as cooperating, collaborating, co-opting, and overtly or covertly resisting.

- Know your options.

- Know the risk of doing something—and of doing nothing.

- Check your moral compass.[50]

Never for a moment overestimate follower power. But never for a moment underestimate it either. There are times, even recent times, when the dam breaks, when follower power, people power, becomes so great, it can no longer be contained. The antiwar, civil rights, and women's movements in the United States; the end of apartheid in South Africa; the fall of the Berlin wall and the liberation of Soviet bloc countries such as Poland, Hungary, and Czechoslovakia in Eastern Europe; and of course, the wave of self-expression and self-actualization in China—all are of recent vintage. As Nobel Peace Prize winner and Czech writer Václav Havel put it, "To assert the truth, to behave authentically by breaking through the all-englobing web of lies—in spite of everything, including the risk that one might find oneself up against the whole world—is an act of extraordinary political importance."[51] It is also, with the first sweet smell of success, an act of extraordinary electricity and exhilaration. Here is a description of what it felt like in Poland, to participate in the political protests early on, in 1970, when the Soviet Union was still in its prime and dominated East Europe: "[I experienced] something that can't be written about. You have to have lived it in order to understand how in that band of people we felt our power. For the first time in our lives we had taken a stand against the state. Before it was a taboo, something absolutely unattainable . . . I didn't feel I was protesting just the price rise, although that's what sparked it. It had to do with overthrowing at least in part everything we hated."[52]

Having repeatedly made the point that followers who do something are generally preferred to followers who do nothing, and having repeatedly made the point that even the apparently powerless are not without power and influence, I need finally to reiterate the importance of purpose. Standing up and speaking out is not, of itself, good enough. Being a Participant, an Activist, or a Diehard does not, of itself, merit a badge of honor. For regarding good followership, there are always two questions instead of only one: is something being done? And if something is being done—to what end?

Then and Now

Followers have always mattered more, far more, than those of us fixated on leaders have been ready to say. I am reminded of William Wilberforce, who, in the history books as well as in Michael Apted's recent film *Amazing Grace*, was credited with virtually single-handedly getting the British to end the slave trade. But in recent decades scholars have seen the history of British abolition in a somewhat different light, as involving far more than one man fighting the good fight, against all odds. Change was also fueled by this: in 1787 and 1788, not incidentally around the time of the American and French Revolutions, "a huge grassroots movement against the slave trade burst into life in Britain, startling abolitionists and slave traders alike."[53]

And now subordinates with less power, authority, and influence than their superiors are coming into their own, more consistently and insistently than ever before. The evidence is everywhere around us. Here is another case in point: Dubai is inching toward labor reform, not because leaders in business and government woke up one day and decided to be nice, but because they woke up one day and were afraid. They were afraid of restive foreign labor. "After several years of unprecedented labor unrest, the government is seeking peace with this army of sweat-stained migrants who make local citizens a minority in their own country," reported the *New York Times*. For years, it was migrants like these, in the main from India and Pakistan, who made possible what became one of the world's largest building booms. But most were all along abused by their employers, stuck in a circumstance that critics likened to indentured servitude, until recently when they began to resist by walking off their jobs in droves, blocking traffic, and smashing cars. The result is halting change that now includes enforced midday sun breaks, improved health benefits, upgraded living conditions, and a crackdown on employers who were so brazen as to stop paying workers at all.[54]

Consider this other example of a shift from those at the top to those down below, one of an altogether different nature, more trivial than the previous, but telling nonetheless. This time, power and influence are flowing from the experts to the masses, from industry moguls to consumers who previously played no part whatsoever in the decision-making process. "Inspired by the success of 'American Idol' and by the open culture of the Internet, voter-based competitions are proliferating in every corner of the entertainment world."[55] Fans, followers, ordinary people are being asked to weigh in on everything from who gets a record contract, to who gets to create a music video, to who gets to star in a Broadway revival of *Grease*. People everywhere are simply less willing than they were before to be spoon-fed. And they are more able than they were to weigh in via YouTube, for instance, or Stickam. Incidentally, fan-followers are not shy. Italians incensed by the sky-high ticket prices charged to hear Barbra Streisand sing live called the situation "absurd and shameful." And they demanded that the concert, which was originally scheduled to be held on public property, be moved (which it was) since public property "cannot be used for immoral deals that are shameful to a civilized country."[56]

By now, some smart leaders understand follower power, both intuitively and intellectually. When Wal-Mart came under attack, CEO Lee Scott made the decision to respond not by lashing back but by connecting with those who might otherwise take him down. "He reached out to his opponents, took polls of opinion leaders and hired political consultants. He also embraced environmentally friendly policies, improved employee health-care coverage and began advocating policies like an increase in the minimum wage."[57] Similarly, when Hillary Clinton first announced her intention to run for the Senate from the state of New York (1999), the first thing she did was to go on a "listening tour." She traveled around the state not to tell her would-be constituents what *she* thought about issues such as education and health care, but to ask them what *they* thought. By the time Senator Clinton announced she would be a candidate for president of the United States, she had her act down pat. The very first thing she did was to invite American voters to participate in a series of live conversations on the Web. Knowing full well that the distance between leaders and followers had narrowed, she said, "So, let's talk. Let's chat, let's start a dialogue about your ideas and mine because conversation in Washington has been just a little bit one-sided lately, don't you think?"[58]

This shift—away from leaders and toward followers with growing demands and higher expectations—is by and large a positive development. It is also a major development. It signals that to fixate on leadership at the expense of followership is to whistle against the wind.

Notes

Introduction

1. George Orwell, "Shooting an Elephant," in *New Writing* (London: GB, 1936). The quotes in this section are from this story. I am grateful to Andrew Dover for drawing Orwell's tale to my attention. Thanks too to Robert E. Kelley, who in *The Power of Followership: How to Create Leaders People Want to Follow and Followers Who Lead Themselves* (New York: Doubleday, 1992) pointed me to Bertolt Brecht's poem "A Worker Reads History." An excerpt from the poem introduces this book.

2. Douglas A. Ready and Jay A. Conger, "Why Leadership-Development Efforts Fail," *MIT Sloan Management Review* 44, no. 3 (Spring 2003): 83–88.

3. I use the term *leadership industry* to refer to the big business that is leadership education. I particularly refer to the numberless schools, centers, institutes, courses, workshops, seminars, and experts that now provide one or another form of leadership training and development.

4. Kelley, in *The Power of Followership*, was the first to bestow on *followership* a measure of legitimacy. However, between then (1992) and now, the word and the ideas that underpin it have received scant attention.

5. Bernard M. Bass, *Bass & Stogdill's Handbook of Leadership: A Survey of Theory and Research* (New York: Free Press, 1990), 11.

6. For more on this, see Barbara Kellerman, *Bad Leadership: What It Is, How It Happens, Why It Matters* (Boston: Harvard Business School Press, 2004).

7. In recent years there have, in addition, been groups, organizations, and networks that consider themselves to be leaderless and therefore, presumably, also followerless. For a discussion of the "leaderless organization," see, for example, Ori Brafman and Rod A. Beckstrom, *The Starfish and the Spider: The Unstoppable Power of Leaderless Organizations* (New York: Penguin, 2006).

8. Jean-Jacques Rousseau, *The Social Contract and Discourses* (Markham, ON: Fitzhenry & Whiteside, 1973), 247.

Chapter 1

1. Audi of America, April 14, 2004. For further information on the "Never Follow" ad campaign, see www.google.com, "Audi, 'Never Follow.'"

2. As Max Lerner pointed out, the task of squaring Americans' "basic nonconformism with the stability required by property, investment, and law" fell to the Founders. See *America as a Civilization* (New York: Simon & Schuster, 1957), 718.

3. See http://www.labour.org.uk/leadership/tony_blair_resigns.

4. The quotes and the point more generally are in Charles C. Mann, "The Founding Sachems," *New York Times*, July 4, 2005.

5. Bernard Bailyn, *The Ideological Origins of the American Revolution* (Cambridge, MA: Harvard University Press, 1967), 302–304. This paragraph and several to follow also borrow from my book *The Political Presidency: Practice of Leadership* (New York: Oxford University Press, 1984), chapter 1.

6. Bailyn, *The Ideological Origins of the American Revolution*, 304.

7. Ibid., 306.

8. Samuel P. Huntington, *American Politics: The Promise of Disharmony* (Cambridge, MA: Harvard University Press, 1981), 33.

9. Louis Hartz, *The Liberal Tradition in America: An Interpretation of American Political Thought Since the Revolution* (New York: Harcourt, Brace, 1955), 111.

10. The quotes in this paragraph are from Alexis de Tocqueville, *Democracy in America* (New York: Doubleday, 1969), 430.

11. John Gardner, *The Nature of Leadership: Introductory Considerations*, Leadership Papers/1 (Washington, DC: Independent Sector, 1986), 5, 6.

12. The term is used by Patsy Baker Blackshear on p. 2 of her unpublished paper, "The Followership Continuum: A Model for Increasing Organizational Diversity." For more on her thinking, see a similar published article titled, "The Followership Continuum: A Model for Finetuning the Work Force," *Public Manager* 32 (Summer 2003): 25–30.

13. Michael Useem, *Leading Up: How to Lead Your Boss So You Both Win* (New York: Crown, 2001). The quote is on p. 1.

14. The point of this paragraph is made even more clearly in books such as Larraine R. Matusak's *Finding Your Voice: Learning to Lead . . . Anywhere You Want to Make a Difference* (San Francisco: Jossey-Bass, 1997). The message this book sends is similar to the one most commonly delivered by leadership educators both inside and outside the academy: you too can be a leader! Matusak writes that "you don't need an elevated position or a title of great importance to assume a leadership role" (p. 1). However, seen from another angle, all the emphasis is on leaders and leadership. There is no discussion of followership or of what constitutes the good follower.

15. Joseph C. Rost, *Leadership for the Twenty-First Century* (New York: Praeger, 1991), 107–112.

16. David Collinson, "Rethinking Followership: A Post-Structuralist Analysis of Follower Identities," *Leadership Quarterly* 17, no. 2 (April 2006): 179.

17. No one has written more trenchantly about power relationships that persist than Robert Michels. Early in the twentieth century, the young German sociologist developed the "iron law of oligarchy," which he wrote about at length in *Political Parties: A Sociological Study of the Oligarchical Tendencies of Modern Democracy* (New York: Free Press, 1962).

18. Joanne Ciulla, "Leadership and the Problem of Bogus Empowerment," in *Ethics: The Heart of Leadership*, ed. Joanne Ciulla (New York: Praeger, 1998), 63.

19. Bill George and Peter Sims, *True North: Discover Your Authentic Leadership* (San Francisco: Jossey-Bass, 2007), 176.

20. Rost, *Leadership for the Twenty-First Century*, 109.

21. Quoted by Michiko Kakutani, "Styron Visible: Naming the Evils That Humans Do," *New York Times*, November 3, 2006.

22. Daniel Jonah Goldhagen, *Hitler's Willing Executioners: Ordinary Germans and the Holocaust* (New York: Knopf, 1996).

23. Milton Himmelfarb, "No Hitler, No Holocaust," *Commentary*, March 1984, 37–43.

24. Ibid., 37.

25. The phrase is James R. Meindl's. See "The Romance of Leadership as a Follower-Centric Theory: A Social Constructionist Approach," *Leadership Quarterly* 6, no. 3 (1995). I am using the term somewhat differently from Meindl, but it nevertheless nicely captures my point as well.

26. For early insights on the ways in which people make causal attributions about people's behavior, see Fritz Heider's classic discussion of "the naive analysis of action" in *The Psychology of Interpersonal Relations* (New York: John Wiley & Sons, 1958), especially chapter 5.

27. For a good brief discussion of leader attribution, see James G. (Jerry) Hunt, "What Is Leadership?" in *The Nature of Leadership*, eds. John Antonakis, Anna T. Cianciolo, and Robert J. Sternberg (Thousand Oaks, CA: Sage Publications, 2004), 38, 39. Also see R. G. Lord and C. G. Emrich, "Thinking Outside the Box by Looking Inside the Box: Extending the Cognitive Revolution in Leadership Research," *Leadership Quarterly* 11 (2000): 551–579.

28. This paragraph borrows freely from Sonja M. Hunt, "The Role of Leadership in the Construction of Reality," in *Leadership: Multidisciplinary Perspectives*, ed. Barbara Kellerman (Englewood Cliffs, NJ: Prentice-Hall, 1984); see especially 169–175.

29. Richard Hackman, *Leading Teams: Setting the Stage for Great Performances* (Boston: Harvard Business School Press, 2002), 199, 200.

30. John Byrne, quoted in Barbara Kellerman, *Bad Leadership: What It Is, How It Happens, Why It Matters* (Boston: Harvard Business School Press, 2004), 135. The material on Dunlap is taken from chapter 7.

31. Matthew Shifrin, quoted in Kellerman, *Bad Leadership*, 135.

32. Ibid., 146.

33. This is from Albert O. Hirschman's classic text, *Exit, Voice, and Loyalty: Responses to Decline in Firms, Organizations, and States* (Cambridge, MA: Harvard University Press, 1970), 30.

34. Daniel Goleman, Richard Boyatzis, and Annie McKee, *Primal Leadership: Realizing the Power of Emotional Intelligence* (Boston: Harvard Business School Press, 2004), 3.

35. John Kotter, *The Leadership Factor* (New York: Free Press, 1988); and Warren Bennis, *On Becoming a Leader* (Reading, MA: Addison-Wesley, 1989).

36. Ronald Heifetz, *Leadership Without Easy Answers* (Cambridge, MA: Harvard University Press, 1994); and James M. Kouzes and Barry Z. Posner, *The Leadership Challenge* (San Francisco: Jossey-Bass, 1995).

37. Rudolph Giuliani, *Leadership* (New York: Hyperion, 2002), xii.

38. For a brief discussion of this point, and for the names of several researchers who earlier identified it, see Taly Dvir and Boas Shamir, "Follower Developmental Characteristics as Predicting Transformational Leadership: A Longitudinal Field Study," *Leadership Quarterly* 14 (2003), especially pp. 327, 328. In their abstract Dvir and Shamir write, "The leadership literature has focused on the effects of leaders whereas much less attention has been given to the followers' role in shaping their leader's style." And they quote Gary Yukl, who earlier wrote that "most research and theory on leadership has favored a definition of leadership that emphasizes the primary importance of unilateral influence by a single, 'heroic' leader."

39. See, for example, Mary Parker Follett, "The Giving of Orders," in *Mary Parker Follett: Prophet of Management*, ed. Pauline Graham (Boston: Harvard Business School Press, 1995), 121–140. Also see Chester I. Barnard, *The Functions of the Executive* (Cambridge, MA: Harvard University Press, 1938), especially chapter 12, in which the relationship between leaders ("executives") is directly addressed.

40. For a description of some of these experiments, with which the name Kurt Lewin was most closely associated, see Bernard M. Bass, *Bass & Stogdill's Handbook of Leadership: A Survey of Theory and Research* (New York: Free Press, 1990), 415–435.

41. Quoted by Alessandra Stanley, "The Darkest Behaviors in the Name of Obedience," *New York Times*, June 1, 2006.

42. The quote is from Michael Massing. See his essay titled "Trial and Error," *New York Times Book Review*, October 17, 2004, 17.

43. Erich Fromm, *Escape from Freedom* (New York: Holt, 1941).

44. This paragraph is based on a discussion in Nevitt Sanford, "Authoritarian Personality in Contemporary Perspective," in *Handbook of Political Psychology*, ed. Jeanne N. Knutson (San Francisco: Jossey-Bass, 1973), 139–170.

45. Theodore Adorno, Elsie Frenkel-Brunswick, Daniel Levinson, and Nevitt Sanford, *The Authoritarian Personality* (New York: Harper, 1950).

46. Sanford, "Authoritarian Personality in Contemporary Perspective," 153.

47. So far as behaviors of dominance and deference are concerned, there are, however, some cultural as well as national differences. For example, in Japan there is the tradition of Bushido, a code of honor, especially held among the warrior class, which requires the strictest kind of obedience to those in higher positions of authority. See, for example, Inazo Nitobe, *Bushido: The Soul of Japan* (New York: Filiquarian Publishing, 2007).

48. Hannah Arendt, *Eichmann in Jerusalem: A Report on the Banality of Evil* (New York: Viking Press, 1963).

49. For detailed analysis and description of the experiments, see Stanley Milgram, *Obedience to Authority: An Experimental View* (New York: Harper & Row, 1974). Also see Herbert C. Kelman and V. Lee Hamilton, *Crimes of Obedience: Toward a Social Psychology of Authority and Responsibility* (New Haven, CT: Yale University Press, 1989), 148–156.

50. The quotes in this section are in Milgram, *Obedience to Authority*, 1, 2.

51. Ibid., 4.

52. Ibid., 6.

53. For a complete discussion of this syndrome, see Philip Zimbardo, *The Lucifer Effect: Understanding How Good People Turn Evil* (New York: Random House, 2007).

54. Zbigniew Brzezinski, *Second Chance: Three Presidents and the Crisis of American Superpower* (New York: Basic Books, 2007), 201–205.

55. All the quotes in this section are from the paper of one of my students at Harvard, Dana Savoray. I am grateful to her for providing me with such a telling tale of followership.

56. Most of Savoray's sources are based on accounts in the Israeli press. For example, Weisglass was quoted in *Haaretz* on October 8, 2004.

57. David M. Herszenhorn, "In the Garden, Graduates Boo McCain. Kerrey, Too," *New York Times*, May 20, 2006.

58. Brooks Barnes, Emily Steel, and Sarah McBride, "Behind the Fall of Imus, a Digital Brush Fire," *Wall Street Journal*, April 13, 2007.

59. Quoted in Weston Kosova, "The Power That Was," *Newsweek*, April 23, 2007, 31.

60. Ibid., 29.

61. The quotes on this story are from Julia Preston, "Grass Roots Roared and Immigration Plan Collapsed," *New York Times*, June 10, 2007.

62. David Henry, Mike France, and Louis Lavelle, "The Boss on the Sidelines: How Auditors, Directors, and Lawyers Are Asserting Their Power," *BusinessWeek*, April 25, 2005, 88–94.

63. Nanette Byrnes, "The Great CEO Exodus," *BusinessWeek*, October 30, 2006, 78.

64. Kevin P. Coyne and Edward J. Coyne Sr., "Surviving Your New CEO," *Harvard Business Review*, May 2007, 62.

65. Nanette Byrnes and David Kiley, "Hello, You Must Be Going," *BusinessWeek*, February 12, 2007, 30.

66. Geraldine Fabrikant, "One Misstep and They're Out the Door," *New York Times*, May 15, 2007.

Chapter 2

1. The heading that follows is from Van Gosse and Richard Moser, eds., *The World the Sixties Made: Politics and Culture in Recent America* (Philadelphia: Temple University Press, 2003).

2. Although the plight of Native Americans was also much discussed during this same period—for example, recall that Dee Brown's 1971 book, *Bury My Heart at Wounded Knee*, was an instant sensation—this situation seems to remain stagnant.

3. Todd Gitlin, "Afterword," in *Reassessing the Sixties: Debating the Political and Cultural Legacy*, ed. Stephen Macedo (New York: W. W. Norton, 1997), 289.

4. For more on this, see Richard Moser, "Autoworkers at Lordstown: Workplace Democracy and American Citizenship," in Gosse and Moser, *The World the Sixties Made*, 289–315.

5. For more on this, see Barbara Epstein, *Political Protest and Cultural Revolution: Nonviolent Direct Action in the 1970s and 1980s* (Berkeley: University of California Press, 1991), chapter 2.

6. For more on this, see Andrew Feffer, "The Land Belongs to the People: Reframing Urban Protest in Post-Sixties Philadelphia," in Gosse and Moser, *The World the Sixties Made*, 67–99.

7. Walter Berns, "The Assault on the Universities: Then and Now," in Macedo, *Reassessing the Sixties*, 157.

8. "The Graduate Poll: Pomp and Circumstances," *New York*, May 29, 2006, 17.

9. Epstein, *Political Protest and Cultural Revolution*, 23.

10. Harvey Mansfield, "The Legacy of the Late Sixties," in Macedo, *Reassessing the Sixties*, 21.

11. Stephen Macedo, "Introduction to *Reassessing the Sixties*," in Macedo, *Reassessing the Sixties*, 16.

12. Harlan Cleveland, *Leadership and the Information Revolution* (San Francisco: World Academy of Art and Science, 1997). Published in collaboration with the International Leadership Academy.

13. Ibid., 24.

14. Peter F. Drucker, *The Effective Executive* (New York: Harper & Row, 1966).

15. Jonathan D. Glater, "To: Professor@University.edu—Subject: Why It's All About Me," *New York Times*, February 21, 2005.

16. See James Surowiecki, *The Wisdom of Crowds: Why the Many Are Smarter Than the Few and How Collective Wisdom Shapes Business, Economies, Societies and Nations* (New York: Doubleday, 2004).

17. See, for example, Steven Levy and Brad Stone, "The New Wisdom of the Web," *Newsweek*, April 3, 2006, 47–54.

18. Ken Auletta, "Critical Mass," *New Yorker*, May 14, 2007, 82.

19. Eric Denzenhall, as quoted by Michelle Conlin in "Web Attack," *BusinessWeek*, April 16, 2007, 54.

20. Ibid., 54.

21. Christina Passariello, Keith Johnson, and Suzanne Vranica, "A New Force in Advertising—Protest by Email," *Wall Street Journal*, March 22, 2007. The story about Dolce & Gabbana and all quotes in this paragraph are taken from this article.

22. Steve Lohr, "A Cyberfueled Growth Spurt: The Web Upends Old Ideas About the Little Guy's Role," *New York Times*, February 21, 2006.

23. For an impassioned column on the plight of China's cyberdissidents, see Nicholas D. Kristof, "China's Cyberdissidents and the Yahoos at Yahoo," *New York Times*, February 19, 2006.

24. Nicholas D. Kristof, "In China It's ★★★★★★ vs. Netizens," *New York Times*, June 20, 2006. Also see Jim Yardley, "A Hundred Cellphones Bloom, and Chinese Take to the Streets," *New York Times*, April 25, 2005.

25. For more on this, see Clive Thompson, "Google's China Problem (And China's Google Problem)," *New York Times Magazine*, April 23, 2006, 64–71; 153–156.

26. Geoffrey A. Fowler, "Chinese Censors of the Web Face 'Hacktivists' Abroad," *Wall Street Journal*, February 13, 2006.

27. Andrew Browne, "Blogger Hits Home by Urging Boycott of Chinese Property," *Wall Street Journal*, June 12, 2006.

28. Howard W. French, "Homeowner Stares Down Wreckers, at Least for a While," *New York Times*, March 27, 2007.

29. For more on this, see Yardley, "A Hundred Cellphones Bloom." I should add that in less developed areas of the world, such as the Middle East, dissident bloggers have a very hard time. See Dan Ephron, "Unwanted Attention: Arab Bloggers Face Government Clampdowns," *Newsweek*, June 11, 2007, 33.

30. Adam Nagourney, "Internet Injects Sweeping Change into U.S. Politics," *New York Times*, April 2, 2006.

31. Jeff Zeleny and Patrick Healy, "Obama Shows His Strength in a Fund-Raising Feat on a Par with Clinton," *New York Times*, April 5, 2007.

32. Daren Briscoe, "Net Roots Gets Meta," *Newsweek*, March 5, 2007, 39.

33. Steve Stecklow, "Virtual Battle: How a Global Web of Activists Gives Coke Problems in India," *Wall Street Journal*, June 7, 2005.

34. David E. Sanger, Sarah Lyall, Craig S. Smith, and Ian Fisher, "It's Hard out There for a Leader in the West," *New York Times*, April 2, 2006.

35. The Wolfowitz case is reminiscent of what happened to the director of the National Hurricane Center, X. William Proenza, just a few months later. More than twenty of Proenza's nearly fifty employees signed a letter calling for his dismissal—and within a week he was out.

36. Krishna Guha, "The Marathon Man," *Financial Times (London)*, June 2, 2007.

37. Jeannine Aversa, "World Bank President Admits 'Mistake' in Helping Friend with Job Transfer," Associated Press, April 12, 2007.

38. Steven R. Weisman, "Wolfowitz Loses Ground in Fight for World Bank Post," *New York Times*, April 27, 2007.

39. Micheline Maynard, "U.A.W. Facing Tough Choices, Leader Warns," *New York Times*, June 12, 2006.

40. Kris Maher, "The New Union Worker," *Wall Street Journal*, September 27, 2005.

41. For more on this particular argument, see William Pfaff, "The Children's Hour," *New York Review of Books*, May 11, 2006, 40–43.

42. Jeffrey Goldberg, "Selling Wal-Mart," *New Yorker*, April 2, 2007, 35.

43. James Surowiecki, "Board Stiffs," *New Yorker*, March 8, 2004, 30.

44. Phyllis Plitch, "Breaking the Code of Silence," *Wall Street Journal*, April 10, 2006.

45. Tom Lauricella, "Independent Directors Strike Back," *Wall Street Journal*, July 5, 2006; Kaja Whitehouse, "Move Over CEO—Here Come the Directors," *Wall Street Journal*, October 9, 2006; and Joanne S. Lublin, "Ten Ways to Restore Investor Confidence in Compensation: What Boards Can Do to Ease Shareholder Anger Over Pay Packages," *Wall Street Journal*, April 9, 2007. Also see, Alan Murray, *Revolt in the Boardroom: The New Rules of Corporate Power in America* (New York: HarperCollins, 2007).

46. See, for example, the survey on executive compensation, "Pay Package: Notes from Recent SEC Filings," *Wall Street Journal*, April 10, 2006.

47. Richard Siklos, "Rebuked, Even Sued, a Board Remains in Place," *New York Times*, September 26, 2005.

48.   Kaja Whitehouse, "Stiffed Board," *Wall Street Journal*, April 9, 2007.

49.   Jennifer Levitz, "Getting the Message," *Wall Street Journal*, October 9, 2006.

50.   Gretchen Morgenson, "Finally, Shareholders Start Acting Like Owners," *New York Times*, June 11, 2006.

51.   Erin White and Aaron O. Patrick, "Shareholders Push for Vote on Executive Pay," *Wall Street Journal*, February 26, 2007.

52.   Gretchen Morgenson, "Investors Get a Voice on Pay at Verizon," *New York Times*, May 19, 2007.

53.   Andrew Ross Sorkin, "To Battle, Armed with Shares," *New York Times*, January 4, 2006.

54.   Kurt Eichenwald and Alexei Barrionuevo, "Tough Justice for Executives in Enron Era," *New York Times*, May 27, 2006.

55.   See, for example, Rebecca Hamilton and Chad Hazlett, "It's the Genocide, Stupid," *Baltimore Sun*, June 18, 2007.

56.   This paragraph was based on C. J. Chivers, "Youth Movement Underlies the Opposition in Ukraine," *New York Times*, November 28, 2004; and especially on Timothy Garton Ash and Timothy Snyder, "The Orange Revolution," *New York Review*, April 28, 2005, 28–31. The Orange Revolution has had, not surprisingly, a difficult aftermath. Revolutions often do. In this case, less than three years later there were fierce debates over whether Parliament should be disbanded and new elections scheduled.

57.   Somini Sengupta, "A Tectonic Shift: Nepalese, Often Jaded About Politics, Now Say Enough Is Enough," *New York Times*, April 17, 2006. Also see Samrat Upadhyay, "A King in Check," *New York Times*, April 25, 2006.

58.   Howard W. French, "Riots in a Village in China as Pollution Protest Heats Up," *New York Times*, July 19, 2005.

59.   Joseph Kahn, "Harsh Birth Control Steps Fuel Violence in China," *New York Times*, May 22, 2007.

60.   Zbigniew Brzezinski, *Second Chance: Three Presidents and the Crisis of American Superpower* (New York: Basic Books, 2007), 204.

61.   Robert E. Kelley, *The Power of Followership: How to Create Leaders People Want to Follow and Followers Who Lead Themselves* (New York: Doubleday, 1992); and Ira Chaleff, *The Courageous Follower: Standing Up to and for Our Leaders* (San Francisco: Berrett-Koehler, 1995).

62.   S. Alexander Haslam and Michael J. Platow, "The Link Between Leadership and Followership: How Affirming Social Identity Translates Vision into Action," *Personality and Social Psychology Bulletin* 27, no. 11 (2002): 1469–1479.

63.   Jane M. Howell and Boas Shamir, "The Role of Followers in the Charismatic Leadership Process: Relationships and Their Consequences," *Academy of Management Review* 30, no. 1 (2005): 96–112.

64.   David Collinson, "Rethinking Followership: A Post-Structuralist Analysis of Follower Identities," *Leadership Quarterly* 17, no. 2 (April 2006): 179–189.

65.   Stever Robbins, "Understand What Motivates Your Boss," *HBS Working Knowledge*, March 13, 2006; and Sarah Jane Gilbert, "Do I Dare Say Something?" *HBS Working Knowledge*, March 20, 2006.

66.   The author of the article was Larry Bossidy, former CEO of AlliedSignal. See "What Your Leader Expects of You: And What You Should Expect in Return," *Harvard Business Review*, April 2007, 58–65.

67.   Nannerl Keohane, "On Leadership," *Perspectives on Politics* 3, no. 4 (December 2005): 705–722.

68.   Ellen Byron, "Call Me Mike," *Wall Street Journal*, March 27, 2006.

69.   Diane Brady, "Charm Offensive: Why America's CEOs Are Suddenly So Eager to Be Loved," *BusinessWeek*, June 26, 2006, 76.

70.   Arthur Levitt Jr., "The Imperial CEO Is No More," *Wall Street Journal*, March 17, 2005.

Chapter 3

1.   Quoted in Jason Epstein, "Mystery in the Heartland," *New York Review of Books*, October 7, 2004, 8.

2.   Frans de Waal, *Our Inner Ape: A Leading Primatologist Explains Why We Are Who We Are* (New York: Riverhead Books, 2005), 1.

3.   Ibid., 55.

4.   L. David Mech, *The Wolf: The Ecology and Behavior of an Endangered Species* (Garden City, NY: Natural History Press, 1970), 68.

5. L. David Mech and Luigi Boitani, eds., *Wolves: Behavior, Ecology, and Conservation* (Chicago: University of Chicago Press, 2003), 60.

6. De Waal, *Our Inner Ape*, 59.

7. Ibid., 60.

8. Ibid., 61.

9. For a discussion of the connection between primates and political authority in particular, see Fred H. Willhoite Jr., "Primates and Political Authority," in *Political Leadership: A Source Book*, ed. Barbara Kellerman (Pittsburgh, PA: University of Pittsburgh Press, 1986), 139.

10. Ibid., 156.

11. Robert Michels, *Political Parties: A Sociological Study of the Oligarchal Tendencies of Modern Democracy* (New York: Free Press, 1962).

12. Sara Evans, *Personal Politics: The Roots of Women's Liberation in the Civil Rights Movement and the New Left* (New York: Vintage Books, 1979), 222–223.

13. For some further discussion of the link between hardwiring and human behavior specifically as it pertains to leadership and management, see Nigel Nicholson, *Executive Instinct: Managing the Human Animal in the Information Age* (New York: Crown Business, 2000); and Nigel Nicholson, "How Hardwired Is Human Behavior," *Harvard Business Review*, July–August 1998, 135–147.

14. Richard Hackman, *Leading Teams: Setting the Stage for Great Performances* (Boston: Harvard Business School Press, 2002), 71.

15. For more on the relationship between leaders and followers when the former are in some way bad, see Barbara Kellerman, *Bad Leadership: What It Is, How It Happens, Why It Matters* (Boston: Harvard Business School Press, 2004); and Jean Lipman-Blumen, *The Allure of Toxic Leaders: Why We Follow Destructive Bosses and Corrupt Politicians—and How We Can Survive Them* (New York: Oxford University Press, 2005).

16. Sigmund Freud, "Moses and Monotheism," in *Political Leadership*, ed. Kellerman, 113.

17. Ian Buruma, "The Indiscreet Charm of Tyranny," *New York Review*, May 12, 2005, 37. For a comment on Freud as he now relates, also see Mark Edmundson, "Freud and the Fundamentalist Urge," *New York Times*, April 30, 2006.

18. Quoted in Kellerman, *Bad Leadership*, 123.

19. Quoted in Lipman-Blumen, *The Allure of Toxic Leaders*, 87. Also see Michael Maccoby on transference. Transference is a Freudian, or psychoanalytic, concept that derives from the strong connection between the analyst and the analysand. While I would argue that transference is potentially relevant to the leader-follower relationship only when that relationship is extraordinarily strong, Maccoby considers transference the emotional glue between leaders and followers. For more, see Michael Maccoby, *The Leaders We Need: And What Makes Us Follow* (Boston: Harvard Business School Press, 2007).

20. Lipman-Blumen, *The Allure of Toxic Leaders*, 38–43. This paragraph is based on Lipman-Blumen's insights.

21. Several of these items are from Boas Shamir in David Collinson, "Rethinking Followership: A Post-Structuralist Analysis of Follower Identities," *Leadership Quarterly* 17, no. 2 (April 2006): 183.

22. Jeffrey Kluger, "The New Science of Siblings," *Time*, July 10, 2006, 47.

23. Sigmund Freud, *Group Psychology and the Analysis of the Ego* (New York: W.W. Norton, 1959), 12.

24. Ibid., 76. For more by Freud on this general theme, also see his *Civilization and Its Discontents* (New York: W.W. Norton, 1961).

25. From Jared Diamond, "The Religious Success Story," *New York Review of Books*, November 7, 2002.

26. See, for example, the otherwise dauntingly complete Bernard M. Bass, *Bass & Stogdill's Handbook of Leadership: A Survey of Theory and Research* (New York: Free Press, 1990).

27. Richard M. Valelly, "Power Reconsidered: The Workings of Power," in *2006 APSA Annual Meeting Program* (Washington, DC: American Political Science Association, August–September 2006), 13.

28. Jane Mansbridge, "Cracking Through Hegemonic Ideology: The Logic of Formal Justice," *Social Justice Research* 18, no. 3 (September 2005): 336.

29. This paragraph is based on John Gaventa, *Power and Powerlessness: Quiescence and Rebellion in an Appalachian Valley* (Urbana: University of Illinois Press, 1980), 38.

30. Saul Alinsky, *Rules for Radicals: A Practical Primer for Realistic Radicals* (New York: Vintage, 1971), 3.

31. The phrase is Nicholas Kristof's. See "Wretched of the Earth," *New York Review of Books*, May 31, 2007, 35.

32. Ibid.

33. Quote in Ann Ruth Willner, *The Spellbinders: Charismatic Political Leadership* (New Haven, CT: Yale University Press, 1984), 23.

34. Ibid.

35. The social nature of followership (although this word was not used) was vividly demonstrated in 1971 by psychology professor Philip Zimbardo and a few of his colleagues at Stanford University. In a simulated prison situation, several of the student volunteers, all of whom were either Americans or Canadians and all of whom were male, quickly began to act as if the situation were real. Those who were told to play the role of "guards" became mean and even vicious, while those who were told to play the role of "prisoners" became frightened and depressed. As mentioned earlier in this chapter, we follow not only our leaders but other followers.

36. Timothy Garton Ash, "The Stasi on Our Minds," *New York Review of Books*, May 31, 2007, 4.

37. For explanations of why leadership studies have accentuated the positive and nearly eliminated the negative, see my book *Bad Leadership*.

38. Geraldine Umugwaneza, "Followers as Supporters of Status Quo: Rwanda's Willing Executioners" (unpublished paper, Kennedy School of Government, Harvard University, Cambridge, MA, 2006). Umugwaneza, who was a student of mine in a course titled "Followership," relied on sources including Gerard Prunier, *The Rwanda Crisis: History of a Genocide, 1959–1994* (Kampala, Uganda: Fountain Publishers, 1995).

39. Amy Joyce, "Big Bad Boss Tales," *Washington Post*, May 29, 2005.

40. Ibid. For the quote on Emett, see Bill Buford, "The Taming of the Chef," *New Yorker*, April 2, 2007, 52.

41. Quoted in Benedict Carey, "In the Execution Chamber, the Moral Compass Wavers," *New York Times*, February 7, 2006. Bandura has identified eight mechanisms that people use to justify immoral behavior. They are moral justification, euphemistic labeling, advantageous comparison, displacement of responsibility, diffusion of responsibility, disregard or distortion of the consequences, dehumanization, and blaming the victim.

42. John R. P. French Jr. and Bertram Raven, "The Bases of Social Power," in *Studies in Social Power*, ed. Dorwin Cartwright (Ann Arbor, MI: Institute for Social Research, 1959).

43. Joseph S. Nye Jr., *Soft Power: The Means to Success in World Politics* (New York: Public Affairs, 2004), 2.

44. For a discussion that is more clearly in the psychoanalytic tradition, see Abraham Zaleznik and Manfred F. R. Kets de Vries, *Power and the Corporate Mind* (Boston: Houghton Mifflin, 1975). For example, there is this sentence: "The potential source of conflict here is the balance achieved in the individual between his wishes to control and overpower authority figures, and, at the other extreme, his equally strong wishes to be dominated and controlled by these same figures" (p. 152).

45. Ibid., 146.

46. For an interesting piece of historical note on the relation between superiors and subordinates in corporate America, see Abraham Zaleznik, "The Dynamics of Subordinacy," *Harvard Business Review*, May–June 1965, 119–120.

47. This paragraph is based largely on Isaiah Berlin, "Equality," *Proceedings of the Aristotelian Society* 56 (1955–1956): 301–326.

48. James C. Scott, *Domination and the Arts of Resistance: Hidden Transcripts* (New Haven, CT: Yale University Press, 1990), 23.

49. Ibid., 3.

50. Ibid., 2.

51. Ibid., 227.

52. For more on the differences between democratic and authoritarian leaders in corporate America, see Bass, *Bass & Stogdill's Handbook of Leadership*, part V.

53. The seminal work on transactional and transformation leadership is James MacGregor Burns, *Leadership* (New York: Harper & Row, 1978).

54. Ibid., 20.

55. Ibid., 452. For more on the impact of Burns's ideas on leadership and management in the corporate sector, see Marshall Sashkin, "Transformational Leadership Approaches: A Review and Synthesis," in *The Nature of Leadership*, eds. John Antonakis, Anna T. Cianciolo, and Robert J. Sternberg (Thousand Oaks, CA: Sage Publications, 2004), 171–196.

56. George C. Homans, *The Human Group* (London: Routledge and Kegan Paul, 1951), 246.

57. Quoted in Robert Cottrell, "Death Under the Tsar," *New York Review of Books*, June 14, 2007, 42.

58. Dorwin Cartwright and Alvin Zander, eds., *Group Dynamics: Research and Theory* (New York: Harper & Row, 1968), 139.

59. For more on what is sometimes called the contagion effect, see the original and still important book on the subject, G. Le Bon, *The Crowd* (Harmondsworth, UK: Penguin Books, 1977; originally published in 1895), especially pp. 486–488.

60. Irving Janis, *Groupthink: Psychological Studies of Policy Decisions and Fiascoes* (Boston: Houghton Mifflin, 1982), vii. For more on this general subject, see Richard H. Willis, "Conformity, Independence, and Anticonformity," *Human Relations* 18, no. 4 (1965): 373–388.

61. Thomas E. Ricks, *Fiasco: The American Military Adventure in Iraq* (New York: Penguin Press, 2006).

62. Bass, *Bass & Stogdill's Handbook of Leadership*, 579.

63. Nannerl Keohane, "On Leadership," *Perspectives on Politics* 3, no. 4 (December 2005): 715.

64. Group for the Advancement of Psychiatry, *Leaders and Followers: A Psychiatric Perspective on Religious Cults* (Washington, DC: American Psychiatric Press, 1992). The white, middle-class, idealistic young people who form the majority in most cults are often lonely and depressed, dependent, and in need of affection. Cults provide their members with strong leaders and communities, both of which apparently provide, at least for a time, a sense of self-worth and a feeling of belonging.

65. Jane M. Howell and Boas Shamir, "The Role of Followers in the Charismatic Leadership Process: Relationships and their Consequences," *Academy of Management Review* 30, no. 1 (2005): 99. The quote is based on findings of research conducted on charismatic leadership processes, not cult leadership processes. But they apply to the latter as well.

66. S. Alexander Haslam and Michael J. Platow, "The Link Between Leadership and Followership: How Affirming Social Identity Translates Vision into Action," *Personality and Social Psychology Bulletin* 27, no. 11 (2001): 1477.

67. In this general regard, I will name only three books: Robert E. Kelley, *The Power of Followership: How to Create Leaders People Want to Follow and Followers Who Lead Themselves* (New York: Doubleday, 1992); Ira Chaleff, *The Courageous Follower: Standing Up to and for Our Leaders* (San Francisco: Berrett-Koehler, 2003); and Lipman-Blumen, *The Allure of Toxic Leaders.*

68. Chaleff, *The Courageous Follower*, xix.

Chapter 4

1. Francis Bacon, "Of Followers and Friends," excerpt in Robert Kelley, "Followership," in *Encyclopedia of Leadership*, eds. George R. Goethals, Georgia J. Sorenson, and James MacGregor Burns (Thousand Oaks, CA: Sage Publications, 2004), vol. 2, 513.

2. All of the quotes from this section on Zaleznik are from Abraham Zaleznik, "The Dynamics of Subordinacy," *Harvard Business Review*, May–June 1965, 118.

3. Abraham Zaleznik and Manfred F. R. Kets de Vries, *Power and the Corporate Mind* (Boston: Houghton Mifflin, 1975), chapter 7.

4. Ibid., 145.

5. Ibid.

6. Robert E. Kelley, *The Power of Followership: How to Create Leaders People Want to Follow and Followers Who Lead Themselves* (New York: Doubleday, 1992), 1.

7. Ibid., 12.

8. Ibid., 25.

9. Ibid., 26.

10. For a discussion of the first six motivations, see Kelley, *The Power of Followership*, chapter 3; for a discussion of the seventh, see chapter 4.

11. For a discussion of the five followership styles, see Kelley, *The Power of Followership*, chapters 5 and 6.

12. Kelley, "Followership," 504–513.

13. Ira Chaleff, *The Courageous Follower: Standing Up to and for Our Leaders* (San Francisco: Berrett-Koehler, 1995; 2nd ed., 2003). All the quotes cited here are from the second edition.

14. Ibid., 4.

15. For a full discussion of Chaleff's "followership styles," see Chaleff, *The Courageous Follower*, 38–43.

16. Ibid., xvii.

17. I wrote a book on this subject, titled *Reinventing Leadership: Making the Connection Between Politics and Business* (Albany: State University of New York Press, 1999).

18. For a book on followers who were close to the top, to political leaders in this case, see Jeff Schubert, *Dictatorial CEOs and Their Lieutenants* (Sidney, Australia: Ocean Publishing, 2006).

19. U.S. Census Bureau, *Current Population Survey*, Washington, DC, November 2004. Other reasons for not voting included "too busy," illness or disability, and the like. But some 10.7 percent declared themselves "not interested," and another 9.9 percent reported liking neither the candidates nor the issues.

20. Anthony Downs's book is *An Economic Theory of Democracy* (1957). Downs was quoted by Louis Menand in "Fractured Franchise," *New Yorker*, July 9–16, 2007, 88. For more on this, also see Bryan Caplan, *The Myth of the Rational Voter: Why Democracies Choose Bad Politics* (Princeton, NJ: Princeton University Press, 2007).

21. Ruy A. Teixeira, *Why Americans Don't Vote: Turnout Decline in the United States, 1960–1984* (Westport, CT: Greenwood Press, 1987); and Kevin Chen, *Political Alienation and Voting Turnout in the United States, 1960–1988* (San Francisco: Mellon Research University Press, 1992).

22. Chen, *Political Alienation and Voting Turnout*, 173.

23. Ibid., 95.

24. Cliff Zukin, Scott Keeter, Molly Andolina, Krista Jenkins, and Michael X. Delli Carpini, *A New Engagement? Political Participation, Civic Life, and the Changing American Citizen* (Oxford: Oxford University Press, 2006), 68.

25. Michael X. Delli Carpini, "In Search of Informed Citizens: What Americans Know About Politics and Why It Matters" (paper presented at Siegenthal Conference on Citizenship, Nashville, TN, November 1999). Delli Carpini writes that "informed citizens are demonstrably better citizens, as judged by the standards of democratic theory and practice underpinning the American system" (p. 35).

26. Zukin et al., *A New Engagement?* 83.

27. Ibid., 92, figure 4.1.

28. Ibid., 110.

29. It is estimated that in the Canadian federal election of 2004, only 37 percent of those aged eighteen to twenty-four turned out to cast a ballot, while those aged fifty-eight to sixty-seven voted in nearly twice the numbers. Paul Howe, "Political Knowledge and Electoral Participation in the Netherlands: Comparisons with the Canadian Case," *International Political Science Review* 27, no. 2 (2006): 137.

30. Quoted by Lawrence F. Kaplan, "American Idle," *New Republic*, September 12, 2005, 19.

31. Poll number cited in Adam Cohen, "Look on the World, Not on Yourself So Much," *New York Times*, May 7, 2006, 11.

32. Figures cited by Norman Ornstein, "Vote—Or Else," *New York Times*, August 10, 2006.

33. This paragraph is based on Ornstein's op-ed titled "Vote—Or Else."

34. I am grateful to Todd Rogers for making this point.

35. Those who might have a further interest in Isolates should see John Brehm, *The Phantom Respondents: Opinion Surveys and Political Representation* (Ann Arbor: University of Michigan Press, 1993). Brehm does not distinguish between Isolates and Bystanders. But he does address the problem of nonresponse to surveys, particularly in the political realm, arguing that it distorts survey results in important ways. Brehm writes, "We might think of the problems nonresponse poses to political representation, in terms of *who* is represented, and *what* effect nonresponse has on politics" (p. 185).

36. Barbara Kellerman, *Bad Leadership: What It Is, How It Happens, Why It Matters* (Boston: Harvard Business School Press, 2004), 35–40.

Chapter 5

1. Hannah Arendt, quoted in Wolf Lepenies, *The Seduction of German Culture in German History* (Princeton, NJ: Princeton University Press, 2006), 128. Jaspers's book was titled *Die Schuldfrage* [The question of guilt].

2. Hermann Cohen, quoted in Lepenies, *The Seduction of German Culture*, 149.

3. Frederic Spotts, *Hitler and the Power of Aesthetics* (Woodstock, NY: Overlook Press, 2003), 44.

4. Kurt Luedecke and Leni Riefenstahl are both quoted by Spotts, *Hitler and the Power of Aesthetics*, 44, 45.

5. William Shirer, quoted in Spotts, *Hitler and the Power of Aesthetics*, 49.

6. Ian Kershaw, *Hitler: 1889–1936: Hubris* (New York: W. W. Norton, 1998), 187.

7. Lepenies, *The Seduction of German Culture*, 208.

8. Kershaw, *Hitler: 1889–1936: Hubris*, 180.

9. Ibid., 182.

10. This paragraph is based on Kershaw, *Hitler: 1889–1936: Hubris*, 183.

11. *Mein Kampf* is, of course, full of anti-Semitic references. The book was first published in Germany in 1925. Adolph Hitler, *Mein Kampf*, trans. Ralph Manheim (Boston: Houghton Mifflin, 1972).

12. Inga Clendinnen, *Reading the Holocaust* (Cambridge: Cambridge University Press, 1999), 101. The section on Speer is based largely on Clendinnen.

13. Quoted by Clendinnen, *Reading the Holocaust*, 101. Also see Albert Speer, *Inside the Third Reich: Memoirs*, trans. Richard and Clara Winston (New York: Macmillan, 1970). On pp. 16–17, Speer expounds on what he recognized early on as Hitler's "peculiar magic."

14. Leni Riefenstahl, *Leni Riefenstahl: A Memoir* (New York: St. Martin's Press, 1992), 252.

15. All quotes in this paragraph in Kershaw, *Hitler: 1889–1936: Hubris*, 277.

16. Robert Gellately, *Backing Hitler: Consent and Coercion in Nazi Germany* (Oxford: Oxford University Press, 2001), 9.

17. Ibid., 15. This paragraph is based on Gellately's discussion.

18. Ibid., 121.

19. Ian Kershaw, *Hitler: 1936–1945: Nemesis* (New York: W.W. Norton, 2000), 183–184.

20. Ibid., 184.

21. Neil J. Mitchell, *Agents of Atrocity: Leaders, Followers, and the Violation of Human Rights in Civil War* (New York: Palgrave Macmillan, 2004), 5.

22. Benjamin A. Valentino, *Final Solutions: Mass Killing and Genocide in the Twentieth Century* (Ithaca, NY: Cornell University Press, 2004), 33, 34.

23. The quotes in this sentence are from Saul Friedlander, quoted in Valentino, *Final Solutions*, 34.

24. Ibid., 35.

25. Daniel Jonah Goldhagen, quoted in Valentino, *Final Solutions*, 36.

26. Daniel Jonah Goldhagen, *Hitler's Willing Executioners: Ordinary Germans and the Holocaust* (New York: Knopf, 1996), 418.

27. Ibid., 355.

28. Christopher R. Browning, *Ordinary Men: Reserve Police Battalion 101 and the Final Solution in Poland* (New York: HarperPerennial, 1998).

29. Ibid., 184.

30. Quotes in this paragraph are from Kershaw, *Hitler: 1889–1936: Hubris*, 437.

31. Gellately, *Backing Hitler*, 13.

32. Ibid., 121.

33. Fritz Stern, *Five Germanys I Have Known* (New York: Farrar, Straus and Giroux, 2006), 427.

34. Gellately, *Backing Hitler*, 149. For more on what was known, or could be known, in Germany during the war, see Victor Klemperer, *I Will Bear Witness: A Diary of the Nazi Years, 1933–1941* (New York: Random House, 1998).

35. This paragraph is based on Kershaw, *Hitler: 1936–1945: Nemesis*, 552. White Rose is now legendary in Germany, and its leading members are widely regarded as heroes. Among other testimonials, there have been films about White Rose and about Sophie Scholl, one of its leading members.

36. This quote is from the back cover of a book that chronicles this story in full. See Nathan Stoltzfus, *Resistance of the Heart: Intermarriage and the Rosenstrasse Protest in Nazi Germany* (New Brunswick, NJ: Rutgers University Press, 2001).

37. Ibid., xxv.

38. Ibid., 147.

39. The estimate of one thousand is cited in Stolzfus, *Resistance of the Heart*, 243.

40. Leopold Gutterer, quoted in Stolzfus, *Resistance of the Heart*, 244.

41. Ibid., 272.

42. Browning, *Ordinary Men*, 61.

43. For a full description of this episode, see Browning, *Ordinary Men*, chapter 7.

44. Ibid., 188.

45. Kershaw, *Hitler: 1936–1945: Nemesis*, 659.

46. Ibid., 657.

47. Ibid., 671.

48. Ibid., 754.

49. Kristen Renwick Monroe, *The Hand of Compassion: Portraits of Moral Choice During the Holocaust* (Princeton, NJ: Princeton University Press, 2004), x.

50. Ibid., 23.

51. Ibid., 30.

52. Ibid., 187, 188.

53. As quoted by Günter Grass in an excerpt from his book titled "How I Spent the War," *New Yorker*, June 4, 2007, 71. Grass's memoir was published by Harcourt, Inc., in 2007.

54. See Walter Laqueur, foreword to Stolzfus, *Resistance of the Heart*, x.

55. This figure is cited by Herbert A. Strauss, "Jewish Emigration from Germany: Nazi Policies and Jewish Responses," in *The Nazi Holocaust: Historical Articles on the Destruction of European Jews*, ed. Michael R. Marrus (Westport, CT: Meckler, 1989), vol. I, 164.

56. Werner Rosenstock, "Exodus 1933–1939: A Survey of Jewish Emigration from Germany," in *The Nazi Holocaust*, ed. Marrus, 143.

57. Strauss, "Jewish Emigration from Germany," 179.

58. Ibid.

59. Ibid.

60. This section was based on Strauss, who described the phases of emigration as I did here. His article in *The Nazi Holocaust*, ed. Marrus, is on pp. 161–210.

61. Klemperer, *I Will Bear Witness*, 277–278.

62. Victoria J. Barnett, *Bystanders: Conscience and Complicity During the Holocaust* (Westport, CT: Greenwood Press, 1999), 6. It was Raul Hilberg who first (in 1961) divided Germans during the Holocaust into three groups—perpetrators, victims, and bystanders. See his monumental study, *The Destruction of the European Jews* (New York: Holmes & Meier, 1985) and his other works.

63. This paragraph is based on Barnett, *Bystanders*, 6.

64. Ibid., 9.

65. Ervin Staub, quoted in Barnett, *Bystanders*, 10.

66. This distinction was made by Barnett, *Bystanders*.

67. Ibid., 6.

68. The quote is in Barnett, *Bystanders*, 7.

69. Ibid., 17.

70. Ibid., 18, 19.

71. Ibid., 37.

72. For the definitive work on this, see Robert J. Lifton, *The Nazi Doctors: Medical Killing and the Psychology of Genocide* (New York: Basic Books, 2000); originally published in 1986.

73. Ian Buruma, *Murder in Amsterdam: The Death of Theo van Gogh and the Limits of Tolerance* (New York: Penguin Press, 2006), 19.

74. Additional quotes also from Buruma, *Murder in Amsterdam*, 74, 238.

75. David Cesarani and Paul A. Levine, "Conclusion," in *Bystanders to the Holocaust: A Reevaluation*, eds. David Cesarani and Paul A. Levine (London: Frank Cass, 2002), 269.

76. Tony Kushner, "'Pissing in the Wind?' The Search for Nuance in the Study of Holocaust 'Bystanders,'" in *Bystanders to the Holocaust*, eds. Cesarani and Levine, 70.

77. Barnett, *Bystanders*, 46.

78. David S. Wyman, *The Abandonment of the Jews: America and the Holocaust, 1941–1945* (New York: Pantheon Books, 1984).

79. Ibid., x–xi.

80. Ibid., 311.

81. Michael J. Cohen, "Churchill and the Jews: The Holocaust," in *The Nazi Holocaust*, ed. Marrus, 346.

82. Gilbert is quoted by Cohen, "Churchill and the Jews," 348.

83. Robert N. Rosen defends Roosevelt against the charge that he was a Bystander in his book *Saving the Jews: Franklin D. Roosevelt and the Holocaust* (New York: Thunder's Mouth Press, 2006). The Auschwitz debate is aired from both sides in Michael J. Neufield and Michael Berenbaum, eds., *The Bombing of Auschwitz: Should the Allies Have Attempted It?* (New York: St. Martin's Press, 2000). Also see Henry Feingold, "Who Shall Bear Guilt for the Holocaust: The Human Dilemma," in *The Nazi Holocaust*, ed. Marrus, 121–142.

84. Feingold, "Who Shall Bear Guilt for the Holocaust," 131.

85. David Remnick, "The Seventh Day: Why the Six-Day War Is Still Being Fought," *New Yorker*, March 28, 2007.

86. Monroe, *The Hand of Compassion*, 260.

87. Stern, *Five Germanys I Have Known*, 240.
88. See Barnett, *Bystanders*, 1–5, for her description of what happened in Sonderburg under Nazi rule.
89. Ibid., 3.
90. Ibid.

Chapter 6

1. See, for example, Peter F. Drucker, *The Effective Executive* (New York: Harper & Row, 1966), 3–5.
2. Marcia Angell, "Your Dangerous Drugstore," *New York Review*, June 8, 2006, 38.
3. Ibid.
4. Fran Hawthorne, "Merck at Risk," *Chief Executive (US)*, June 1, 2003, 54–57.
5. Bill George with Peter Sims, *True North: Discover Your Authentic Leadership* (San Francisco: Jossey-Bass, 2007), 165.
6. The information on Gilmartin is taken from "Business Biographies," Reference for Business, http://www.referenceforbusiness.com/biography/.
7. Ibid.
8. Gilmartin's speech at the annual stockholders' meeting, April 27, 2004, http://www.merck.com/newsroom/executive_speeches/042704a.html.
9. "Business Biographies," Reference for Business, http://www.referenceforbusiness.com/biography/.
10. Marcia Angell, *The Truth About the Drug Companies: How They Deceive Us and What to Do About It* (New York: Random House, 2004), 3.
11. Several different timelines relate the story of Vioxx. I rely most on the one by Robert Steyer, "Vioxx Timeline 1998–2005," TheStreet.com, August 22, 2005, http://www.thestreet.com/stocks/biotech/10239081.html?pub_tscs. Further details are available on the Food and Drug Administration (FDA) Web site, "Sequence of Events with VIOXX, since opening of IND," Fda.gov, http://www.fda.gov/ohrms/dockets/ac/05/briefing/2005–4090B1_04_E-FDA-TAB-C.htm; the official Merck timeline is available on Merck's Web site: "Vioxx® (rofecoxib) Information Center," Merck.com, http://www.merck.com/newsroom/vioxx/. There are other timelines available as well, for example, on the National Pubic Radio, *New York Times*, and *USA Today* Web sites.
12. Carolyn Abraham, "The Painful Battle over the 'Wonder': Carolyn Abraham Reports on the Canadian Doctor Who Found Herself Smack in the Middle of the Controversy over Vioxx," *Globe and Mail (Canada)*, February 19, 2005.
13. Ibid.
14. Raymond Gilmartin's full statement can be found on the following Web page: http://www.nytimes.com/2004/09/30/business/30WIRE-MERK.html?ex=1254283200&en=84f4ea5ff7fb269d&ei=5090&partner=rssuserland.
15. This particular ad appeared in the *New York Times* on November 12, 2004. It was part of a larger campaign that eventually featured ads in seven leading newspapers. See "Merck Now Offers Vioxx Defense," *Boston Globe*, November 22, 2004.
16. Angell, *The Truth About the Drug Companies*, xix.
17. Robert Burton, "How Merck Stacked the Deck," *Salon*, March 31, 2005.
18. *New York Times*, editorial, "Punishment for Merck," August 23, 2005.
19. *Chicago Tribune*, editorial, "A Sin of Omission," December 17, 2005.
20. Peter Kang, "Merck Faces New Vioxx Suits," Forbes.com, September 13, 2006, http://www.forbes.com/health/2006/09/13/merck-vioxx-kidneys=health=pharmaceuticals-ex_pk_0913merck.html.
21. As of September 30, 2006, Merck had won five of the nine cases that went to trial. Robert Cryan, Edward Chancellor, and David Vise, "How Deep Do Merck's Wounds Go?" *Wall Street Journal*, September 30–October 1, 2006. By February 2007 the tally was as follows: in the eighteen cases scheduled during all of 2006, juries decided in Merck's favor nine times. The company lost four cases, and another five were withdrawn from trial calendars. See John Simons, "Merck Is on the Mend," *Fortune*, February 5, 2007, 110. For the latest information, check the Web, where various sites constantly update legal claims against Merck based on the taking of Vioxx.
22. From Bloomberg News, "California and the West: Merck Knew of Vioxx Dangers," *Los Angeles Times*, June 28, 2006.
23. Senate Committee on Finance, *Withdrawal from the Market of Vioxx Arthritis Pain Medication*, Congressional Quarterly Inc., November 18, 2004.

24. Merck has since developed a new drug, Arcoxia, which is similar to Vioxx. However, FDA approval was not easy to secure, precisely because "safety issues" lingered. See Sarah Rubinstein and Anna Wilde Mathews, "Vioxx Successor Faces FDA Hurdles," *Wall Street Journal*, April 4, 2007.

25. Angell, "Your Dangerous Drugstore," 39.

26. John Abramson, *Overdo$ed America: The Broken Promise of American Medicine* (New York: Harper-Collins, 2004), 36.

27. This point has been made more than once. See, for example, Leonard J. Weber, *Profits Before People? Ethical Standards and the Marketing of Prescription Drugs* (Bloomington: Indiana University Press, 2006).

28. Ed Silverman, "Former Merck Scientist Becomes Lightning Rod," *Star-Ledger (Newark)*, September 25, 2005.

29. Dani Veracity, "Leaked Documents Show Merck Knew of Vioxx Dangers, Yet Hid Them for Years," NewsTarget.com, August 6, 2005, http://www.newstarget.com/010613.html.

30. Anna Wilde Mathews and Barbara Martinez, "E-Mails Suggest Merck Knew Vioxx's Dangers at Early Stage," *Wall Street Journal*, November 1, 2004.

31. Anne Belli, "Ex-Merck Scientist's Views on Vioxx Changed," *Knight Ridder Tribune News*, December 6, 2005.

32. Quoted in Belli, "Ex-Merck Scientist's Views."

33. Silverman, "Former Merck Scientist."

34. Jeff May, "Merck Witness Has Dent in Armor," *Star-Ledger (Newark)*, January 8, 2006.

35. Quoted in May, "Merck Witness Has Dent in Armor."

36. Heather Won Tesoriero and Barbara Martinez, "Top Merck Witness May Become Liability in New Vioxx Trials," *Wall Street Journal*, December 12, 2005.

37. May, "Merck Witness Has Dent in Armor."

38. Ibid.

39. Mathews and Martinez, "E-Mails Suggest Merck Knew."

40. Tesoriero and Martinez, "Top Merck Witness."

41. Ibid.

42. John Curran, "Expert: Merck Ignored Vioxx Safety Risks," Associated Press, September 17, 2005.

43. Anna Wilde Mathews and Barbara Martinez, "E-Mails Suggest Merck Knew Vioxx's Dangers at an Early Stage," *Wall Street Journal,* November 1, 2004.

44. Ibid.

45. Quoted in May, "Merck Witness Has Dent in Armor."

46. Mark Donald, "Deconstructing Vioxx: How Mark Lanier Took on Merck and Won," *Texas Lawyer* 21, no. 26 (August 29, 2005).

47. This paragraph is also based on Donald, "Deconstructing Vioxx."

48. The information is from Sherwood's biographical summary at the Institute of Medicine of the National Academies' Web site, http://www.iom.edu/CMS/3740/4881/10279/10300.aspx. Also see information on Sherwood at Informedix, http://03tilt.com/informedix/company_advisors.html.

49. This story is available at http://www.npr.org/templates/story/story/php?storyId-4696711. The NPR story is the source for all the material on Sherwood.

50. Mathews and Martinez, "E-Mails Suggest Merck Knew."

51. Ibid.

52. From the full transcript of the NPR broadcast of *All Things Considered*, June 9, 2005.

53. Ibid.

54. Ibid.

55. All quotes in this paragraph and the immediately preceding one are from the transcript of *All Things Considered*, June 9, 2005.

56. The quotes in this paragraph are from the prepared statement delivered by Gurkirpal Singh, MD, to the Senate Committee on Finance, chaired by Charles Grassley in November 2004.

57. From an article, "Part I: Documents Suggest Merck Tried to Censor Vioxx Critics," posted on NPR's Web site, http://www.NPR.org/, and reported by Snigda Prakash. http://www.npr.org/templates/story/story.php?storyId=4696609, and "Part II: Did Merck Try to Censor Vioxx Critics?" http://www.npr.org/templates/story/story.php?storyId=4696711.

58. Ibid.

59. Associated Press, "Cardiologist Accuses Merck of Misconduct," December 5, 2005.

60. Alex Berenson, "Doctor Links Merck Trial to His Demotion," *New York Times*, December 10, 2005.

61. Ibid.

62. The descriptions of Graham are in John Simons, "Blowing the Whistle at the FDA," *Fortune*, January 24, 2005, 32. The quote is from *Medical News Today*, quoting ABC TV's *Nightline*, "FDA Forced Dr. D. Graham to Blow the Whistle," MedicalNewsToday.com, November 24, 2004, http://www .medicalnewstoday.com/articles/16846.php.

63. Michael Scherer, "The Side Effects of Truth," *Mother Jones*, May–June 2005.

64. David J. Graham, "Blowing the Whistle on the FDA" *Multinational Monitor* 25, no. 12 (December 2004): 22.

65. Taken from testimony of David J. Graham, MD, MPH, Senate Committee on Finance, November 18, 2004.

66. James Surowiecki makes an interesting distinction between the FDA's authority before a drug comes to market and after. In particular he charges that "the U.S. has no rational system for 'post-market surveillance'—the evaluation of drugs after they've been approved." See his article, "A Drug on the Market," *New Yorker*, June 25, 2007, 40.

67. Scherer, "The Side Effects of Truth."

68. Angell, *The Truth About the Drug Companies*, 3.

69. Weber, *Profits Before People?*, 182.

70. Anna Wilde Mathews, "Drug Firms Use Financial Clout to Push Industry Agenda at FDA," *Wall Street Journal*, September 1, 2006.

71. Barry Meier, "Reviews Cite Flaws at Guidant," *New York Times*, March 21, 2006. It should be noted that the panel was commissioned by Guidant.

72. Anna Wilde Mathews, "Sequel for Vioxx Critic: Attack on Diabetes Pill," *Wall Street Journal*, May 22, 2007.

73. All quotes in this paragraph are from Max Bazerman and Dolly Chugh, "Decisions Without Blinders," *Harvard Business Review*, January 2006, 90.

74. The paraphrase is from Alex Berenson, "Merck Inquiry Backs Conduct over Vioxx," *New York Times*, September 7, 2006.

75. See John Carreyou and Heather Won Tesoriero, "Merck Vioxx Probe Clears Officials," *Wall Street Journal*, September 7, 2000; and Berenson, "Merck Inquiry Backs Conduct."

76. Drucker, *The Effective Executive*, 5.

77. Mathews, "Sequel for Vioxx Critic."

78. See, for example, Stephanie Saul and Gardiner Harris, "Diabetes Drug Still Has Risks, Doctors Warn," *New York Times*, June 6, 2007.

79. A supervisor in the drug safety office of the FDA, Dr. Rosemary Johann-Liang, said that in March 2006 she approved a recommendation from an agency safety reviewer that Avandia (and another similar drug named Actos, made by another company) be required to carry the strongest warning "because they posed a risk of unusual swelling that could lead to heart failure." For her troubles, she was ordered by her superiors to retract her approval of the warning, lost her authority to approve such assessments, and was no longer allowed to supervise reviews of the two drugs. See Saul and Harris, "Diabetes Drug Still Has Risks."

Chapter 7

1. James L. Franklin, "Breaking the Silence: The Church and Sexual Abuse," *Boston Globe*, November 22, 1992.

2. A. W. Richard Sipe, *Sex, Priests, and Power: Anatomy of a Crisis* (New York: Brunner-Routledge, 1995), 11, 12.

3. Ibid., 12.

4. Ibid., 26.

5. All quotes in this paragraph are from Franklin, "Breaking the Silence."

6. Laurie Goodstein and Sam Dillon, "Scandal Is Stirring Lay Catholics to Push Church for More Power," *New York Times*, November 10, 2002.

7. Margaret R. Miles, foreword to Sipe, *Sex, Priests, and Power*, xi.

8. Jason Berry, *Lead Us Not into Temptation: Catholic Priests and the Sexual Abuse of Children* (Urbana: University of Illinois Press, 2000), 179.

9. James A. Brundage, quoted in Berry, *Lead Us Not into Temptation*, 180.

10. For further discussion of the history of celibacy in the church, both distant and more recent, see Thomas P. Doyle, A. W. Richard Snipe, and Patrick J. Wall, *Sex, Priests, and Secret Codes: The Catholic Church's 2000-Year Paper Trail of Sexual Abuse* (Los Angeles: Volt Press, 2006).

11. Berry, *Lead Us Not into Temptation*, xii.

12. Ibid.

13. The estimate was made by the Reverend Andrew Greeley in the March 20, 1993 issue of *America*, a Jesuit magazine. See Berry, *Lead Us Not into Temptation*, x.

14. Berry, *Lead Us Not into Temptation*, xii.

15. Andrew Greeley, foreword to Berry, *Lead Us Not into Temptation*, xx.

16. Michael Rezendes, "Church Allowed Abuse by Priest for Years: Aware of Geoghan Record, Archdiocese Still Shuttled Him from Parish to Parish," *Boston Globe*, January 6, 2002.

17. The Investigative Staff of the *Boston Globe*, *Betrayal: The Crisis in the Catholic Church* (Boston: Little, Brown, 2002), 53.

18. This is based on an article on the same story that appeared in the *Globe* one day after the first. Also prepared by the Globe Spotlight Team, "Geoghan Preferred Preying on Poorer Children," *Boston Globe*, January 7, 2002.

19. Sacha Pfeiffer and Kevin Cullen, "AG Wants Church to Report Past Sex Abuse," *Boston Globe*, January 17, 2002.

20. Ibid.

21. Andrew M. Greeley, *Priests: A Calling in Crisis* (Chicago: University of Chicago Press, 2004), 1.

22. Investigative Staff, *Betrayal*, 33. All the quotes in this paragraph are from the same source.

23. Ibid., 143.

24. Ibid.

25. Ibid., 147.

26. Cardinal John J. O'Connor, quoted in Investigative Staff, *Betrayal*, 148.

27. Michael Novak, "The Boston Disease," *National Review Online*, December 13, 2002, http://www.nationalreview.com/novak/novak.

28. Quoted in Investigative Staff, *Betrayal*, 153.

29. Ibid., 155.

30. For a fuller account of this meeting, see Investigative Staff, *Betrayal*, 154–156.

31. Novak, "The Boston Disease."

32. Investigative Staff, *Betrayal*, 184.

33. Mary Jo Bane, "A Challenge to Lay Catholics," *Boston Globe*, February 3, 2002.

34. Terence Smith, "Challenging the Church," *Online Newshour*, March 26, 2002.

35. Quoted in Smith, "Challenging the Church."

36. Peter Pollard, "Clerical Abuse: A Case Against Forgiving or Forgetting," *Boston Globe*, April 7, 2002.

37. Investigative Staff, *Betrayal*, 66, 67.

38. *Boston Herald*, editorial, "Shanley Case Shows Legacy of Church Lies," April 9, 2002.

39. Quoted in Eileen McNamara, "Reclaiming Their Church," *Boston Globe*, April 14, 2002.

40. Quoted in Michael Paulson, "Catholics Drawn to Splinter Group in Wellesley," *Boston Globe*, May 1, 2002. I have drawn on this article for the facts cited in this paragraph; it contains further information about the genesis of Voice of the Faithful as well.

41. McNamara, "Reclaiming Their Church."

42. Paulson, "Catholics Drawn to Splinter Group."

43. Ralph Ranalli, "Judge at Center of Geoghan Case Considered a 'Fresh-Air Person,'" *Boston Globe*, May 8, 2002.

44. Ibid.

45. Kevin Cullen and Michael Rezendes, "A Grand Jury Is Said to Weigh Case Against Law," *Boston Globe*, June 19, 2002.

46. Mark Jurkowitz, "When 'Two Alien Cultures' Face Off," *Boston Globe*, July 28, 2002.

47. Maggie Mulvihill, "Law Losing His Power Pals: Supporters Are Divided on What His Future Holds," BostonHerald.com, April 10, 2002.

48. Michael Rosenwald, "Law's Supporters Counter Protests Outside the Cathedral," *Boston Globe*, April 22, 2002.

49. All the quotes in this paragraph are from Michael Rezendes and Sacha Pfeiffer, "Law Distances Self on Shanley," *Boston Globe*, May 20, 2002.

50. All quotes about this meeting are from Michael Paulson, "Activist Group Told to Work 'With and Under' Law," *Boston Globe*, May 24, 2002.

51. Thomas Farragher, "Small Group Has Big Goals," *Boston Globe*, July 21, 2002.

52. Ibid.

53. This quote and the paragraph more generally are based on Michael Paulson, "Catholic Group to Rate Bishops," *Boston Globe*, July 20, 2002.

54. This brief biographical description and all the quotes from Post's speech on that occasion were posted on BishopAccountability.org, 2004.

55. Eric Convey and Robin Washington, "Laity Get Tough on Law: Petition Urges Pope to Punish Bishops," *Boston Herald*, July 22, 2002.

56. Eric Convey, "Theologians Back Lay Catholics' Bid for Greater Voice," *Boston Herald*, July 20, 2002.

57. Michael Paulson, "Lay Catholics Issue Call to Transform Their Church," *Boston Globe*, July 21, 2002.

58. Ibid.

59. Convey, "Theologians Back Lay Catholics' Bid."

60. MassNews staff, "Is 'Voice of the Faithful' Unfaithful to Catholic Principles?" *Massachusetts News*, July 22, 2002.

61. Investigative Staff, *Betrayal*, 197.

62. The paragraph was based on Sacha Pfeiffer and Matt Carroll, "Law to Reject Donations from Voice of the Faithful," *Boston Globe*, July 23, 2002.

63. Sacha Pfeiffer and Stephen Kurkjian, "Catholic Charities Shifts on Lay Group's Fund-raising," *Boston Globe*, July 26, 2002.

64. Paul R. Dokecki, *The Clergy Sexual Abuse Crisis: Reform and Renewal in the Catholic Community* (Washington, DC: Georgetown University Press, 2004), 88. Dokecki includes in his book a good review of the role of VOTF during the 2002 crisis in the Boston Archdiocese. See pp. 83–96.

65. Rod Dreher, "Law Faces the Law," *National Review Online*, August 15, 2002.

66. *Boston Globe*, editorial, "The Cardinal's Oath," August 17, 2002.

67. Dokecki, *The Clergy Sexual Abuse Crisis*, 92. For a profile of Father Walter Cuenin, see Paul Wilkes, "A Priest's Battle for a More Open Church," *New Yorker*, September 2, 2002.

68. Eric Convey and Robin Washington, "Reilly Says Archdiocese Is Still Holding Out," *Boston Herald*, October 23, 2002.

69. Matt Carroll, "Judge Warns Archdiocese of Heavy Fines," *Boston Globe*, October 31, 2002.

70. Dokecki, *The Clergy Sexual Abuse Crisis*, 93.

71. Margery Eagan, "Crackdown on Voice of the Faithful Shows Cardinal's Intolerance," *Boston Herald*, October 6, 2002.

72. Thomas H. O'Connor, emeritus professor at Boston College, quoted in Michael Paulson, "Quietly, Cardinal Back in Public Eye After Long Silence," *Boston Globe*, November 3, 2002.

73. Paulson, "Quietly, Cardinal Back in Public Eye."

74. Tom Mashberg, "Cardinal Apologizes for His Role in Scandal," *Boston Herald*, November 4, 2002.

75. From the text of the remarks delivered by Cardinal Bernard F. Law, at the start of Mass at the Church of the Holy Cross on November 3, 2002. The text appeared in the *Boston Globe* on November 4, 2002.

76. The quotes and the material in this paragraph are in Walter V. Robinson, "Judge Finds Records, Law at Odds," *Boston Globe*, November 26, 2002.

77. Thomas Farragher and Sacha Pfeiffer, "More Clergy Abuse, Secrecy Cases," *Boston Globe*, December 4, 2002.

78. Ibid.

79. Michael Paulson, "A Church Seeks Healing: Pope Accepts Law's Resignation in Rome," *Boston Globe*, December 14, 2002.

80. Cardinal William Keeler, quoted in Investigative Staff, *Betrayal*, 215.

81. Rod Dreher, "State of Law," *National Review Online*, December 13, 2002.

82. Quoted in Dokecki, *The Clergy Sexual Abuse Crisis*, 95.

83. Pam Belluck, "Cardinal Law Says Resigning Was the Best Way to Serve the Church," *New York Times*, December 17, 2002.

84. Francis X. Rocca, "Our Man in Rome," *Boston*, September 2006, http://www.bostonmagazine.com/article/our-man-in-rome. The quotes in this paragraph are taken from the article.

85. Martin Evans, "Bishop Accused of Hoarding," *Newsday*, September 13, 2006.
86. Regine Laboissiere, "Catholic Group Calls for Change," *Hartford Courant*, September 24, 2006.
87. Gillian Flaccus, "L.A. Archdiocese to Pay $660M Over Clergy Abuse," *USA Today*, July 16, 2007.
88. "Financial Disclosure of the Archdiocese of Boston Regarding Settlements and Related Costs," April 2006.

Chapter 8

1. Center for Defense Information, "Terrorism Project," October 5, 2001.
2. Spelling on names such as Al Qaida varies from text to text. In general, I have used the same spelling as Sean Naylor, who wrote the definitive book on Operation Anaconda (see note 3).
3. Sean Naylor, *Not a Good Day to Die: The Untold Story of Operation Anaconda* (New York: Berkley Books, 2005), 10. This chapter draws on Naylor's book, which is an indispensable guide through the labyrinth that was Operation Anaconda.
4. Philip Smucker, "How bin Laden Got Away, *Christian Science Monitor*, March 4, 2002.
5. "Operation Anaconda: A Day by Day Guide to the First Week of Fighting," *Time,* March 10, 2002, http://www.time.com/time/covers/1101020318/popup/.
6. Richard T. Cooper, "The Untold War: Fierce Fight in Afghan Valley Tests U.S. Soldiers and Strategy," *Los Angles Times*, March 24, 2002. This chapter draws on Cooper's excellent article.
7. Richard W. Stewart, *Operation Enduring Freedom: The United States Army in Afghanistan*, U.S. Army brochure, updated March 17, 2006.
8. Cooper, "The Untold War."
9. Mark Danner, "Iraq: The War of the Imagination," *New York Review of Books*, December 21, 2006.
10. Cooper, "The Untold War."
11. Naylor, *Not a Good Day to Die*, 24.
12. Ibid., 19.
13. Ibid., 47.
14. "10th Mountain Division (Light Infantry)," GlobalSecurity.org, http://www.globalsecurity.org/military/agency/army/10mtn.htm.
15. This paragraph is based on Naylor, *Not a Good Day to Die*, 12, 13.
16. Robert H. McElroy, with Patrecia Slayden Hollis, "Afghanistan: Fire Support for Operation Anaconda: Interview with Major General Franklin L. Hagenbeck, *Field Artillery*, September–October 2002, 7.
17. Naylor, *Not a Good Day to Die*, 53.
18. Ibid., 55.
19. Ibid., 61.
20. Military mission statement for Operation Anaconda, quoted in Naylor, *Not a Good Day to Die*, 118.
21. Ibid., 123.
22. Ibid., 130.
23. Ibid., 131.
24. Ibid., 146.
25. Ibid., 180, 181.
26. *Time*, March 10, 2002, http://www.time.com/. The day-by-day account of Operation Anaconda is based mostly on this source.
27. Sean Naylor, "Operation Anaconda" (presentation at Security Studies Program Seminar, http://web.mit.edu/ssp/seminars/wed_archives_06spring/naylor.htm, March 22, 2006).
28. It was General Hagenbeck who later provided the information. See Benjamin S. Lambeth, *Air Power Against Terror: America's Conduct of Operation Enduring Freedom* (Santa Monica, CA: Rand Research, 2005), 191.
29. The number of enemy dead as a result of Anaconda varies. Some estimates were as low as between two hundred and three hundred.
30. Wikipedia, "Operation Anaconda," http://www.en.wikipedia.org/wiki/Operation_Anaconda.
31. *Time*, March 10, 2002, http://www.time.com/.
32. Cooper, "The Untold War."

33. Quoted in Michel Elliott, "Deadly Mission," *Time*, March 18, 2002, 34.

34. Ibid.

35. Rory McCarthy and Peter Beaumont, "Battle for Gardez: A Bloody Duel to the Death in Eastern Afghanistan Could Prove a Decisive Turning Point in the War on Terror," *Observer (UK)*, March 10, 2002.

36. All quotes in this paragraph are from *Army Magazine*, "Operation Anaconda: Taking the Fight to the Enemy in Afghanistan," April 1, 2002, http://www.ausa.org/webpub/DeptArmyMagazine.nsf/byid/CCRH-6CCCS3H.

37. Elaine Grossman, "Was Operation Anaconda Ill-Fated from the Start?" *Inside the Pentagon*, Defense and the National Interest, July 29, 2004, http://www.d-n-i.net/.

38. Lambeth, *Air Power Against Terror*, 165.

39. Ibid.

40. Stewart, *Operation Enduring Freedom*, section 43.

41. Quoted by Lambeth, *Air Power Against Terror*, 174.

42. The quotes in the paragraph are in Lambeth, *Air Power Against Terror*, on pp. 166, 217, and 230, respectively.

43. I am grateful to Michele Macaloon for making this point.

44. All the quotes extracted from this interview are in Austin Bay, "A Full Report on Operation Anaconda—America's First Battle of the 21st Century. A Complete After Action Interview with Col. Weircinski [sic]," StrategyPage.com, June 27, 2002, http://www.strategypage.com/.

45. Naylor, *Not a Good Day to Die*, 234.

46. Ibid., 229.

47. News transcript, U.S. Department of Defense, http://www.defenselink.mil/transcripts/2002/t03072002.

48. Staff Sgt. Dave Enders and Sgt. 1st Class (Ret.) Phil Tegtmeier, "Soldiers Use 'Big Four' Battle Drills to Maintain Combat Edge," *NCO Journal*, January 2003, 7–10.

49. Ann Scott Tyson, "Anaconda: A War Story," *Christian Science Monitor*, August 1, 2002.

50. Ibid.

51. Ibid.

52. Gerry Gilmore, "Combat Veterans Recount Grit, Valor, Air Support in Defeating Terror Troops," American Forces Information Service, October 23, 2002.

53. Mark Thompson, "Sudden Warrior," *Time*, September 9, 2002, 78.

54. Naylor, *Not a Good Day to Die*, 233.

55. Thompson, "Sudden Warrior."

56. Ibid.

57. Both Grippe and Kraft are quoted in Naylor, *Not a Good Day to Die*, 254–255.

58. Randal Perez, interview by Martin Savidge, *CNN Live at Daybreak*, March 18, 2002.

59. Quoted in Thompson, "Sudden Warrior."

60. All of the information and all the quotes on Rivera are from John Sack, "Anaconda," *Esquire*, August 2002, 116.

61. Ibid.

62. Ibid.

63. H. R. McMaster, *Dereliction of Duty: Lyndon Johnson, Robert McNamara, the Joint Chiefs of Staff, and the Lies That Led to Vietnam* (New York: HarperCollins, 1997), 311, 312.

64. Martin L. Cook, *The Moral Warrior: Ethics and Service in the U.S. Military* (Albany: State University of New York Press, 2004), 64.

65. McMaster, *Dereliction of Duty*, 300–334.

66. Lewis Sorley, *Honorable Warrior: General Harold K. Johnson and the Ethics of Command* (Lawrence: University Press of Kansas, 1998), 303.

67. The phrase *drain the swamps* is from Stewart, *Operation Enduring Freedom*, section 1.

68. There is a rich literature on what constitutes a "just war." For a brief discussion on this, see Cook, *The Moral Warrior*, chapter 1.

69. Ibid., 32.

70. Sean Naylor argues that Operation Anaconda should have taught us ten lessons. They are (1) know your enemy; (2) know your friends; (3) think twice before you plug and play; (4) the eye in the sky is not all-seeing; (5) high tech is not all that it's cracked up to be; (6) jointness has its limits; (7) remember Patton's three principles: audacity, audacity, and audacity; (8) always trust the guy on the ground;

(9) combat-focused training saves lives; and (10) the "troops won't let you down." Naylor, "Operation Anaconda."

71. Mark Danner, "Iraq: The War of the Imagination," *New York Review of Books*, December 21, 2006, 83.

72. United States Marine Corps, Marine Corps University, *User's Guide to Marine Corps Values*," http://www.MATSGFL.USMC.MIL/mATSG%20sECTIONS/training/chapter19.htm.

73. See, for example, the article by Marine Corps General Michael J. Jernigan, "The 'Emperor's New Clothes' Approach to Leadership," in *Military Leadership: In Pursuit of Excellence*, eds. Robert L. Taylor and William E. Rosenbach (Cambridge, MA: Westview Press, 2005), 109–113. Reprinted from the *Marine Corps Gazette*.

74. See, for example, Michael Duffy, "The Revolt of the Generals," *Time*, April 16, 2006; and Evan Thomas and John Barry, "Anatomy of a Revolt," *Newsweek*, April 24, 2006.

75. For more on this reasoning, see Nathaniel Fick, "General Dissent: When Less Isn't More," *USA Today*, April 24, 2006.

76. Deputy Secretary of Defense Paul Wolfowitz called Shinseki "wildly off the mark." Wolfowitz was quoted by, among others, Dave Moniz, "Ex-Army Boss: Pentagon Won't Admit Reality in Iraq," *USA Today*, June 3, 2003.

77. Quoted by Phillip Carter, "War by Video Conference: How al Qaeda Fought Us to a Draw in the Biggest Battle in Afghanistan," review of Naylor, *Not a Good Day to Die*, *Washington Monthly*, July–August 2005, http://www.washingtonmonthly.com/features/2005/0507.carter.html.

78. Quoted by Hendrik Hertzberg, "Webbcast," *New Yorker*, February 5, 2007, 25.

79. Maureen Dowd, "Better Never Than Late," *New York Times*, May 2, 2007. Also see excellent review article of George Tenet's memoir by Thomas Powers. Tenet's book is *At the Center of the Storm: My Years at the CIA* (New York: HarperCollins Publishers, 2007). Powers' article is "What Tenet Knew," *New York Review of Books*, July 19, 2007, 70–74.

Chapter 9

1. Quoted by President George W. Bush at the funeral of Coretta Scott King, on February 7, 2006.

2. The Kitty Genovese case became very well known and has by now been described and analyzed in countless social science textbooks. The quotes in this paragraph are from a contemporaneous account. See Martin Gansberg, "Thirty-Eight Who Saw Murder and Didn't Call the Police," *New York Times*, March 27, 1964.

3. Nicholas D. Kristof, "If Not Now, When?" *New York Times*, October 29, 2006.

4. Nicholas D. Kristof, "Heroes of Darfur," *New York Times*, May 7, 2006; and "Car Washes and Genocide," *New York Times*, January 16, 2007.

5. *Boston Globe*, editorial, "Shaming China on Darfur," also appeared in the *International Herald Tribune*, June 1, 2007.

6. Phrase is title of an editorial on the subject, *New York Times*, August 3, 2007.

7. See, for example, Andrew Rosenthal, "There Is Silence in the Streets: Where Have All the Protesters Gone?" *New York Times*, August, 31, 2006.

8. As was pointed out to me by Dave Simonson, every popular or protest movement aspires to "graduate" followers, from Bystanders to Participants, and from Participants to Activists, and so on.

9. John Cassidy, "Alien Nation," *New Yorker*, April 10, 2006, 25.

10. Rex Wockner, "Pride Around the World" in *The Bottom Line: San Diego,* July 20, 2007, http://www.sdbottomline.com/index1.html.

11. For more on this particular issue, see Kim Severson, "Bringing Moos and Oinks into the Food Debate," *New York Times,* July 25, 2007. Severson notes that in a 2006 survey of five thousand people aged thirteen to twenty-four, PETA was the nonprofit organization most would like to volunteer for. Severson also comments on the role played in the animal rights movement by technology, for example, mass e-mails, easily concealed cameras, and online images, including grim if not gruesome pictures of slaughterhouses.

12. Steve Stecklow, "Environmentalists, Loggers Near Deal on Asian Rainforest," *Wall Street Journal*, February 23, 2006.

13. Claudia Deutch, "Companies and Critics Try Collaboration," *New York Times*, May 17, 2006. Stories dedicated to related subjects constituted a special section of the *Times*, section E.

14. Marc Gunther, "The Green Machine," *Fortune*, August 2, 2006, 57.

15. Heather Green, "The Greening of America's Campuses," *Business Week*, April 9, 2007, 64.

16. This paragraph is based on Jerry Adler, "Going Green," *Newsweek*, July 17, 2006, 42–52.

17. Ethan Wilensky-Lanford, "Political Activism Beginning to Take Hold in Kyrgyzstan," *New York Times*, December 12, 2005.

18. Hassan M. Fattah, "Workers in Arab Emirates Protest, and Win," *New York Times*, September 25, 2005.

19. Seth Mydans, "Haunted by Past Horrors, Cambodians Speak Out," *New York Times*, January 30, 2006.

20. Steven Lee Myers and C. J. Chivers, "Protesters Charge Fraud in Belarus Presidential Election," *New York Times*, March 20, 2006. Also see Steven Lee Myers, "Bringing Down Europe's Last Ex-Soviet Dictator," *New York Times Magazine*, February 26, 2006, http://www.nytimes.com/2006/02/06magazine/26belarus.htm.

21. The quote is from Craig S. Smith, "French Premier Considers Easing Job Law," *New York Times*, March 28, 2006.

22. Elaine Sciolino and Craig S. Smith, "Protests in France over Youth Labor Law Turn Violent," *New York Times*, March 29, 2006.

23. Elaine Sciolino, "Chirac Will Rescind Labor Law That Caused Wide French Riots," *New York Times*, April 11, 2006.

24. Roddy Scheer, "Money Matters: Boring from Within," *Earth Action Network*, January–February 2006.

25. Marcella Bombardieri and David Abel, "Summers Gets Vote of No Confidence," *Boston Globe*, March 16, 2005.

26. Ibid.

27. Marcella Bombardieri, "Summers Should Go, Ex-Harvard Dean Says," *Boston Globe*, February 16, 2006.

28. "John Harvard's Journal: A Presidency's Early End," *Harvard Magazine*, May–June 2006, 64.

29. Ibid., 60, 61.

30. Evan H. Jacobs and Anton S. Troianovski, "Summers Resigns," *Harvard Crimson*, February 22, 2006.

31. This paragraph is based on the wonderful article by Helen Epstein and Julia Kim, "AIDS and the Power of Women," *New York Review of Books*, February 15, 2007, 39–41.

32. Jane Gross, "Living with Alzheimer's," *New York Times*, March 29, 2007.

33. Anne Applebaum, "Hero," *New York Review of Books*, October 20, 2005, 18.

34. Laura Landro, "Patients, Families Take Up the Cause of Hospital Safety," *Wall Street Journal*, May 30, 2007.

35. Deborah Sontag, "Israel Honors Mothers of Lebanon Withdrawal," *New York Times*, June 3, 2000.

36. Elisabeth Bumiller, "In the Struggle over the Iraq War, Women Are on the Front Line," *New York Times*, August 29, 2005.

37. *New York Times*, editorial, "One Mother in Crawford," August 9, 2005.

38. Anne E. Kornblut, "Mother's Grief-Fueled Vigil Becomes Nexus for Antiwar Protesters," *New York Times*, August 13, 2005.

39. C. Fred Alford, *Whistleblowers: Broken Lives and Organizational Power* (Ithaca, NY: Cornell University Press, 2001), 19, 20.

40. Mark Hayhurst, "I Knew What Was About to Happen," *Guardian Unlimited*, January 23, 2001, http://www.guardian.co.uk/science/2001/jan/23/spaceexploration.g2.

41. See *Time*, "The Interview," December 30, 2002, 58.

42. Bethany McLean and Peter Elkind, *The Smartest Guys in the Room: The Amazing Rise and Scandalous Fall of Enron* (New York: Portfolio, 2003), 355.

43. Ibid., 355.

44. John Wiener, "Saving History from the Shredder," *Nation*, September 6–13, 1999, 20–24.

45. Alex Berenson, "At Pfizer, the Isolation Increases for a Whistleblower," *New York Times*, June 6, 2005.

46. Greenhouse is cited in *New York Times*, editorial, "Banished Whistle-Blowers," September 1, 2005.

47. Erik Eckholm, "Army Contract Official Critical of Halliburton Pact Is Demoted," *New York Times*, August 29, 2005.

48. Judy Greenwald, "Whistleblower Retaliation Claims Challenging Employers," *Business Insurance*, September 26, 2005, 4.

49. Chris Strohm, "Report Finds Government Whistleblowers Lack Adequate Protections," GovernmentExecutive.com, January 10, 2006, http://www.govexec.com/dailyfed/0106/011006c1.htm.

50. Gina Holland, "High Court Trims Whistleblower Rights," Associated Press, May 30, 2006, http://sfgate.com/cgi-bin/article.cgi?f=/n/a/2006/05/30/national/w132119D75.DTL&type=politics.

51. The word *quirky* is Alford's, *Whistleblowers*, 31.

52. Ibid., 32.

53. Ibid., 35.

54. To read more about Jon Oberg, see Sam Dillon, "Whistler-Blower on Student Aid Vindicated," *New York Times*, May 7, 2007.

55. In response to the apparently growing political clout of illegal immigrants, Joseph Turner, armed with only $100 and a computer, formed a group he called Save Our State. His goal was to save California from turning into a "Third World cesspool." Needless to say, some consider Turner a hate monger. He is, in any case, an Activist, fighting for a cause in which he deeply believes. See Miriam Jordan, "In Immigrant Fight, Grass-Roots Groups Boost Their Clout," *Wall Street Journal*, September 28, 2006.

56. Ian Buruma, "Kimworld," *New Yorker*, August 22, 2005, 64.

57. Jean Lipman-Blumen, *The Allure of Toxic Leaders: Why We Follow Destructive Bosses and Corrupt Politicians—and How We Can Survive Them* (New York: Oxford University Press, 2005), 43.

58. Ibid., 44.

59. Ibid., 174.

60. Barbara Kellerman, *Bad Leadership: What It Is, How It Happens, Why It Matters* (Boston: Harvard Business School Press, 2004), 165.

61. Both quotes on the Smithsonian are in Robin Pogrebin, "Report Faults Oversight by Smithsonian Regents," *New York Times*, June 19, 2007. The second quote is from a report prepared by the Smithsonian.

62. Lewis Sorley, *Honorable Warrior: General Harold K. Johnson and the Ethics of Command* (Lawrence: University Press of Kansas, 1998), 268.

63. All the quotes in this paragraph are from Kelley Holland, "The Silent May Have Something to Say," *New York Times*, November 5, 2006.

64. Ian Buruma, "The Indiscreet Charm of Tyranny," *New York Review of Books*, May 12, 2005, 36.

65. Quoted by Michael Massing, "Trial and Error," *New York Review of Books*, October 17, 2004, 17.

66. Ibid.

67. Ibid.

68. Kellerman, *Bad Leadership*, chapter 6.

69. John R. Emshwiller, "Lesser Known Enron Executive Is Key Witness," *Wall Street Journal*, March 20, 2006.

70. Ibid.

71. Alexei Barrionuevo, "Enron Executive Points a Finger at Former Chiefs," *New York Times*, March 8, 2006.

72. Alexei Barrionuevo, "Data Modified, Jury Is Told," *New York Times*, February 22, 2006.

73. Robert E. Kelley, "In Praise of Followers," *Harvard Business Review*, November–December 1988, 142–148.

74. Robert E. Kelley, *The Power of Followership: How to Create Leaders People Want to Follow and Followers Who Lead Themselves* (New York: Doubleday, 1992).

75. Ibid. See especially chapter 6, 125–147.

76. Ira Chaleff, *The Courageous Follower: Standing Up to and for Our Leaders*, 2nd ed. (San Francisco: Berrett-Koehler, 2003).

77. Ibid., 159.

78. Katharine Q. Seelye and Jennifer Steinhauer, "At Los Angeles Times, a Civil Executive Rebellion," *New York Times*, September 21, 2006.

79. Katharine Q. Seelye, "Los Angeles Times Publisher Is Ousted," *New York Times*, October 6, 2006.

80. Katharine Q. Seelye, "Los Angeles Paper Ousts Top Editor," *New York Times*, November 8, 2006.

81. Ibid.

Chapter 10

1. William Gardner, Bruce Avolio, Fred Luthans, Douglas R. May, and Fred Walumba, "Can You See the Real Me? A Self-Based Model of Authentic Leader and Follower Development," *Leadership Quarterly* 16 (2005): 343–372.

2. David Collinson, "Rethinking Followership: A Post-Structuralist Analysis of Follower Identities," *Leadership Quarterly* 17, no. 2 (April 2006): 185.

3. Ibid., 186.

4. Robert B. Cialdini, *Influence: The Psychology of Persuasion* (New York: William Morrow, 1993).

5. Ibid., 230.

6. Abhijit V. Banerjee, "A Simple Model of Herd Behavior," *Quarterly Journal of Economics*, August 1992, 797.

7. Stephen Worchel, "Come One, Come All: Toward Understanding the Process of Collective Behavior, in *The SAGE Handbook of Social Psychology*, eds. Michael A. Hogg and Joel Cooper (Thousand Oaks, CA: Sage Publications, 2003), 487.

8. The quotes and information relating to Debian are from Siobhan O'Mahony and Fabrizio Ferraro, "Governance in Production Communities" (unpublished paper presented at the Center for Public Leadership, Cambridge, MA, 2006). See especially pp. 17–19.

9. Ibid., 38.

10. Ori Brafman and Rod A. Beckstrom, *The Starfish and the Spider: The Unstoppable Power of Leaderless Organizations* (New York: Penguin, 2006).

11. Ibid., 129, 131.

12. Barron H. Lerner, MD, "In a Hospital Hierarchy, Speaking Up Is Hard to Do," *New York Times*, April 17, 2007.

13. John Cassidy, "Annals of Economics: Relatively Deprived," *New Yorker*, April 3, 2006, 45.

14. Ibid.

15. Among the findings of a survey of workers conducted by researchers at Florida State University. Quoted by Brent Kallestad, "Just FYI: Bad Bosses Can Do More Than Annoy," *Houston Chronicle*, January 2, 2007.

16. Princeton economist Angus Deaton, quoted by Cassidy, "Annals of Economics," 46.

17. Barbara Kellerman, *Bad Leadership: What It Is, How It Happens, Why It Matters* (Boston: Harvard Business School Press, 2004).

18. Robert E. Kelley, *The Power of Followership: How to Create Leaders People Want to Follow and Followers Who Lead Themselves* (New York: Doubleday, 1992), 102–105.

19. Dan Fost, "Mangling Managers: Survey Finds Many Workers Mistrust Bosses," *San Francisco Chronicle*, January 3, 2007.

20. Todd Pittinsky, Seth Rosenthal, Laura Bacon, L. Matthew Montoya, and Weichun Zhu, *National Leadership Index 2006: A National Study of Confidence in Leadership* (Cambridge, MA: Center for Public Leadership, 2006), 4.

21. The quotes and the account in the paragraph are from Michelle Conlin, "Smashing the Clock," *BusinessWeek*, December 12, 2006, 60–68.

22. Jared Sandberg, "Working for a Boss Who Only Manages Up Can Be a Real Downer," *Wall Street Journal*, May 16, 2006.

23. Stever Robbins, "Understand What Motivates Your Boss," *HBS Working Knowledge*, March 13, 2006; and Sarah Jane Gilbert, "Do I Dare Say Something?" *HBS Working Knowledge*, March 20, 2006.

24. Kevin P. Coyne and Edward J. Coyne Sr., "Surviving Your New CEO," *Harvard Business Review*, May 2007, 62–69.

25. Larry Bossidy, "What Your Leader Expects of You—and What You Should Expect in Return," *Harvard Business Review*, April 2007, 58–65.

26. James Kelly and Scott Nadler, "Leading from Below," *Wall Street Journal*, March 3–4, 2007.

27. Michael Useem, *Leading Up: How to Lead Your Boss So You Both Win* (New York: Crown, 2001) 1.

28. Debra E. Meyerson, *Tempered Radicals: How People Use Difference to Inspire Change at Work* (Boston: Harvard Business School Press, 2001). This paragraph is based on Meyerson's book.

29. Ibid., 138.

30. Matt Vilano, "The Perils of an Office Coup," *New York Times*, June 25, 2006.

31. Ira Chaleff, letter to author, March 12, 2006. I am grateful to Mr. Chaleff for sharing his insights.

32. The importance of this point is difficult to overestimate. It has been made by others as well, including Ira Chaleff and Jean Lipman-Blumen, who point out that, in his dissertation, Tom Peters showed that "even small but consistent wins by a toxic leader can cow would-be challengers." In Jean Lipman-Blumen, *The Allure of Toxic Leaders: Why We Follow Destructive Bosses and Corrupt Politicians—and How We Can Survive Them* (New York: Oxford University Press, 2005), 212.

33. Ibid., 211.

34. Tom Devine, *The Whistleblower's Survival Guide: Courage Without Martyrdom* (Washington, DC: Fund for Constitutional Government, 1997), 14–25.

35. For more on the challenges subordinates face in speaking up to their superiors, see Sarah Jane Gilbert, "Do I Dare Say Something?" *HBS Working Knowledge*, March 20, 2006. Gilbert's article was based on a working paper written by Amy Edmondson and James Detert.

36. The quotes and the information in this paragraph are in Michael Barbaro, "Apologetic, Home Depot Tries to Move Beyond Nardelli's Shadow," *New York Times*, May 25, 2007; and Joe Nocera, "Speaking Up in Fresh Air at Home Depot," *New York Times*, May 26, 2007.

37. Alan Murray, "After the Revolt, Creating a New CEO," *Wall Street Journal*, May 5–6, 2007. The quotes and information in this paragraph are, unless otherwise indicated, taken from Murray's article.

38. The phrase *nobody revolts* is from Joe Nocera, "Running G. E., Comfortable in His Skin," *New York Times*, June 9, 2007. (The article was about Jeffrey Immelt.) The line about the fear of firing is from Michael Orey, "Fear of Firing," *BusinessWeek*, April 23, 2007, 52. And the information about the precarious perches of CEOs is in Roger O. Crockett, "At the Head of the Headhunting Pack," *BusinessWeek*, April 9, 2007, 80.

39. Cliff Zukin, Scott Keeter, Molly Andolina, Krista Jenkins, and Michael X. Delli Carpini, *A New Engagement? Political Participation, Civic Life, and the Changing American Citizen* (Oxford: Oxford University Press, 2006), 188. For those with a further interest in the general subject of citizen participation, this book constitutes an important reference.

40. Susan Page, "Poll: Bush's New Iraq Strategy Fails to Rally Public Support," *USA Today*, January 16, 2007.

41. Frank Rich, "Yes, You Are the Person of the Year!" *New York Times*, December 24, 2006.

42. Zukin et al., *A New Engagement?*, 186.

43. Ibid., 189. Regarding interest in the news by young people in particular, also see Thomas Patterson, "Young People and News," A Report from the Joan Shorenstein Center on the Press, Politics and Public Policy, John F. Kennedy School of Government, Harvard University, July 2007, http://www.ksg .harvard.edu/presspol/carnegie_knight/young_news_web.pdf.

44. See, for example, Adam Nagourney and Megan Thee, "Young Americans Are Leaning Left, New Poll Finds," *New York Times,* June 27, 2007.

45. Zukin et al., *A New Engagement?*, 203.

46. Excerpt from a report written by Thomas Axworthy and Herman Leonard, "Two Simple Mechanisms for Advancing the Democratic Governance of Hong Kong," *South China Morning Post*, August 7, 2006.

47. Howard W. French, "In Chinese Boomtown, Middle Class Pushes Back," *New York Times*, December 16, 2006.

48. Lipman-Blumen, *The Allure of Toxic Leaders*, 186.

49. Quoted by Neil J. Mitchell, *Agents of Atrocity: Leaders, Followers, and the Violation of Human Rights in Civil War* (New York: Palgrave Macmillan, 2004), 43.

50. For more on "the arts of resistance," see James C. Scott, *Domination and the Arts of Resistance: Hidden Transcripts* (New Haven, CT: Yale University Press, 1990).

51. Quoted by Scott, *Domination and the Arts of Resistance*, 206.

52. Polish worker and resistance fighter quoted by Scott, *Domination and the Arts of Resistance*, 212.

53. Adam Hochschild, "English Abolition: The Movie," *New York Review of Books*, June 14, 2007, 73.

54. This paragraph is based on Jason de Parle, "Fearful of Restive Foreign Labor, Dubai Focuses on Reforms," *New York Times*, August 6, 2007.

55. Jeff Leeds, "Democracy Rules, and Pop Culture Is Depending on It," *New York Times*, February 2, 2007.

56. As quoted in "Arts, Briefly," compiled by Lawrence van Gelder, in "Italian Groups Protest Streisand Ticket Prices," *New York Times*, May 24, 2007.

57. Alan Murray, "Behind Nardelli's Abrupt Exit; Executive's Fatal Flaw: Failing to Understand New Demands on CEOs," *Wall Street Journal*, January 4, 2007.

58. Quoted in "Hillary Clinton Launches White House Bid," CNN.com, January 22, 2007, http://www.cnn.com/2007/POLITICS/01/20/clinton.announcement/index.html.

Index

About the Author

B A R B A R A   K E L L E R M A N   is James Macgregor Burns Lecturer in Public Leadership at Harvard University's John F. Kennedy School of Government. She was the founding executive director of the Kennedy School's Center for Public Leadership from 2000 to 2003; from 2003 to 2006 she served as the center's research director. Kellerman has held professorships at Fordham, Tufts, Fairleigh Dickinson, George Washington, and Uppsala universities. She also served as dean of graduate studies and research at Fairleigh Dickinson, and as director of the Center for the Advanced Study of Leadership at the Academy of Leadership at the University of Maryland.

Kellerman received her BA from Sarah Lawrence College, and her MA, MPhil, and PhD (1975, in political science) degrees from Yale University. She was awarded a Danforth Fellowship and three Fulbright fellowships. She holds an honorary degree from Ripon College. At Uppsala (1996–1997), she held the Fulbright Chair in American Studies.

Kellerman is author and editor of many books, including *Leadership: Multidisciplinary Perspectives*; *The Political Presidency: Practice of Leadership*; and *Reinventing Leadership: Making the Connection Between Politics and Business*. Her most recent books are *Bad Leadership: What It Is, How It Happens, Why It Matters* (2004) and a coedited volume (with Deborah Rhode), *Women & Leadership: The State of Play and Strategies for Change* (2007). She appears often on media outlets such as CBS, NBC, PBS, CNN, NPR, and

BBC and Bloomberg Radio. She has contributed articles and reviews to, among others, the *New York Times*, the *Washington Post*, the *Boston Globe*, the *Los Angeles Times*, and the *Harvard Business Review*. Kellerman speaks to audiences around the world, including recently in Berlin, London, Moscow, Rome, São Paolo, and Shanghai.

Other Leadership Books
by Barbara Kellerman

Women & Leadership: The State of Play and Strategies for Change,
coeditor with Deborah Rhode (2007)

Bad Leadership: What It Is, How It Happens, Why It Matters (2004)

*Reinventing Leadership: Making the Connection Between
Politics and Business* (1999)

The President as World Leader, coauthored with Ryan Barilleaux (1991)

Leadership and Negotiation in the Middle East,
coeditor with Jeffrey Z. Rubin (1988)

Political Leadership: A Source Book, editor (1986)

Women Leaders in American Politics,
coeditor with James David Barber (1986)

The Political Presidency: Practice of Leadership (1984)

Leadership: Multidisciplinary Perspectives, editor (1984)